Commerce, morality and the eighteenth-century novel

British culture underwent radical change in the eighteenth century with the emergence of new literary genres and discourses of social analysis. As novelists developed the fictional form, writers of economic tracts and treatises sought a language and a conceptual framework to describe the modern commercial state. In *Commerce, Morality and the Eighteenth-Century Novel*, Liz Bellamy argues that the evolution of the novel in eighteenth-century Britain needs to be seen in the context of the discursive conflict between economics and more traditional systems of social analysis. In a series of fresh readings of a wide range of novels, Bellamy shows how the novel contributed to the debate over public and private virtues and had to negotiate between commercial and anti-commercial ethics. The resulting choices were crucial in determining the structure as well as the moral content of the novel.

LIZ BELLAMY is an associate lecturer at the Open University. She is author of *Jonathan Swift's Gulliver's Travels* (1992), with Tom Williamson *Property and Landscape: A Social History of Land Ownership and the English Countryside* (1987) and with Kate Moorse *The Changing Role of Women* (1996); and she is editor of the journal *Rural History: Economy, Society, Culture*.

COMMERCE, MORALITY AND THE EIGHTEENTH-CENTURY NOVEL

LIZ BELLAMY

CAMBRIDGE
UNIVERSITY PRESS

PUBLISHED BY THE PRESS SYNDICATE OF THE UNIVERSITY OF CAMBRIDGE
The Pitt Building, Trumpington Street, Cambridge CB2 IRP, United Kingdom

CAMBRIDGE UNIVERSITY PRESS
The Edinburgh Building, Cambridge CB2 2RU, United Kingdom
40 West 20th Street, New York, NY 10011-4211, USA
10 Stamford Road, Oakleigh, Melbourne 3166, Australia

© Liz Bellamy 1998

First published 1998

Printed in the United Kingdom at the University Press, Cambridge

Typeset in Baskerville 10/12.5 pt. [VN]

A catalogue record for this book is available from the British Library

ISBN 0 521 62224 7 hardback

Contents

Acknowledgements

In the course of writing this book, I have built up debts to many people and several institutions: to Gillian Beer, Nigel Leask, John Mullan, Suzanne Raitt, Simon Schaffer, Keith Snell and the late Raymond Williams, and to Jesus College, Cambridge for providing a happy working environment. More recently, I have been grateful for the encouragement of Marilyn Brooks and Bob Owens of the Open University, and of friends, colleagues and students at Norwich City College, particularly Tom Betteridge, Garth Clucas, Cathy Davies, George Norton and Val Purton. The final stages of writing were made considerably easier by a research grant from Norwich City College. Linda Bree of Cambridge University Press has proved a supportive editor, while Hilary Hammond has dealt efficiently with the manuscript.

A version of parts of chapters 1 and 3 has previously been published in *Literature and History*, 5:2, in an article entitled 'Private Virtues, Public Vices: Commercial Morality in the Novels of Samuel Richardson', and I am grateful to the editors for permission to include a revised and extended form of this material here.

My primary debt, however, is to three people who have provided an unfailing source of help, support, intellectual stimulation and inspiration while this book has been under construction: Stephen Heath, Tom Williamson, and, above all, my long-suffering supervisor, John Barrell.

CHAPTER I

Introduction

Since the 1980s analysts of the eighteenth-century novel have sought to locate the emergence of the genre in the context of contemporary fictional expectations and concepts of literary form. Writers such as Lennard Davis, Michael McKeon, William Ray and J. Paul Hunter[1] have developed the work of John Richetti in the late 1960s, which examined the relationship between the novel and forms of popular fiction,[2] and have made a concerted effort to reverse the teleological bias that has characterised much criticism since the publication of Ian Watt's *Rise of the Novel* in 1957.[3] As Richetti wrote in *Popular Fiction Before Richardson*:

The beginnings of the novel must be approached as essentially an event in the development of mass culture, a social phenomenon with important consequences for literature proper. What is required is not a critical hunt for lost minor masterpieces . . . but an effort of the historical imagination to understand the values which the eighteenth-century reading public attached to fiction, or, at least the values which the most successful popular narratives advertised and delivered.[4]

J. Paul Hunter has argued along similar lines that:

To understand the origins of the novel as a species and to read individual novels well, we must know several pasts and traditions – even non-fictional and non-narrative traditions, even non-'artistic' and non-written pasts – that at first might seem far removed from the pleasures readers find in modern novels . . . All texts – at least all texts that find or create readers – construct a field in which desires and provisions compete, and the history of texts . . . involves a continuous sorting out of needs, demands, insistences and outcomes.[5]

It is as part of this sorting out process, I would argue, that economic writings should be added to Richetti's whore biographies and rogue tales, Davis' news-sheets and ballads, McKeon's romances and spiritual biographies, and Hunter's journalism, didactic works and travel guides to be recognised as part of the cultural context from which the novel 'rose'. For the development of economic analysis in the eighteenth century was not just a matter of significance to financiers and economists. It had a much wider impact, for it represented the emergence of a new discourse of social analysis which provided a radical challenge to the terms of the existing forms, redefining the relationship between the individual and the state and influencing images of the polity and ideas of social morality. As such it presented a fundamental challenge to the terms in which society could be represented, and to traditional ethical systems.

Much has been written about the eighteenth-century debate over commercial society, particularly in the last twenty-five years. Developing Caroline Robbins' classic study of the growth of liberal thought, *The Eighteenth-Century Commonwealthman*, J. G. A. Pocock has demonstrated the importance of the rhetoric of civic humanism.[6] This discourse was based on a reinterpretation of classical Republican writings, and judged the workings of the economic system in essentially moral terms. Civic humanist writers identified ownership of land as a prerequisite for the possession of political power and political integrity, and the development of commerce and finance was therefore seen as liable to threaten the stability of the state. The owners of wealth in land had a personal stake in the maintenance of the power and wealth of the nation, so their private interest was consonant with the public interest. For owners of other forms of wealth, however, this was not necessarily the case. They were seen as liable to have private interests that were opposed to the interests of the public – most notably the perpetuation of the national debt. Landed wealth was therefore associated with the exertion of public virtue, and other forms of wealth with the lack of this essential quality.[7]

A number of recent critics have analysed the cultural consequences of the dominance of civic humanist ideology. John Barrell has traced its importance within writings on aesthetics, while David Solkin has described how both aesthetic theory and artistic practice responded to the conflict between an heroic ethos and commercial discourse based around politeness.[8] Stephen Copley has indicated how the language of civic humanism was modified by writers such as Defoe, Addison and Steele, who accepted its basic moral framework, with its emphasis on public virtue and the importance of the aristocracy, but incorporated a greater level of acceptance of the realities of the commercial system and an increasing recognition of the role of the middle class.[9] This tradition can be seen as a pre-structure for the emergence of the discourse of political economy from the middle of the eighteenth century. Yet this book will argue that the discursive landscape of the eighteenth century was more complicated than some critical accounts have suggested. In addition to the mediated civic humanist discourse was another, more primitive kind of economic writing, which has tended to fall outside the explanatory paradigms of recent analysts.[10] In the course of the seventeenth and eighteenth centuries a number of writers began to move away from the classical preoccupations to construct a tradition of economic thought which was based on the assessment of the economic consequences of individual actions. By the eighteenth century many writers within this tradition were articulating beliefs which ran directly contrary to the civic humanist rhetoric, assuming, for example, that the maximisation of material wealth was the primary function and duty of individuals as well as of the state. These works can be seen as important precisely *because* of their progressive failure to engage with classical or traditional terms of analysis. They indicate the growth of an autonomous bourgeois model of the state which provided a challenge to conventional ethics through its refusal to endorse or reconcile itself with the classical moral agenda. While these works did not propound an explicit morality, they embodied an implicit code of behaviour that did not resemble the civic humanist model and which was predicated on a very different concept of the relationship between individuals and the state from that presented in either religious writings or works of moral philosophy.

The writers of the civic humanist tradition maintained a clear distinction between a sphere of public, political action, based on the furtherance of the interests of the state, and the private domestic realm, which was concerned with the family or the individual. The latter was conceived as invariably inferior to the former. A willingness to sacrifice the interests of the individual to the interests of the state was almost a defining feature of the civic humanist aristocrat. Yet this narrow political definition of the public was increasingly challenged in the course of the century. As the pursuit of self-interest began to be represented within economics as the duty of the individual, it became increasingly difficult to distinguish between the private and the public. This coincided with the emergence of a much looser, more modern notion of the public, referring not to a realm of political action, but to a general public or popular opinion. This did not usually relate to the totality of society (even in economic writings the labouring majority were still seen as the 'mob' or the 'masses') but rather to a wider notion of the social elite who could perhaps best be described as 'the reading classes'.

In practice the people who actually constituted the reading public of the eighteenth century were more diverse than the civic humanist public in sexual as well as social terms. More and more women were consuming and also producing literature, but the three competing visions of the social structure – of civic humanism, moral philosophy and economic analysis – all presented a view of society and the public that was more or less exclusively masculine. Civic humanism analysed the code of virtue that was appropriate to the aristocratic elite; moral philosophy analysed the behaviour and motivation of the 'refined' and intellectual classes; economics considered the role of the labouring class, but in each case it was assumed that the subjects were men. The novel that emerged in the course of the eighteenth century had to encounter the fragmentation of the social vision that resulted from the discursive conflicts, but it also had to recognise the partial nature of that vision, and reconcile the masculine concepts of the public emerging from the various traditions of social analysis, with the actual sexual diversity of the reading public.

Yet while the novel began to represent some of the interests and preoccupations of an increasingly bourgeois and female readership, the largely masculine critical establishment continued to emphasise ideas of literary form that were inherited from an aristocratic and patriarchal tradition of writing. In particular, the standards of classical epic were upheld and enforced. The conflicts over the kind of virtue that was to be identified as characteristic of eighteenth-century society were therefore underscored by conflicts over the form in which that virtue was to be presented.

There is some irony in the fact that while the early economic tracts and treatises have often been excluded from cultural analysis because they are 'low', the writings on epic seem to have been neglected because they are too 'high'. Both are perceived to fall outside the increasingly dominant discourses of a particular professional cultural elite that rose to prominence by the mid-century and was to form the basis for the bourgeois consciousness that has dominated the literary and critical establishment ever since. The economic writers are seen as tradesmen, tied to the commercial system and unable to appreciate the wider picture. The writers on epic are identified as being preoccupied with moribund standards, and divorced from the really significant developments within contemporary literature. Both have therefore been squeezed out of the picture, and afforded a far less important cultural role than their influence on eighteenth-century thinking appears to warrant.

Some academics have dismissed the writings on epic on the grounds that no great epic poems were produced in the eighteenth century. Yet it could be argued that the persistence of criticism of epic is significant precisely *because* no great epic poems were produced. Critics would obviously write about epic if there were a lot of successful epics about. What is interesting is the fact that they did so when there were not. Those attempting to create contemporary epics were forced to confront the inapplicability of epic standards to what was identified as an increasingly commercial and feminised state, based on the division of labour. Yet the critical establishment still continued to uphold epic as the most important literary form for the embodiment of national aspirations so that those writing in other genres were continually reminded of their inherent inferiority of status. This critical conservatism can be read as a manifestation of the uncertainty within the cultural elite, as it faced a variety of challenges. Faith in the eternal significance of the generic hierarchy was being undermined by both the emergence of new poetic forms and the increasing popularity of narrative fiction. The developing discourse of economic analysis enshrined models of the economic and social structure which challenged neoclassical concepts of literary form and ideas of representation. With both images of the state and perceptions of the role of literature undergoing change, the extent of the divergence between literary practice and critical theory is of considerable significance.

The maintenance of interest in epic standards and epic criteria, long after the emergence and apparent hegemony of the novel, also raises a more general issue concerning the tendency of modern critics to underestimate the importance of 'cultural inertia' within the societies they scrutinise. Despite the attempts over the last fifteen years to counteract the teleological enthusiasm that characterised much of the criticism in the sixties and seventies, there is still a tendency to value change and innovation over stasis and traditionalism. The novels of Daniel Defoe, Samuel Richardson and Henry Fielding are frequently evaluated in terms of their novelty, and the extent of their contribution to the development of the novel form, while works that are perceived to be retrogressive or reactionary receive little critical attention. The critical avoidance of both epic poetry and the preoccupation with the epic ideal in neoclassical criticism can be taken as evidence of this.

J. C. D. Clark has identified a comparable emphasis on change within the study of history, and has traced its origins to the campus radicalism of the 1960s and seventies. Clark argues that social history in particular was dominated by socialist historians, and by a belief that a stress on radical movements in society was necessary for a work of historical exegesis to be itself considered 'radical'.[11] Yet the progressivist tendency within literature seems to have rather different ideological roots. The emphasis on change and innovation is connected with the persistence of liberal humanist notions of the enduring value of literary texts, and of the importance of individual works, either as models of moral and aesthetic excellence, or as contributions to the development of literary forms that will ultimately produce such excellent works. In this vision of literary criticism, Samuel Richardson's epic novel *Clarissa* is more worthy of study than Richard Glover's epic poem *Leonidas*. Such a preference may be justified either on the grounds that Richardson's innovative form ensures that *Clarissa* is 'better' than *Leonidas* (in that it generates more moral, aesthetic and intellectual satisfaction) or because *Clarissa* represents developments in narrative method that will make possible the work of Fanny Burney and thereafter Jane Austen. In contrast, *Leonidas* is not a great influence on subsequent literary form and, in terms of the conventional concept of the canon, Glover's role is limited.

The focus of this book is not, however, the evaluation of contributions to the canon or the celebration of literary excellence. Instead it represents an attempt to recover aspects of the social and cultural environment in which novels were written and read, facilitating the analysis of their meanings and significances, particularly in relation to the construction of images of the social system. In this context it is vital to appreciate the way that literature sought to resist change, as well as the way that it adapted to it. The backward-looking, minor or dead-end discourses constitute a significant aspect of our past. The maintenance of epic standards and aspirations into the eighteenth century can be taken as evidence of conservatism in both literature and society, but it is also important in relation to the development of the novel. By analysing what the writers of epic were trying to do, we can highlight those retrogressive aspects of the novel form that have been subsumed or neglected within progressivist readings.

The novels of the mid-eighteenth century developed within a society that contained a variety of competing images of the role of the individual and his or her relationship to the wider community of the state. There was no simple consensus about how society should be described, or about the sort of values which it should enshrine. Moral and economic discourse propagated divergent ethical models, while the patriarchal epic ideal of heroic conduct was increasingly challenged by more feminised fictional formulations. The mid-century novel therefore developed at a time of social and moral but also literary uncertainty. While moral and economic writers debated how the individual should behave within society, novelists, poets and critics became preoccupied with the contingent issue of the code of conduct that should be represented within literature, and the generic codes that were appropriate for the expression of the aspirations of the modern state. The novel form became both the subject of debate, and the forum within which it was contested. I shall examine four mid-century novels, to indicate the values and morals explicitly advocated, but also the extent to which the structure as well as the themes of narrative fiction manifested anxieties about the role of this morality within an increasingly commercial state, and the ability of the novel to represent that state.

The novels selected include two which are still regularly read and studied (Samuel Richardson's *Clarissa* and Henry Fielding's *Tom Jones*); one that is part of the revised canon that has been constructed by feminist critics (Charlotte Lennox's *The Female Quixote*); and one work which, despite being the favoured reading matter of both Jane Austen and George Eliot, is rarely read today, even within universities (Richardson's *Sir Charles Grandison*). Like Cervantes' *Don Quixote*, both *The Female Quixote* and *Grandison* explored the non-heroic nature of modern society by highlighting the disparity between the modern world and traditional or literary codes of conduct. Lennox exploits the disjunction between the commercial state and the world of romance in order to achieve a comic effect. In *Grandison* the questioning of the codes of honour and chivalry sometimes appear to subvert the rationale of the text itself.

In relation to the more canonical works of Richardson and Fielding, the identification of a network of economic, moral and aesthetic uncertainties serves to undermine a number of established ideas and interpretations. The image of Fielding as the great patrician, constructing an authoritative narrative predicated on the subordination of the reader, and of Richardson as the great innovator, developing a new and ultimately subversive form, is opened up for revision. The mid-eighteenth-century novel can ultimately be seen as an embodiment of the ethical tensions that conditioned the period, shaped by the artistic consequence of the divide between old civic humanist concepts of the public and more modern, private terms of analysis of moral behaviour.

The final section of this book will consider how this divide affected various types of fiction that developed in the second half of the century. In the first half of the century the novel consisted of an assortment of very diverse individual works. Thereafter it remained equally diverse, but the diversity became more classifiable, as the form fragmented into a variety of sub-genres, each with its own structures and conventions. One species of writing that has received little attention from the modern critical establishment, but which clearly defined itself as a distinct literary form, was what I have elsewhere termed the 'novel of circulation'.[12] This involved the portrayal of the adventures of a non-human protagonist – an object or animal – which was passed through society by a series of acts of exchange, and was thereby able to experience at first-hand the diversity of the modern community. The format of the 'novel of circulation' inevitably provided the context for a critique of the economic system that was frequently based on civic humanist rhetoric, while at the same time it drew on the concept that trade was a mechanism for uniting the diverse parts of a divided community. But as the novel of circulation attempted to provide an image of the extensive economy, without the invocation of private morality the main trend of the novel was in the opposite direction, towards a focus on intensive and personal experience.

Ironically, it is in the sentimental novel, with its emphasis on private and affective codes of behaviour, that some of the most thorough and explicit analyses of the economic system can be found. Sentimental writers drew attention to the gap between the private values they sought to celebrate, and the very different ethos and aspirations which they represented as characteristic of society as a whole. The sentimental novel simultaneously rejected the idea of literature as having a simple mimetic function, and highlighted the marginal role for fiction within a commercial society.

The terms of the representation of the role of the novel were, however, rather different in the radical novels that were produced in the 1790s. These have, after Gary Kelly's extensive and definitive study, become generally referred to as 'jacobin' novels.[13] They attempted to invest fiction with a central, cultural position, by emphasising its political as well as its ethical importance. A resolution of the conflict between public and private virtue was sought in the elevation of the private to the status of the public. The philosophical belief that the improvement of society was based on the perfectability of the human mind ensured that the novel of experience inevitably became a polemical vehicle, with phylogeny located in narrative ontogeny. Solutions to social problems

were found in the story of the individual, while institutions were represented as inimical to the propagation of private morality. At the same
time, however, women jacobin writers developed the novel form to
attack the confinement of the female sex within a limited affective
sphere. The dominance of the private, sentimental realm was seen as
having prevented women's participation in the public world, but also
precluded the development of the strength of mind and breadth of
outlook that were seen as necessary for such participation. Irrationality
and irresolution were not natural to women, but were imposed on them
by their restricted social role.

So while the jacobin writers attempted to resurrect some of the
wider cognitive functions of fiction, they also embodied the importance
of gender in the terms in which the role of the individual was conceptualised. The emphasis within male texts on personal moral development was countered by the female recognition of the destructive potential of the dominance of the private and domestic. The male
enthusiasm for the formative nature of individual experience was juxtaposed with a female suspicion that the construction of a separate
private sphere was itself a manifestation of the controlling power of the
institutions of patriarchy. So while the male and female jacobin texts
can be seen as springing from common ideological roots, their gendered perspectives ensured that they offered very different visions of
the role of fiction and its relationship to concepts of public and private.
Yet both shared a desire to problematise and politicise these concepts.
In this respect, they can be read as part of a new fictional genre, but
also as the final phase of an old struggle to give the novel the kind of
public and political significance that was seen by many writers and
thinkers, particularly at the start of the century, as the key to respectability and credibility. Even as they attempted to construct their political fictions, the novel was being shaped by Fanny Burney into the
private and intimate story of individual moral awakening that was to
form the basis of Jane Austen's achievement in the nineteenth century.
In this tradition the elision of the public and the private succeeded
because the idea of a distinct political or ethical sphere was finally
abandoned, and private morality was unproblematically assumed to be
of general interest and relevance.

The eighteenth-century novel therefore represents a kind of Mandevillian Moment, in which the contest between public and private
morality was brought to the fore, and the novel became the ground on
which it was fought. The ensuing discussion will aim to bring out the

importance of the public in novels which have frequently been interpreted retrospectively, in the light of the ultimate triumph of a private, feminised version of morality. But before considering the novel, I will look at the economic, philosophical and literary context to indicate why the ethical conflicts were considered to be so important.

PART ONE

Contexts

CHAPTER 2

The economic context

EARLY ECONOMIC THOUGHT

The second half of the eighteenth century was a period of immense importance in the history of economic thought. It saw the publication of David Hume's essays, of Sir James Steuart's *Inquiry into the Principles of Political Oeconomy* (1767) and, above all, of Adam Smith's *Inquiry into the Nature and Causes of the Wealth of Nations* (1776). It has been hailed as the age which saw the birth of a discourse. To it have been traced the origins of modern economics, and it is often regarded as the period when economics first became 'scientific', or 'analytical'.[1] Yet the works of the 1760s and seventies can be seen as the culmination of an old tradition as much as the start of a new one. They developed from a long history of more primitive, practical tracts, dealing with particular economic issues. Taken together, these tracts represent a vision of society, and even a concept of social mores and ethics, which were to form the bedrock on which the analytical systems of subsequent theorists were built.

The cornerstone of this early economic vision of society was the idea of the balance of trade. Writers expatiated at length on the undeniability of the philosophy that the fundamental purpose of trade was not to increase the general assets of the country, but to maximise the quantity of bullion that flowed in from abroad. As Samuel Fortrey expressed it, in *England's Interest and Improvement* of 1673:

Money, and all forein commodities that come hither, are onely bought by the exchange of our own commodities; wherefore by how much our own store doth exceed those necessaries we want from abroad, by so much will the plenty of money be increased amongst us.

Our care should therefore be to increase chiefly those things which are of least charge at home, and greatest value abroad.[2]

The economic system therefore dictated that production should be increased as far as possible, and consumption should be controlled as far

13

as possible. Minimising the consumption of foreign goods would limit
the outflow of bullion, and restricting the consumption of domestic
goods would increase the surplus which could be exported. In this
respect the economic vision fitted in with the civic humanist model of
society, for the rhetoric inherited from classical republicanism emphasised the dangers of consumption, and upheld austerity and frugality as
crucial public as well as private virtues. As Bishop George Berkeley
wrote in *An Essay towards Preventing the Ruin of Great Britain* of 1721:

Frugality of manners is the nourishment and strength of bodies politic. It is that
by which they grow and subsist, until they are corrupted by luxury, the natural
cause of their decay and ruin. Of this we have examples in the Persians,
Lacedemonians, and Romans: not to mention many later Governments which
have sprung up, continued a while, and then perished by the same natural
causes. But these are, it seems, of no use to us; and, in spite of them, we are in a
fair way of becoming ourselves, another useless example to future ages.[3]

John Brown concluded in his *Estimate of the Manners and Principles of the
Times* (1757) that the character of the manners of the times was of 'a *vain,
luxurious*, and *selfish* EFFEMINACY'.[4] Luxurious spending was identified as
particularly rife amidst the middle and lower classes, and was identified
with licentiousness and insubordination. Without an adequate control
of consumption, the distinction of ranks could not be maintained, and
social disintegration would result.

The terms of the eighteenth-century debate over luxury have been
extensively analysed by John Sekora in his book *Luxury: The Concept in
Western Thought, Eden to Smollett*, which identifies the eighteenth century
as a period of crucial change in the definition of the concept: 'In 1700 the
edifice of laws and attitudes surrounding the concept seems wholly
intact; yet by 1800 it is rubble.'[5] From being a public, political vice,
associated primarily with the lower classes, luxury gradually began to be
seen as a private, individual vice, associated with the upper classes.[6]
From being a central concern of political and moral writers, it became
increasingly marginalised.

Yet the primary focus of Sekora's study is on those writers who
participated in the moral debate over luxury, attacking or defending
this vice, rather than with those who did not discuss it. And while the
role of the 'mercantile writers' is recognised,[7] the account of their works
is relegated to an endnote.[8] For many of the primitive economic
writers, the subject of luxury is simply not on the agenda, and their
handling of the theme of consumption forms an interesting counter-

point to the discussion of luxury in the classical tradition described by Sekora.

Other writers of early tracts invoked the language of morality, condemning luxury and effeminacy in order to buttress the case against consumption. The author of *Britannia Languens: Or, A Discourse of Trade* (1680) presents a catalogue of vice and debauchery that is liable to result from a consumptive trade, including drunkenness, idleness, 'promiscuous copulation' and 'claps and poxes'.[9] This locates the danger of luxury firmly within the lower class and it reinforced the concept that the purpose of trade was to strengthen the nation, rather than to satisfy the greed of individuals, for since economic theory disavowed individual spending, the only justification for economic expansion was the consolidation of the interests of the state. Thus within these early works the interests of the public were identified with the interests of the state.

Although in theory the doctrine of the balance of trade was based on minimising all consumption, in practice many writers believed that the main threat to the wealth of the state lay in the purchase of foreign goods. The sixteenth-century tract, *A Discourse of the Common Weal of this Realm of England*, thought to have been written by John Hales,[10] contains a complaint against foreign 'trifles', which was to recur in economic writings of the next two centuries.[11] The primary speaker of the dialogues laments: 'what nombre first of trifles commeth hether from beyonde the seas, that we might ether clene spare, or els make them with in oure owne Realme, for the which we paie enestimable treasure everie yeare, or els exchange substanciall wares and necessarie for them, for the which we might receive great treasure.'[12] For both Samuel Fortrey and the author of *Britannia Languens* the main threat to prosperity lies not so much in consumption *per se*, but rather in the unrestrained consumption of foreign goods. The latter laments 'the late Increase of our Importations, our National Luxury and folly being such, that our Merchants find a home-vent for almost all sorts of Forreign Goods and trifles in the Universe',[13] and for many writers on commerce the word *luxury* came to be associated with imported goods.

Thus from as early as the late seventeenth century, some economic writers are identifying luxury with the upper classes rather than the lower orders, for it is the aristocracy and gentry who consume French wines and brandies, exotic spices and silks, not the poor or the middle classes. Sekora has shown that in the writings which engage with the civic humanist agenda, the location of luxury at the top rather than the bottom of the social order does not occur until the late eighteenth or early nineteenth century.[14] But many moral writers draw on the economic association of luxury with foreign goods, to provide a critique of aristocratic consumption that is informed by a xenophobic *animus*. In *The Rape of the Lock* Pope at once celebrates the exoticism of Belinda's toilet, and condemns its luxury, in stressing its origins in countries which were associated in the eighteenth century with both mystery and depravity:

> This casket India's glowing gems unlocks,
> And all Arabia breathes from yonder box.[15]

The economic writers' identification of the undesirability of foreign 'trifles' contrasts with their portrayal of the 'substanciall wares and necessarie' produced within this country. British goods are described as fundamentally wholesome, in contrast to the decadence and effeminacy of foreign products.

Writers were convinced of the value of good old English woollens and beers compared to the frippery of French silks and wines, although the conviction did not always extend as far as their wardrobes and cellars. Samuel Fortrey suggested that the king should 'commend to his people, by his own example, the esteem and value he hath of his own commodities, in which the greatest courtier may be as honourably clad, as in the best dress *Paris* or a *French* Taylour can put him in'.[16] The fact that the superiority of British goods is of a moral rather than a physical character is hinted at in the idea of being 'honourably' rather than elegantly, richly or finely clad. A similar idea informs John Philips' poem *Cyder* of 1708. The poet appeals to Simon Harcourt, the dedicatee of the second book of the poem, urging him not to reject the choice and honest beverage of his native land in favour of the 'Massic grape'.[17] Such arguments reinforce the suggestion that prior to the recent corruption that was caused by foreign luxuries, Britain was an organic and self-sufficient economy, and was basically healthy and honest.

This view had no relation to the actual economic condition of Britain over at least the preceding millennium. The country had been deeply and inextricably involved in trade for centuries, but this kind of rhetoric indicated an emotional concept of the state, an escapist nationalism, that lay behind some of the ideas of the economic system. There was, however, a significant difference between the moral and economic attitudes to consumption. For although the early economic writers did not advocate unrestrained luxury, the restrictions they proposed were determined by economic considerations rather than moral precepts. As the economic model changed, and consumption was seen to have an important function, the writers ceased to advocate frugality and restraint. This change was signalled by Thomas Mun in his works *A Discourse of Trade, from England unto the East Indies* of 1621, and *England's Treasure by Forraign Trade*, written in 1623 and published in 1664.[18] Mun's work does not depart from the basic concept of the balance of trade, but it tempers the aggressively competitive edge. He suggests that:

All kind of Bounty and Pomp is not to be avoided, for if we should become so frugal, that we would use few or no Forraign Wares, how shall we then vent our own commodities? what will become of our Ships, Mariners, Munitions, our poor Artificers and many others? doe we hope that other Countreys will afford us money for All our wares, without buying or bartering for Some of theirs? this would prove a vain expectation; it is more safe and sure to run a middle course by spending moderately, which will purchase treasure plentifully.

Again, the pomp of Buildings, Apparel and the like, in the Nobility, Gentry and other able persons, cannot impoverish the Kingdome; if it be done with curious and costly works upon our Materials, and by our own people, it will maintain the poor with the purse of the rich, which is the best distribution of the Common-wealth.[19]

Mun recognises that a total ban on imported goods would hinder the continuation of international trade, and suggests that the moderate consumption of home-produced goods can be beneficial. As such, *England's Treasure* recognises the interdependence of the international commercial system, and provides an early articulation of the theory that the level of economic activity is important in determining the prosperity of the state. Mun assumes that luxurious spending is largely confined to the 'Nobility, Gentry and other able persons', but also that the maintenance of the poor is an end of the economic system, rather than an impediment to its working.

Sir Dudley North extended this idea in his 'Discourse of Coyned Money' of 1691, to suggest that luxurious consumption, far from being undesirable, was essential for the maintenance of the economic system:

The main spur to Trade, or rather to Industry and Ingenuity, is the exorbitant Appetites of Men, which they will take pains to gratifie, and so be disposed to work, when nothing else will incline them to it; for did Men content themselves with bare Necessaries, we should have a poor World.[20]

Jacob Vanderlint argues, in *Money Answers All Things* of 1734, that 'instead of urging the People to be less Consumers, Things should be made so plentiful, that they might be greater Consumers, that Business

might increase, and not abate amongst the People'.[21] Vanderlint puts
forward an economic argument in favour of the expansion of the
economy through increased money, increased spending, and, implicitly,
an increased rate of circulation (although he proposes to bring about this
stimulation of the economy through a reduction in prices).[22] This will
increase employment and the greater demand for labour will increase
the real value of wages. Vanderlint therefore assumes that the increased
spending of the upper and middle classes is not only acceptable but
desirable, provided it is contained within the bounds of the social
hierarchy:

I don't call that State, Equipage, or Way of Living, which is suitable to the Rank
or Condition of a Man, Luxury hurtful to Society, how pompous soever, if it be
contained within the Limits of his Estate . . . for I think such a State and Way of
Living necessary and usefull to Society, whilst it's confined within the Bounds
aforesaid.[23]

So instead of identifying a system of moral precepts which individuals
should obey, the early economists analysed the consequences of their
actions, in order to ascertain how people should behave within a
commercial state. And once accumulation and personal consumption
were recognised as being in the interests of the state, there was little
point in emphasising the distinction between the public and the private.
Edward Misselden asks, in *The Circle of Commerce*:

Is it not lawfull for Merchants to seeke their *Privatum Commodum* in the exercise
of their calling? Is not gaine the end of trade? Is not the publique involved in the
private, and the private in the publique? What else makes a Common-wealth
but the private-wealth, if I may so say, of the members thereof in the exercise of
Commerce amongst themselves, and with forraine Nations?[24]

As the economic writers began to consider the mechanisms by which
private wealth became public, they started to look with new eyes at the
economic infrastructure. This did not lead directly to a recognition of
the value of financial speculation, but it brought about a greater appreciation of the function of financial systems. In *England's Treasure* there
are indications that Mun was conscious of the possibility that wealth
could be spread through society by mechanisms other than consumption. For Mun implicitly suggests that the inflow of money from trade is
only beneficial if the money is employed as financial capital. If it is
merely accumulated, prices will rise and trade will decline.[25] Money can
provide investment as well as consumption, so that private wealth can
be used for the benefit of the public.

This idea was developed by Richard Cantillon,[26] the physiocrats and David Hume, and it represented not only an acceptance of the complexity of commercial society, but also a recognition of the role of the figure who was to become known as the capitalist. The investor could be seen as someone who fulfilled a useful function within the economic system, encouraging effort and ingenuity, supporting improvements and innovations, and making possible the trade and industry on which national wealth and strength were based. These individuals began to be appreciated as essential to economic progress, rather than being represented as merely passive parasites, who reaped the profits from the labour of others, and constituted a drain on the nation's resources. This had political consequences, for as the economic role of capital and investment was increasingly recognised, there was progressively less reason why wealthy capitalists should be seen as necessarily debarred from the elite groups that controlled the country.

The social model produced by the early economic writers was thus very different from that generated in other discourses of social analysis. Writers on civic humanism and natural jurisprudence were concerned with the morality of the economic system, and with whether it were possible for commercial society to embody the values and virtues of the classical social ideal. The economic writers posed no such questions. They wanted to explain rather than to justify the economic system, and by analysing its workings they indicated how economic progress could best be achieved. They were primarily interested in trade and the mechanisms of exchange, rather than the systems of finance and speculation which preoccupied political economists and provided the metaphors for the indictment of the commercial economy.

Trade was associated in economic writings with wealth, and with the health, happiness and strength of the nation. It brought work and affluence to labourers, and bound society in a network of acts of exchange. It made possible the maintenance of a professional army, which was conceived not as a threat to domestic stability, but as a symbol of the spread of national wealth and national power. In contrast, many of the moral writers saw affluence as almost indistinguishable from corruption – where 'wealth accumulates' 'men decay'. Wealth perverted the integrity of government, and disrupted the traditional balance of interests of the political system. It necessitated the creation of a standing army, which destabilised the balance of power, and introduced 'blest paper credit', the 'last and best supply' which, as Alexander Pope reminds us, 'lends corruption lighter wings to fly'.[27]

In *The Machiavellian Moment* J. G. A. Pocock has analysed the debates over land, trade and credit, and the maintenance of the standing army which took place from the seventeenth to the eighteenth century, and has highlighted the civic humanist critique of the commercial system.[28] Yet although Pocock has outlined the terms of the Whig defence of commerce, his concern has tended to be with moral or political works, by writers such as John Locke, Daniel Defoe, Joseph Addison, Andrew Fletcher and Charles Davenant. These writers engaged directly with the classical arguments, and sought to produce an image of the commercial system which was consonant with civic humanist values.[29] Within the primitive and practical tracts, in contrast, there is hardly any attempt to defend commercial society against the moral attack. The economic writers sometimes support their economic arguments by the invocation of moral concepts, but the nature of those arguments is dictated by economic concerns. There is no suggestion in economic literature that government corruption is a consequence of the luxury introduced by trade. Where corruption is considered it is seen rather as a force opposing trade, impeding its benevolent influence. Emphasis is given to the need to liberate commerce from the corrupt control of unenlightened government, to enable it to go on its way, bringing universal benefit.

The failure to encounter the problems detailed by Pocock may be seen as an indication of the primitive nature of economic theory in the eighteenth century, and its inability to construct a credible answer to the critique of commercial society. It would certainly be wrong to overstate the coherence or the analytical sophistication of the early tracts, but their avoidance of the issues of factional political economy may be more than simply a sign of their discursive inadequacy. It indicates the relative autonomy of this strand of economic discourse from a realm in which, as Pocock has indicated, bourgeois ideology was hampered by the terms and omnipresence of civic humanist values.[30] The development of a primitive, marginal but essentially bourgeois discourse may indicate that despite the problems encountered by economic thought in the more 'classical' form discussed by Pocock, in the early eighteenth century this thought was more significant than his conclusions suggest.

Pocock identifies 'frugality' as the source of economic virtue in Whig ideology,[31] yet the most striking feature of economic writing from the mid-seventeenth century is the increasing stress on consumption. In a sense this can be seen as a ratification of the critique of trade of the writers in the civic humanist tradition, for the decline of the accumulative models of the economic system emphasised the primacy of private rather than public interests. Yet it also represents an acceptance of the economic status quo, and an assumption that economic progress is for the good of society. The maximisation of that progress could be identified as public virtue, and this made possible the evolution of a code of personal behaviour and values which served as a system of commercial morality.

In 1705 Bernard Mandeville published his poem *The Grumbling Hive, or Knaves Turned Honest*, reissued with prose exposition in 1714 as *The Fable of the Bees or, Private Vices, Public Benefits*.[32] This put into rather doggerel verse the economic idea which Mun had developed in the 1620s, that luxurious consumption was important within the economic system because most of the economy was based on the production of goods or services which could be regarded as unnecessary. Philip Pinkus has emphasised the non-judgemental nature of Mandeville's observations, in that 'he does not say that this is good or evil, he simply demonstrates that . . . the corruptions inherent in society, provide the fuel that makes society thrive'.[33] While Swift and other satirists condemn the iniquities of modern society, Mandeville merely notes them, and leaves the reader to inject the condemnation. The paradox is that many of Mandeville's contemporaries did not supply the appropriate moral judgements, but instead identified the text as an endorsement of the commercial values it portrayed. As a result, Mandeville was represented as an advocate of unrestrained commercialism, and the abandonment of traditional moral codes. He became the modern Machiavelli, in that his name was used as a byword for all forms of depravity, iniquity and excess.

The storm of protest that greeted Mandeville's work was in sharp contrast to the tacit acceptance of the economic doctrines of Mun. Part of the explanation for the difference in reception may be related to the literary forms in which the two wrote. For while Mun accepted the marginal role of economic analysis, and expressed his theories within tracts and treatises of limited circulation and appeal, Mandeville exposed the importance of consumption in a poem, albeit a poem of very limited literary merit. Moreover in his revisions and annotations he increasingly engaged with moral issues and concerns. The extended edition of 1723 of *The Fable of the Bees* contains a sustained attack on Shaftesbury's social philosophy, and in particular the concept of natural human benevolence.[34]

The purpose of Mandeville's fable was to indicate the disjunction between on the one hand an economic system based on complex exchange, in which growth, profit and trade were identified as inherently good and beneficial, and on the other a system of personal morality which stressed frugality and economy. While contemporary ethics was predicated on an assumption that society had an organic and need-based structure, the commercial economy exploited the fact that this was far from the case. Mandeville therefore juxtaposed the economic insights of writers such as Mun with both the philosophical deism of Shaftesbury and the tenets of orthodox Christianity. The resultant paradox of private vices/public benefits reverberated through the eighteenth century, as economists, philosophers and novelists sought a resolution of its terms.

Yet the poem and, more particularly, the prose exposition were not attacked because of the economic theory of consumption itself, but because they expressed economic theory in terms of moral discourse – a tradition that was essentially opposed to economic analysis – and they did so by engaging directly with moral writers. The controversy provoked by Mandeville therefore reveals the extent of the discursive divide that existed in seventeenth- and eighteenth-century culture. The expression of commercial morality was legitimate within primitive and marginalised writings on commerce. It was only when such ideas impinged on the dominant discursive forms – on writings on morality, civic humanism or political economy – that they became controversial. In modern analyses of early economics it is the 'high' discourses, the works which engaged with the terms of the moral tradition, which have been picked out as important and accorded a cultural hegemony which is perhaps illusory. The existence of these conflicting discourses reveals the extent of the acceptance of commercial society within eighteenth-century culture. The writers on commerce not only took for granted the economic status quo, but saw growth as a political benefit, and equated moral and economic good. They discussed the means by which growth could be maximised, and identified increased consumption amongst the lower classes as a sign of the health rather than the corruption of the economic system. If 'luxury' was considered as a vice at all, it was seen as a venal failing of the upper classes, and many writers hailed luxurious spending as a symptom of increasing wealth and economic strength. All this was perfectly acceptable within their marginalised and primitive discourse. It was more problematic in 'high', or more respectable, literary forms.

Those who debated about the nature of commercial society within the terms of civic humanism were in practice dependent on its material benefits. Despite the anti-commercial rhetoric, there was no rigorous divide between landed and financial interests in the eighteenth century.

Landowners borrowed and speculated, and speculators attempted to acquire land. Howard Erskine-Hill has indicated the interdependence of land and wealth, as well as revealing the extent of the involvement of many country party heroes in the most notorious adventure in speculative investing, the South Sea Island Bubble.[35] What is more, the existence of economic discourse indicates a tacit recognition of the complexity of the economic infrastructure. The subject clearly required its own analytical discourse, its own terminology, its own rules and its own debates, and these were developed from the seventeenth century by the writers of the practical tracts. Nonetheless the cultural elites of the eighteenth century did not incorporate the terms of commercial morality into the realm of political discourse, and this is a sign of their reluctance to admit the mercantile classes into both the positions and the discourses of power. The civic humanist tradition embodies the moral reservations of the cultural elite concerning the new economic system. It condemns the impact of market relations and complex financial structures on the social system of the country, but this condemnation is derived from a basically classical model. As Sir James Steuart wrote in his *Inquiry into the Principles of Political Oeconomy* of 1767:

I have already . . . taken notice of the great difference between the political oeconomy of the ancients and that of modern times; for this reason, among others, that I perceive that the sentiments of the ancients which were founded upon reason and common sense . . . have been adopted by some moderns, who have not perhaps sufficiently attended to the change of our manners, and to the effects which this change must operate upon everything relative to our oeconomy.[36]

The development of economic morality in many ways filled an ideological vacuum that resulted from the inapplicability of classical morality to the realities of a capitalist economic system. But within the dominant culture of the eighteenth century this economic morality was far from being overwhelmingly embraced or accepted. It was constantly countered by the terms of moral analysis, the persistence of which embodied the uneasiness felt in society about the developing economic structure. Old values seemed to have been swept away, and replaced by a system at once incomprehensible and uncontrollable. The reservations of the ruling classes with regard to capitalism were essentially conservative and reactionary, but within eighteenth-century culture they provided a strong challenge to the development of commercial morality. The extent and cultural implications of this conflict between moral and economic terms of analysis are revealed in the work of two writers who contributed to both moral and economic discourse, David Hume and Adam Smith.

DAVID HUME

David Hume is now regarded as one of the foremost philosophical thinkers of the eighteenth century, yet his most famous work, *A Treatise of Human Nature* (1739–40), was barely read by his contemporaries, and the *Dialogues Concerning Natural Religion* (1779) were not published until after his death. In his own day Hume was known as an historian and polite essayist, who wrote on politics, economics, literature and morals. These belles-lettristic interests grew out of his philosophical enterprises, for he explained in the Advertisement to the *Treatise* that once he had completed the analysis of human understanding and human passions that formed the basis of this epistemological work, he would 'proceed to the examination of *morals, politics*, and *criticism*'.[37] The 'Essays, Moral, Political and Literary' which formed a part of Hume's *Essays and Treatises on Several Subjects* (1758) can be seen as a partial fulfilment of this promise. Yet it is difficult to establish any clear analytical continuity between the *Treatise* and the *Essays*. The former is written from the abstruse and speculative metaphysical perspective of the moral philosopher. The latter is cast within the framework of 'normal' perceptions, which Hume identifies in both the *Treatise* and the *Enquiry Concerning Human Understanding* as very different from the pattern of philosophical thinking.[38] This abandonment of the point of view of the philosopher for the analysis of the social system is significant in that it indicates the specialised and marginal role of philosophy within a commercial and materialist state. It also suggests that although David Hume, like Adam Smith, was a writer of both moral philosophy and economics, the two disciplines had very different terms of reference, and presented very different visions of the social system and its ethical code.

The distinction between moral philosophy and forms of social analysis such as politics and economics is developed in Hume's essay 'Of the Rise and Progress of the Arts and Sciences'. Hume contrasts the deterministic study of mass behaviour with the actual complexity of choice and motivation which is revealed in the study of individuals:

What depends upon a few persons is, in a great measure, to be ascribed to chance, or secret and unknown causes: What arises from a great number, may often be accounted for by determinate and known causes.[39]

The actions of the majority have a predictability which cannot be discerned in the actions of individuals, and are therefore susceptible to the schematic analysis of discourses of politics and economics, rather than the more flexible and abstruse techniques of moral philosophy:

When any *causes* beget a particular inclination or passion, at a certain time, and among a certain people: though many individuals may escape the contagion, and be ruled by passions peculiar to themselves, yet the multitude will certainly be seized by the common affection, and be governed by it in all their actions.[40]

Moreover,

Those principles or causes, which are fitted to operate on a multitude, are always of a grosser and more stubborn nature, less subject to accidents, and less influenced by whim and private fancy, than those which operate on a few only. The latter are commonly so delicate and refined, that the smallest incident in the health, education, or fortune of a particular person, is sufficient to divert their course, and retard their operation; nor is it possible to reduce them to any general maxims or observations. Their influence at one time will never assure us concerning their influence at another.[41]

This suggests that economics has a different methodological base not only from moral philosophy, but also from other disciplines devoted to the 'polite arts', and to the construction of histories of individual endeavour. The latter can be generalised far less easily than the former, but the distinction between the two also has a clear class basis. The mercantile and labouring classes can be described by the crude generalising terms of economic analysis which are seen as inappropriate to those of the polite and cultured classes that can be discriminated as individuals:

It is more easy to account for the rise and progress of commerce in any kingdom than for that of learning . . . Avarice, or the desire of gain, is an universal passion, which operates at all times, in all places, and upon all persons: but curiosity, or the love of knowledge, has a very limited influence, and requires youth, leisure, education, genius, and example, to make it govern any person.[42]

Hume goes on in the essay to suggest that it is in practice possible to construct some general principles in relation to the rise and progress of the arts and sciences, but the terms of his analysis confirm the orthodox model of the discursive hierarchy. The study of economics is denigrated because of its association not only with the commercial classes, but also with what are commonly regarded as the baser instincts of mankind. Yet while the applicability of economics to the multitude detracted from the social and intellectual respectability of the genre, it also confirmed its importance to society and its empirical validity. Philosophy, on the other hand, was not only socially exclusive. It also made its practitioners increasingly less susceptible to those impulses and affections which justify the generalising principles of economic discourse. It makes them individuals, rather than members of the multitude. The philosopher will find that:

The bent of his mind to speculative studies must mortify in him the passions of interest and ambition, and must, at the same time, give him a greater sensibility of all the decencies and duties of life. He feels more fully a moral distinction in characters and manners; nor is his sense of this kind diminished, but on the contrary, it is much encreased, by speculation.[43]

The more you study philosophy, the more you will be removed from those basic economic impulses which govern the rest of mankind. The spread of philosophical reasoning will therefore make society increasingly difficult to define and describe within the inherently generalising formulae of the discourses of social analysis.

Yet such speculative studies are clearly perceived to be beyond the scope of the vast majority who are not sensible of intricate moral distinctions, and whose behaviour can be safely predicted and analysed. The awareness of the social dimension in the discursive divide ensures, however, a certain defensiveness in Hume's tone in the introduction to his essay 'Of Commerce', when he justifies the application of his refined reasoning to the prosaic subject of commerce:

I thought this introduction necessary before the following discourses on *commerce, money, interest, balance of trade* &c. where, perhaps, there will occur some principles which are uncommon, and which may seem too refined and subtile for such vulgar subjects. If false, let them be rejected: But no one ought to entertain a prejudice against them, merely because they are out of the common road.[44]

In practice, however, Hume's observations in the essay are not really 'out of the common road' at all. 'Of Commerce' indicates the beneficial consequences of luxurious spending within advanced states and advocates the evolution of a high-wage economy. This acceptance of the economic desirability of material expansion is combined with an oblique reference to Hume's reservations about the moral consequences of unlimited economic growth. Hume is not prepared to recognise that the economic principles articulated in the essay are necessarily universally applicable, and this leads to an endorsement of the existence of the discursive divide between economics and moral philosophy:

There may be some circumstances, where the commerce and riches and luxury of individuals, instead of adding strength to the public, will serve only to thin its armies, and diminish its authority among the neighbouring nations. Man is a very variable being, and susceptible of many different opinions, principles, and rules of conduct. What may be true, while he adheres to one way of thinking, will be found false, when he has embraced an opposite set of manners and opinions.[45]

This reluctance to embrace the moral implications of his own economic arguments is also manifested in the essay on 'Luxury' of 1752, which became known after 1760 as 'Of Refinement in the Arts'. In the essay, Hume addresses the Mandevillian paradox, by arguing '*first*, that the ages of refinement are both the happiest and most virtuous; *secondly*, that whenever luxury ceases to be innocent, it also ceases to be beneficial; and when carried a degree too far, is a quality pernicious, though perhaps not the most pernicious, to political society.'[46]

The first aspect of this argument represents a confident assertion of the value of material expansion, and Duncan Forbes has stressed the positive side of the work:

This is Hume at his least sceptical: he had none of the doubts and misgivings which Adam Smith and the other leading thinkers of the Scottish Enlightenment had about the all-round benefits of commercial civilization.[47]

Thomas A. Horne has suggested that Hume was the first writer of the eighteenth century to provide a coherent answer to Mandeville. He locates this answer in Hume's identification of commerce as a force that 'so far from being incompatible with virtue . . . actually . . . promotes it'[48] and argues that this enthusiasm for commercial activity provided a final denial that there could be a conflict between private codes of morality and the public interest. Yet although 'Of Refinement in the Arts' is significant in the history of economic writing as a eulogy of commerce expressed within a work addressed to a cultured social elite, the second part of Hume's argument, that luxury ceases to be beneficial when it is no longer virtuous, undermines the coherence of the first.

Since Hume follows Francis Hutcheson in employing a relative notion of luxury, rather than the absolute luxury of Mandeville, it is necessary for him to identify at what point the virtue becomes a vice:

No gratification, however sensual, can of itself be esteemed vicious. A gratification is only vicious, when it engrosses all a man's expence, and leaves no ability for such acts of duty and generosity as are required by his situation and fortune.[49]

Hutcheson has argued in a similar vein in his *Remarks on the Fable of the Bees* that luxury should be defined as 'using more curious and expensive habitation, dress, table, equipage than the person's wealth will bear, so as to discharge his duty to his family, his friends, his country, or the indigent'.[50]

Thus 'in each constitution, station, or degree of wealth'[51] there is a level of legitimate luxury, and a level beyond which luxury becomes vicious. Both Hume and Hutcheson can therefore argue that this vicious luxury cannot be beneficial to the public, for such spending is at the expense of a public virtue such as charity, which would benefit the public more directly than personal consumption. Retrenchment of vicious expenditure would not cause a stagnation of the economy, but by increasing redistributive charity would spread the capacity to consume. As Hume argues 'that labour, which, at present, is employed only in producing a slender gratification to one man, would relieve the necessitous, and bestow satisfaction on hundreds'.[52]

But although Hume and Hutcheson confine this argument to vicious luxury, it can also be applied to virtuous or innocent luxury, which both writers had previously justified. As Hutcheson indicates:

Unless . . . all mankind are fully provided not only with all necessaries, but all innocent conveniences and pleasures of life, it is still possible without any vice, by an honest care of families, relations, or some worthy persons in distress, to make the greatest consumption.[53]

If the existence of need can be seen as an indictment of luxurious consumption, how do we distinguish between vice and virtue? At what point can an individual say 'Now I have done my duty – let the luxury commence'? This is not made clear by either Hume or Hutcheson, and as a result the utilitarianism of their definition of morality is disrupted. Indeed the use by both writers of the terms *station* and *situation* suggests an ultimate reliance on a concept of morality and duty that is derived from traditional distinctions of social class. Moreover the appeal to charity cannot be seen as an adequate response to Mandeville, for in his *Essay on Charity Schools* Mandeville had argued that charity had only a marginal role within a complex economy. The message of *The Fable of the Bees* is that, in a commercial state, with a vast labouring population, the multitude can only be supported by the expansion of the economy, which depends on the maintenance of levels of consumption. Direct charity, far from having a positive economic function, is regarded by Mandeville as frequently pernicious. It satisfies the vanity of the donor,

and encourages idleness in the recipient. Above all, Mandeville suggested that a paternalistic community will never be able to rival a commercial state in the quality of its provision for the poor.[54]

The end of 'Of Refinement' represents the collapse of Hume's argument. A *de facto* acceptance of the economic function of vicious luxury is
combined with a refusal to embrace the terms of Mandeville's paradox.
On the one hand Hume asserts that:

It seems upon any system of morality, little less than a contradiction in terms to
talk of a vice, which is in general beneficial to society.[55]

and on the other that:

Luxury, when excessive, is the source of many ills; but is in general preferable to
sloth and idleness, which would commonly succeed in its place, and are more
hurtful both to private persons and to the public.[56]

While Hume is anxious to define morality in terms of public utility, he
has reservations about the moral codes that can be derived from
economic analysis. While economic analysis determines the structures
of society, and moral philosophy is becoming increasingly concerned
with the rarefied realms of metaphysics, the practical judgement of
individual behaviour is seen to be based on the duties defined by an
inherited social hierarchy. Hume recognised that society could no
longer be structured around primitive codes of personal morality, but he
was unwilling to accept the Hobbist model of the wholly acquisitive
individual. His utilitarian concept of the determining nature of the
economic system is tempered by a recognition of the importance of
manners, politeness and taste in defining the character and controlling
the behaviour of the individuals within the state. Yet although Hume
represents the development of the arts as a means by which individuals
will cease to be determined by the crude dictates of the economic
system, his aesthetic and moral writings do not provide a challenge to
the validity of economic discourse. For as was indicated in 'Of the Rise
and Progress of the Arts and Sciences', the beneficent influence of
culture is not to be extended to the mass of the people, who are defined
by the economic structure, but only to those with 'leisure, education and
genius'.[57]

The incorporation of economic analysis in the 'high' discourse of
Hume's *Essays* is therefore combined with a definition of its social
relevance. While economics described the behaviour of the mass of the
people, and articulated the principles of general social phenomena, the

discipline of moral philosophy considered the principles of human perception on the basis of the experience of egregious individuals. Hume therefore provided a justification for the separation of economic and moral discourse on the basis of social class, but in doing so undermined the claims for universal applicability that were central to economic writings. Moreover, in suggesting that members of the social elite were motivated by different concerns from those which affected ordinary working people, Hume implicitly questioned the relevance of economic morality within fiction, since the majority of mid-eighteenth-century novels were located amongst those classes who were seen to be beyond the determining influence of economics. Yet at the same time the existence of economic discourse provides a continual reminder of the limited relevance of other codes of social behaviour.

Adam Smith's dual role, as moral philosopher and economist, has caused considerable confusion to the analysts of both disciplines. In *The Theory of Moral Sentiments* (1759) Smith emphasises the social function of the principle of sympathy – that faculty which can 'interest [a man] in the fortune of others, and render their happiness necessary to him, though he derives nothing from it except the pleasure of seeing it'.[58] In the *Inquiry into the Nature and Causes of the Wealth of Nations*, however, he identifies not sympathy but self-interest as the essential principle of human behaviour:

Man has almost constant occasion for the help of his brethren, and it is in vain for him to expect it from their benevolence only. He will be more likely to prevail if he can interest their self-love in his favour, and show them that it is for their own advantage to do for him what he requires of them . . . It is not from the benevolence of the butcher, the brewer, or the baker, that we can expect our dinner, but from their regard to their own interest.[59]

Numerous writers on Smith's work have tried to reconcile these apparently opposing doctrines, and the conclusions of *The Wealth of Nations* have frequently been interpreted with reference to *The Theory of Moral Sentiments*.[60] For instance, in the introduction to their collection of essays on Adam Smith, Andrew Skinner and Thomas Wilson have indicated the importance of finding a connection between the two texts,[61] and Istvan Hont and Michael Ignatieff have suggested, in the introductory essay of *Wealth and Virtue: The Shaping of Political Economy in the Scottish Enlightenment*, that Smith's project in *The Wealth of Nations* can only be appreciated through an appraisal of the totality of his literary output:

We should be able to understand the relation between Smith's concerns as a moral philosopher, as a professor of jurisprudence and as a political econom-ist . . . There was a central question about modern 'commercial society' which Smith identified in his moral philosophy, in his jurisprudence lectures, and in the 'early draft', and which the final version of the *Wealth of Nations* was intended . . . to answer.[62]

This is, in effect, a modern reworking of the old 'Adam Smith problem', yet despite Smith's sporadic attempts to relate the insights within his various works, his writing is informed by a reluctant recognition of the diversity of the various discourses in which he worked. Although it may be interesting to relate passages of *The Theory of Moral Sentiments* to passages of *The Wealth of Nations*, the former must always be read as moral philosophy, and the latter as economics. The two should not be assimilated merely because they were both written by Adam Smith.

The disjunction between moral and economic discourse was made inevitable by the departures in *The Theory of Moral Sentiments* from the utilitarian concept of human nature that was propagated by Hume and Hutcheson. Far from being consonant, the interests of society are frequently shown to be in conflict with natural human sentiments and codes of morality.[63] For example, at various points Smith identifies moral vices which are a public necessity. One such is the tendency to look up to and emulate social superiors:

This disposition to admire, and almost to worship, the rich and the powerful, and to despise, or, at least, to neglect persons of poor and mean condition, though necessary both to establish and to maintain the distinction of ranks and the order of society, is, at the same time, the great and most universal cause of the corruption of our moral sentiments.[64]

Smith demonstrates in *The Theory of Moral Sentiments* the mechanisms and beliefs which lead human beings to associate wealth with happiness, although as is clear from Smith's eulogies on the middle state and the simple life, he does not believe that wealth is intrinsically desirable. The admiration of and desire for wealth is constructed as a sentiment at once erroneous and natural to the human condition. It is only under the unnatural circumstances of 'the languor of disease and the weariness of old age' that 'the pleasures of the vain and empty distinctions of greatness disappear':[65]

But though this splenetic philosophy, which in time of sickness or low spirits is familiar to every man, thus entirely depreciates those great objects of human desire, when in better health and in better humour, we never fail to regard them under a more agreeable aspect. . . The pleasures of wealth and greatness . . . strike the imagination as something grand and beautiful and noble, of which the attainment is well worth all the toil and anxiety which we are so apt to bestow upon it.

And it is well that nature imposes upon us in this manner. It is this deception which rouses and keeps in continual motion the industry of mankind.[66]

Nature is therefore a force which works against the moral instincts of humanity, in order to further their material condition. It is as though economic expansion has a supernatural sanction, which overrules the moral cavils against luxury and wealth. A similar concept informs the passage in which Smith contrasts the moral tendency to value honesty and virtue with the 'natural course of things' in which industry is rewarded. While 'Nature' tends to favour the industrious knave, 'the natural sentiments of mankind' will prefer the indolent good man: 'Thus man is by Nature directed to correct, in some measure, that distribution of things which she herself would otherwise have made.' While nature rewards or punishes men in such a way as to encourage virtue and discourage vice, men judge merit or demerit in terms of sentiments and passions. Unlike nature, men 'would endeavour to render the state of every virtue precisely proportioned to that degree of love and esteem, and of every vice to that degree of contempt and abhorrence, which he himself conceives for it'.[67]

In distinguishing between the code of virtue followed by nature and that which is upheld by the 'sentiments and passions of man', Smith contrasts a system of human morality based on benevolence with a natural world which is strictly utilitarian. The former is formulated in the discourse of ethics, while the latter is expressed in the discourses of economics and natural jurisprudence. Smith therefore has to construct a mechanism to explain the workings of the 'natural' world which is distinct from established ethical systems. He can rely neither on the theocentric model of Locke, nor on the secular benevolence which Shaftesbury emphasised and which was utilised by Hume in his *Enquiries*. The doctrines of *laissez-faire* economics and of the 'invisible hand' can be seen as an inevitable consequence of Smith's moral philosophy, since only an impersonal force could make sense of the economic system, in the absence of controlling divine or human agents.

In many respects, however, the systemic structure of the *Wealth of*

Nations gave it an appearance of autonomy which was not maintained throughout the text. As Smith's near contemporary Francis Horner wrote in his journal:

Did not Adam Smith judge amiss in his premature attempt to form a sort of system upon the wealth of nations, instead of presenting his valuable speculations to the world under the form of separate dissertations? As a system, his work is evidently imperfect; and yet it has so much the air of a system, and a reader becomes so fond of every analogy and arrangement, by which a specious appearance of system is made out, that we are apt to adopt erroneous opinions, because they figure in the same fabric with approved and important truths.[68]

Much of Smith's analysis is predicated on the assumption that there was a distinction between the terms of moral and economic analysis, but in practice the mechanistic approach was frequently combined with an explicit articulation of moral values and beliefs. This does not mean, as some critics have suggested,[69] that Smith's economic writings should be interpreted as works primarily devoted to issues of morality and natural jurisprudence. Smith's system is based not on moral but on economic desiderata, on empirical analysis and not on traditional precepts. Nonetheless, the recurrent utilisation of the terms of traditional morality which has been identified by writers such as Michael Ignatieff and Istvan Hont indicates the tension within the developing discourse resultant from the marginalisation of moral philosophy.

The relationship between the values derived from Smith's economic system, and those imposed upon it, is revealed in *The Wealth of Nations* in the attempt to answer one of the traditional moral criticisms of commercial society – that it encouraged upward mobility. It was thought that economic development, and in particular the extension of the division of labour, would introduce an increasingly meritocratic society. Moreover, as people began to realise the complex structure of society, and that it was bound not by the traditional ties of paternalism, but by a series of acts of exchange, there was a fear that the circulation of money would be matched by a circulation of labour – and that the 'value in use' of labour would be matched by its 'value in exchange'. Yet in *The Wealth of Nations* Smith presented the division of labour in such a way as to allay anxieties of this kind. Smith followed Adam Ferguson in suggesting that the division of labour will not increase social mobility, the talented individual will not be able to pass through the various aspects of his profession to a level of greater responsibility and power, because the consciousness and abilities of the workforce are dictated by the nature of the labour they perform. Adam Ferguson had written in his *Essay on the History of Civil Society* that 'many mechanical arts . . . require no capacity; they succeed best under a total suppression of sentiment and reason, and ignorance is the mother of industry as well as superstition'.[70] Adam Smith makes the same point more strongly in the prelude to the famous passage on the philosopher and the street porter in *The Wealth of Nations*:

The difference in natural talents in different men is, in reality, much less than we are aware of; and the very different genius which appears to distinguish men of different professions, when grown up to maturity, is not upon many occasions so much the cause, as the effect of the division of labour.[71]

Thus while recognising an equality in the natural abilities of men, Smith and Ferguson are able to justify the hierarchical structure of society, and reverse the traditional fear that the division of labour will create social mobility. While Smith and Ferguson appreciate the problems of an increasingly stratified society, they represent this society as having a stability that is tantamount to a caste system. This emphasis on the mentally and spiritually limiting nature of labour in an advanced commercial society reinforced the validity of economic discourse. Smith's labourers, like Hume's multitude, were essentially predictable, because they were the products of their labour, and were determined by the economic system. As a result they lacked that individuality which could put them outside the generalising terms of economic analysis.

Yet this lack of individuality was not welcomed by Smith. Imbued as he was with the eighteenth-century Republican ideal of undivided personality, he distrusted the specialised and stupefied blindness of the labouring population since 'the man whose whole life is spent in performing a few simple operations . . . has no occasion to exert his understanding, or to exercise his invention in finding out expedients for removing difficulties which never occur'. This leads to general mental and emotional degeneration, which renders the individual 'not only incapable of relishing or bearing a part in any rational conversation, but of conceiving any generous, noble, or tender sentiment'.[72]

The working man, under the division of labour, is therefore unable to fulfil 'many even of the ordinary duties of private life'.[73] The development of a complex, commercial economy is conceived as a threat not just to the civic humanist, aristocratic ideal of public, political virtue, but also to the preservation of domestic and affective virtue amongst the labouring classes. Smith's dislike of this perceived moral degeneration is partly humanitarian and based on a concern for the health as well as the stability of the social system, but it is validated in the utilitarian terms of *The Wealth of Nations* by an indication of how the stupidity of the labourer can be detrimental to the state. Not only will he be rendered incapable of judging the interests of his country, but 'the uniformity of his stationary life' will make him physically and mentally unfit for assisting in its defence, since 'his dexterity at his own particular trade seems . . . to be acquired at the expence of his intellectual, social, and martial virtues'. But this is the state into which the labouring poor of a civilised society must necessarily fall 'unless government takes some pains to prevent it'.[74]

Smith's moral perspective therefore ensures the disintegration of the self-perpetuating mechanism of the state, which has so often been identified within *The Wealth of Nations*. For his abhorrence of the idea of a member of a complex state, shorn of intellectual, social and martial virtues, stimulates a demand that the economic structure be adjusted by the government, in order to secure the strength of the state and the good of the public. Smith emphasises the importance of the education of the poor in the maintenance of the state, and the terms in which he expresses the public good which will result from this programme indicate the extent to which his economic philosophy is permeated with traditional social values:

An instructed and intelligent people . . . are always more decent and orderly than an ignorant and stupid one . . . They are more disposed to examine, and more capable of seeing through, the interested complaints of faction and sedition, and they are, upon that account, less apt to be misled into any wanton or unnecessary opposition to the measures of government. In free countries, where the safety of government depends very much upon the favourable judgement which the people may form of its conduct, it must surely be of the highest importance that they should not be disposed to judge rashly or capriciously concerning it.[75]

This quotation indicates Smith's adherence to a Lockian concept of the social contract, but it also demonstrates his awareness of the fragility of the social system. Notwithstanding the invisible hand, he perceived the status quo to be threatened by the power of faction, by unwise government, and in particular by class interests. He believed that the spread of education would do something to diminish these threats, for in giving the 'inferior ranks of people' an understanding of the structure of society, it would enable them to appreciate the nature of the public interest. They would therefore be able to ensure that the government acted to improve the condition of the state, and they would appreciate the need to subordinate their class interests to the good of the whole.

It was in these terms that Smith represented the role of the philosopher in *The Wealth of Nations*. For although the division of labour
restricted the capacity of the majority in the commercial state, it also
made possible the refinement of the minority – the 'speculative few'
celebrated by Hume. These individuals could understand the totality of
the system and educate the rest of the population. In the 'Early Draft' of
The Wealth of Nations, written in the 1760s, Smith developed his analysis
of the position of the philosopher in far greater detail than was found in
the final version. He emphasises that it was the disposition to truck and
barter that ensured that men have different capacities, but suggested
that this disposition also made different types of men of benefit to one
another. The porter is of use to the philosopher, and the philosopher is
of use to the porter, because of his ability to improve the mechanic arts,
or to 'deliver down to posterity the inventions and improvements which
had been made before them'.[76] This is a rather more sanguine view of
the economic function of philosophers than that propounded by Mandeville in the version of *The Fable of the Bees* published in 1729. Mandeville
argues that:

They are very seldom the same Sort of People, those that invent Arts and
Improvements in them and those that enquire into the Reason of Things: this
latter is most commonly practis'd by such as are idle and indolent, that are fond
of Retirement, hate Business and take delight in Speculation; whereas none
succeed oftener in the first than active, stirring and laborious Men, such as will
put their Hand to the Plough, try Experiments, and give all their Attention to
what they are about.[77]

Yet, for Smith, the philosopher had a function beyond that of the
provision of technical innovation. The philosopher embodied the
knowledge and culture of his society, and Smith recognised this as a role
that was distinct from the materialistic terms of his economic analysis,
but at the same time susceptible to representation in those terms:

In opulent and commercial societies . . . to think or to reason comes to be, like
every other employment, a particular business, which is carried on by very few
people, who furnish the public with all the thought and reason possessed by the
vast multitudes that labour.

Most people will find that only a very small part of their knowledge is the
result of their own observations and reflections, since 'all the rest has
been purchased, in the same manner as [their] shoes or . . . stockings,
from those whose business it is to make up and prepare for the market
that particular species of goods'.[78]

The suggestion that philosophy is merely a 'particular species of goods' undermines Smith's distinction between productive and unproductive labour in *The Wealth of Nations*,[79] and it may have been for this reason that the passage was dropped from the final version, where philosophy is represented as something rather different from shoes and stockings. But the image of the philosopher as the detached and specialised observer to some extent informs all Smith's writings. In emphasising the dependence of this detached position on the development of commercial society based on the division of labour, Smith indicates the ironic position of the moral philosopher in his own work and that of Hume. For it is the division of labour that has brought about the distinction between the refined elite and the labouring classes,[80] so that the process which rendered the study of moral philosophy possible has also ensured the irrelevance of its findings to the majority of the people. In indicating the role of the division of labour in the constriction of the consciousness of the many, Smith indicates the basis for the separation of the discourses of economics and moral philosophy. The division of labour has produced a division of discourses, between those that are used to describe the motivation of the labouring classes, and those which describe the feelings of the refined elite.

The primitive economic writings of the eighteenth century therefore constitute an autonomous tradition of social analysis, with a particular image of the economic structure and of the role and position of the lower classes. These early works formed a pre-structure for the emergence of the discourse of political economy in the writings of David Hume, James Steuart and Adam Smith. This discourse was to acquire an increasingly hegemonic status in the nineteenth century, with the works of David Ricardo and John Stuart Mill. As is made clear in the writings of both Hume and Smith, far from developing from the tradition of moral analysis, economics derives from an entirely different set of moral, social and epistemological premises. It constitutes an ideology that is opposed to, rather than dependent on, the diverse collection of classically derived discourses – civic humanism, natural jurisprudence and moral philosophy. It deals with people as a mass, rather than with individuals, and it is preoccupied with the lower as much as the upper classes. It develops a system of behaviour based on the assessment of the consequences of individual actions, rather than an abstract preceptual code, and it firmly locates the material wellbeing of the mass of the people as an end to be pursued by society as a whole. The crudeness of the mechanisms proposed by economics was recognised by Hume and Smith, yet the suggestion that the refined and educated elite were capable of rising above these basic forces meant that there was no one discourse or system of morality which could be used to describe contemporary society.

The behaviour of different social groups was not only seen as based on different ethical premises, but was actually articulated within different discursive forms – economics, moral philosophy and civic humanism. Each had its own terms of analysis and representation, and each propagated its own system of ethics and concept of virtue. The public, heroic virtue of civic humanist tradition was increasingly challenged by a more private and exculpatory notion of virtue associated with the rise of economics. The emergence of the novel in the eighteenth century therefore takes place against a background of this discursive and ethical tension and uncertainty. There is no one code for the assessment and portrayal of the relationship between the individual and the social structure. Furthermore each of the competing discourses was predicated on the assumption that its readership was essentially male, and the behaviour it examined or prescribed was appropriate to males. The novel had to develop in the context of a range of forms of social analysis which were both conflicting and fundamentally inadequate for the exploration of a society that was sexually as well as socially diverse, and this provided a considerable challenge to the code of mimesis. In the following sections I will analyse the writings on literary form that were produced in the eighteenth century, to show how they conceptualised this challenge.

CHAPTER 3

The literary context

THEORIES OF EPIC IN THE EIGHTEENTH CENTURY

Epic poetry was generally regarded as the most important and prestigious literary genre in the seventeenth and eighteenth centuries. For Dryden, 'A heroic poem, truly such, is undoubtedly the greatest work which the soul of man is capable to perform',[1] and criticism of epic was regarded as the most important branch of writing about literature. Yet the vast corpus of material on the subject of epic has tended to be dismissed in conventional accounts of the cultural landscape. Because no great epic poem was produced in the eighteenth century, the debates and discussion of epic technique have been regarded as an anachronism and relegated to the status of a curiosity.

This analysis of epic criticism will argue that writings on epic need to be given much greater prominence in accounts of the eighteenth century, and in particular in the story of the rise of the novel. We cannot comprehend the context in which novels were produced without some understanding of contemporary cultural expectations. We need to know what people wanted from their most important literary form, and what they felt their national literature should be doing. In many ways epic formed a standard against which the novel was measured and an understanding of eighteenth-century ideas of epic is therefore crucial in assessing the critical status of the fictional form.

In addition, the incorporation of epic into the story of the rise of the novel causes a substantial modification of the narrative. For although the rise of the novel has often been represented as a literary manifestation of bourgeois hegemony, it is clear that this was not the straightforward process that has sometimes been supposed. The novel gradually replaced the epic as the form which embodied the self-image and aspirations of a developing society, but many of the problems faced by the novelists resulted from their desire to incorporate the values and

functions of the old epic genre, as much as from the need to represent
new systems of perception. The image of the novel as a form increasingly written by women, for women, reflecting the progressive feminisation
of the reading public, needs to be seen in the context of the persistence of
the patriarchal assumptions about the structure and the mimetic function of literature that are to be found within writings on epic. While the
novel was addressing a public that was sexually and socially diverse,
going beyond the narrow, masculine, political elite, the writers on epic
perpetuated a more restricted, civic humanist concept of the public
sphere, and continued to emphasise the importance of literature's connection with, and reflection of, this. Uncertainties over the appropriate
discourse for the analysis of society were therefore overlaid with anxieties over the literary form that was suitable for its portrayal.

The terms in which these anxieties were expressed provide an insight
into the critical and theoretical framework that shaped the novel form.
In the second half of the century in particular, writers on epic frequently
articulated the nature of the challenge that was posed to literary representation by the changing structure of society and the emergence of the
commercial economy. They therefore provide a significant formulation
of the eighteenth-century conception of the relationship between 'literature' and 'reality', and thus give an indication of how contemporaries
perceived the mimetic task which the novel ultimately inherited.

At the start of the eighteenth century there was a great expectation
that a monumental modern epic would be written, to rival the productions of classical Greece and Rome. Shaftesbury epitomised this optimistic mood when he wrote,

We are now in an age when Liberty is once again in the ascendant. And we are
ourselves the happy nation who not only enjoy it at home, but by our greatness
and power give life and vigour to it abroad. . . . 'Tis with us at present as with the
Roman people in those early days, when they wanted only repose from arms to
apply themselves to the improvement of arts and studies.[2]

Debate focussed on how such an epic could best be constructed –
whether by adherence to neoclassical rules of composition, or by following nature.[3]

As the decades went by, however, and nothing that could be described as a great nationalistic poem was produced, the terms of the
discussion began to change, as critics considered not how, but if, a
modern epic would be written, and if not, why not.

Richard Glover's *Leonidas* of 1737 epitomised the problems faced by modern writers of epic. The central character in the poem is a model of both public and private virtue, but his heroism is revealed in the willingness with which he sacrifices the latter to the former. Leonidas is a loving husband, father and friend, and when called upon to give up his life for the sake of his country, he feels some reluctance

> To forsake
> Eternally forsake [his] weeping wife,
> [His] infant offspring, and [his] faithful friends.[4]

But these regrets are instantly repressed as he summons up his public spirit:

> Leonidas awake! Shall these withstand
> The public safety? Lo! thy Country calls.
> O sacred voice, I hear thee! At that sound
> Returning virtue brightens in my heart;
> Fear vanishes before; Death receive
> My unreluctant hand, and lead me on.[5]

This appeal to public virtue had a direct political purpose, for Leonidas represents a country party hero, who gives up his life in order to save the state from the corrupt and tyrannical power of Xerxes and the Persians, symbolising Sir Robert Walpole and the Court administration.[6] But beyond this political allegory, the model of public virtue had little relevance in a complex and interdependent commercial state. In a society based on the division of labour, in which the defence of the country had become the duty of professional soldiers, there was no call for the exertion of that heroic virtue which Leonidas exemplified. The only virtue which existed in such a system was the private duty of fulfilling one's personal responsibilities, and carrying out a specialised and limited professional role. And in the commercial ethics of Mandeville's *Fable of the Bees*, or the early economic tracts, this duty could be extended to include the indulgence of the self in the consumption of unnecessary goods that would stimulate trade and promote the circulation of money. Yet even the more austere and moral ideas of individual duty were totally alien to the epic conception of heroism.

The public role embodied by Leonidas was unnecessary within a complex state, and as an entirely masculine ethic it was also irrelevant to an increasing proportion of the reading public. The celebration of martial and military abilities, and the associated denigration of private affections, were alien to the majority of men as well as women readers, in a society that was increasingly emphasising the domestic role and responsibilities of the individual. David Hume and Adam Smith had identified benevolence and sympathy as the fundamental human qualities – but these were not the virtues associated with epic heroes. John Dennis argued that it was not essential for an epic hero to have qualities such as piety, honesty, fidelity and modesty provided he was fired with courage and patriotism, since 'Publick Virtue makes Compensation for all Faults'.[7] Sir Richard Blackmore argues in the preface to his epic poem *Prince Arthur* (1695) that in heroic verse 'the Action must be *Illustrious* and *Important*: Illustrious in respect of the Person, who is the Author of it, who is always some *Valiant* or *Wise* or *Pious* Prince or great Commander: but let his Character be what it will in other respects (for there is no Necessity the *Hero* should be a good or a wise Person) 'tis always necessary he should have *Courage*'.[8]

The epic writers were therefore faced with the problem of constructing a unifying nationalistic literature, in a form which prioritised a different ethical system, and was predicated on a different gender basis and social structure, from the state they aspired to represent. Epic began to be used to castigate rather than celebrate the contemporary system. The shortcomings of modern society could be gauged by the extent to which it fell short of the epic model. Moreover, the criticism of epic increasingly developed into a discourse of social analysis, as critics compared classical and contemporary society, to identify those aspects of the modern state which impeded literary production. Thomas Blackwell wrote in his *Enquiry into the Life and Writings of Homer* (1735) that '*our private manners* . . . admit not such [epic] representation, nor will our mercenary wars and state intrigues receive the stamp of *simplicity* and *Heroism*'.[9]

In the preface to his heroic poem *Gondibert* (1650), William Davenant justified the location of his work in the past rather than the present by reference to the non-epic nature of modern society, and in particular to the divisions and factions which disrupted or obscured the interests of the public:

Me thinks Government resembles a Ship, where *Divines*, *Leaders* of *Armies*, *Statesmen*, and *Judges* are the trusted Pilots, yet it moves by the means of winds as uncertain as the breath of Opinion, and is laden with people, a Fraight much loosser and more dangerous then any other living Stowage, being as troublesome in fair weather as Horses in a Storm. And how can these Pilots stedily maintain their Course to the Land of Peace and Plenty, since they are often divided at the Helm?[10]

These words would have had a special significance for the readers of the eighteenth century, for they represent an ironic paraphrase of a famous passage of Aristotle's *Politics*. Aristotle compares the citizens within a commonwealth to the sailors on a ship. Each of them has a different function 'for one of them is a rower, another a pilot, and a third a look-out man' etc., but:

They have all of them a common object, which is safety in navigation. Similarly, one citizen differs from another, but the salvation of the community is the common business of them all.[11]

The departure of modern society from this classical ideal has made it unsuitable for representation within epic, and at the same time has made epic irrelevant to it.

For Sir William Temple it was the increasing affluence of society and the spread of the desire of wealth that caused the decay of modern learning. In particular Temple blamed the expansion of trade, and 'the Discoveries and Plantations of the West Indies, and those vast Treasures that have flowed in to these *Western* parts of *Europe* almost every year'.[12] As a result of this increase in commerce the ethos of honour has been replaced by a spirit of acquisition, to the detriment of both individual morality and literary achievement. Like many of his contemporaries, Temple was convinced that success in all realms of human endeavour was dependent on the maintenance of the manners and primitive simplicity of the people, and this required the avoidance of all forms of economic growth. For

Where few are rich, few care for it; where many are so, many desire it; and most in time begin to think it necessary. Where this Opinion grows generally in a Countrey, the Temples of Honour are soon pulled down, and all men's sacrifices are made to those of Fortune . . .

Now I think that nothing is more evident in the World than that Honour is a much stronger principle, both of Action and Invention, than Gain can ever be.[13]

Thus 'Tis no wonder . . . that Learning has been so little advanced since it grew to be mercenary, and that Progress of it has been fettered by the cares of the World, and disturbed by the Desires of being Rich or the fears of being Poor.'[14]

Thomas Blackwell in his *Enquiry into the Life and Writings of Homer* argued that poetry flourished in ancient Greece because at this time the state was free from the vices of the 'Desire of Riches' and 'the Love of Pleasure'. As society grew more materialistic, the increasing division of labour ensured that the citizens became highly specialised and limited. This rendered them inherently incapable of that breadth of vision which was a prerequisite of poetic composition, and which was natural to the integrated individuals of the primitive community:

Whoever confines his thinking to any *one* Subject, who bestows all his Care and Study upon *one* Employment or Vocation, may excel in that; But cannot be qualified for a Province that requires the *freest* and *widest* as well as the most simple and disinterested views of Nature.[15]

John Brown in his *Dissertation on the Rise, Union, and Power, the Progressions, Separations, and Corruptions, of Poetry and Music* (1763) located the decline of poetry and music in the process by which poetry ceased to have a central cultural function, and came to be a specialised art. From being the product of a warrior statesman, enshrining the history, fables and legislative principles of a primitive society, epic poetry was progressively marginalised, until it became 'the *languid Amusement* of the *Closet*', 'studied and attained only by the *sequestered Few*, who were swallowed up by literary Application . . . and little acquainted with Society and Mankind'.[16] Alexander Gerard's *Essay on Taste* (1759) argued in a similar vein that involvement in the production of wealth had become an obstruction to the cultivation of taste. Those who are 'devoted to the exercise of reason, the gratification of appetite, or the pursuits of gain, are', he claimed, 'perfect strangers to the satisfactions or uneasinesses of taste; they can scarce form any idea of them'.[17] This is the opposite of Hume and Smith's argument that the division of labour encouraged the development of the arts by enabling a specialised elite to devote themselves to study and thought.[18] The writers on epic did not believe that literature should result from the lucubrations of the sequestered few, but from active engagement in the varied realms of human endeavour.

The persistence of epic writers, despite the manifest inapplicability of their social model to the community in which they wrote, indicates the absence of a widely accepted code of commercial morality which could challenge the civic humanist paradigm. The separation of the discourses of economics and moral philosophy in the course of the eighteenth century ensured that there was no culturally central genre which could define the nature of the social system, and could provide an image of society which presented its structure as a collection of generally accepted moral mechanisms. The economists analysed social processes and individual actions in terms of their impact on the whole of the polity, but the resultant ethics conflicted with traditional moral standards, and in particular with the feminised private domestic virtue which was increasingly cultivated by the bourgeoisie. The enthusiasm for epic in the early eighteenth century was symptomatic of the desire of many members of the literary establishment to construct a model of the state which was fully invested with masculine ethical values.

The concept of public virtue which was propagated in the eighteenth century basically represented the celebration of physical strength, bloodthirsty valour and the disavowal of personal ties. The continuing appeal of this concept, and the repeated references to public virtue as an indictment of modern society, indicates not so much the brutality of the cultured classes, as their reluctance to accept that separation of social and moral experience which was represented in the discursive divide between economics and moral philosophy. The development of distinct standards, genres and terms for the assessment of personal and social behaviour epitomised the way in which the commercial system had broken the ties between the individual and the community. It was therefore to some extent in reaction to the social implication of the private vices–public benefits paradox that the writers on epic eulogised a social model which was based around the existence of a barbaric public virtue.

There were a number of writers on epic who recognised the irrelevance of the traditional martial form to contemporary society, and attempted to develop a more modern and innovative kind of epic poetry and epic hero. Joseph Trapp suggested in his *Lectures on Poetry* (1742) that the modern poet should not 'think it essential to an Heroic Poem to describe the Anger of some great General, the Return of a King to his own Country, a Colony transplanted from one Region to another . . . or a Hero furbish'd with Celestial Armour'.[19] After the failure of his military heroes, Sir Richard Blackmore, in his *Alfred*, attempted to construct a philosophical epic around a character who embodied the civilised and civilising virtues. But *Alfred*, like Blackmore's other poems, was not popular, and was not regarded as a successful modern epic. The problems of creating a character who could represent a diverse society led Blackmore to endow his heroes with an air of mysticism that provided a kind of symbolic universality, but this universality ensured that the characters lacked individuality and so failed to have any universal appeal.

It was not only the absence of public virtue and martial valour which ensured that modern society was not suitable for portrayal within epic. As many writers recognised in the mid-eighteenth century, epic poetry was developed and perfected in societies which were both individualistic and rigidly hierarchical. The whole structure of the form was therefore manifestly unsuitable for the stratified but interdependent societies which resulted from the development of a complex commercial economy. Epic not only presented a hierarchical social system, dominated by the hero and his moral or military elite, but was a form that was entirely addressed to an elite. This is made absolutely clear in Davenant's preface to *Gondibert*:

> I may now beleeve I have usefully taken from Courts and Camps the patterns of such as will be fit to be imitated by the most necessary men; and the most necessary men are those who become principall by prerogative of blood, which is seldom unassisted with education, or by greatnesse of minde, which in exact definition is Vertue. The common Crowd, of whom we are hopelesse, we desert, being rather to be corrected by laws, where precept is accompanied with punishment, then to be taught by Poesy; . . . Nor is it needfull that Heroick Poesy should be levell'd to the reach of Common men.[20]

This elitist attitude to both society and the reading public indicated the model of the function of literature which was posited within epic verse. The epic genre was based on a form of didacticism which gave little credit to the discriminatory abilities of even those most necessary men to whom it was addressed. Perhaps in part in reaction to the prevalence of satirical and negative moral poetry in the eighteenth century, the epic writers sought to convey their moral theme by the representation of virtue. The hero personified the aspirations of society in his exemplary behaviour, as well as in his success in the many fields of human endeavour. Thus the readers of *Gondibert* were exhorted to imitate the 'patterns' and adhere to the 'precepts' presented, and although Milton's *Paradise Lost* was regarded by many as a more or less successful English epic, the attempts to make it conform to Aristotelian rules ensured that in many accounts of the poem its originality was either suppressed or ignored. For epic theorists continued to stress the importance in life and literature of the great and moral man who could serve as a model for the rest of the people to imitate. They did not consider the literary and social potential of Milton's weak and fallible hero, who was endowed with a universality because he united the reading public in identification with and sympathy for his weakness. It was not so much the religious philosophy of *Paradise Lost* as the attempts to interpret it in terms of classical epic which led to the suggestion that Satan was the martial hero of the work, and to the widespread acceptance of Blake's assertion that Milton was 'of the Devil's party without knowing it'.[21]

The writers of epic reacted to the apparent complexity of society by creating not only an elitist social model, but an aesthetic theory that was both elitist and reactionary. Far from propagating a subjective or consensual concept of taste, the form of the epic, whether strictly formal or otherwise, denied any participatory or evaluative role to the reader. Thus while the mercantile models of capitalising society were resisted by the survival of concepts of classical morality, so the persistence of epic theory provided a challenge to both the increasingly meritocratic social system and the developments in literary criticism which were leading to the articulation of a subjective idea of taste. While the novel was involving the reader in the construction of its plot, and the evaluation of its moral themes and characters, the writers on epic were continuing to produce their exemplary heroes and heroines, to be admired and imitated by the humble subject readers.

The influence and importance of reactionary concepts of literature are revealed in the extraordinary persistence of the neoclassical terms of interpretation. For although many writers from the early eighteenth century stressed the importance of imagination in literary creativity, the neoclassical tradition was maintained by a significant body of critics throughout the century. Writers continued to appeal to the classical rules and theories, and the preface to John Ogilvie's epic *Britannia*, written in 1801, is as Aristotelian as that to Richard Blackmore's *Prince Arthur* of 1695.

The significance of this survival has received little attention from historians of literary criticism. Writers such as René Wellek[22] and H. T. Swedenberg[23] describe the neoclassical attitudes as dissolving by the mid-eighteenth century into a form of emotionalism and sentimentalism which paved the way for the emergence of romantic criticism. But it is important not to underestimate the degree to which the maintenance of neoclassical tenets challenged the more 'bourgeois' critical theories of taste and response which developed in the course of the eighteenth century. The concept of rules of literary creation disrupted the idea of literary consensus which a number of critics have seen as the corner-stone of eighteenth-century literary theory.[24] The reliance on inherited formulae indicated a lack of faith in a distinct and coherent public, with accepted aesthetic assumptions. It revealed a dependence on classical rules and precepts to provide a means of interpreting modern literature and representing modern society. The neoclassical literary theory was therefore based on an ahistoricity which was in contrast to the recognition of social process which began to develop in the eighteenth century, and which has been identified as a feature of bourgeois consciousness. Far from considering literature in terms of established standards of taste, and in terms of the nature of modern society, the neoclassical writers relied only on the orderings sanctioned by the past.

But while the neoclassical terms of interpretation continued virtually unchanged, there were considerable alterations in the way in which other writers were articulating the non-epic nature of the modern state. The critics of the late seventeenth and early eighteenth century had tended to use the image of the primitive and heroic society as the basis for a critique of the present. From the mid-eighteenth century, however, there was some moderation of the negative and minatory tone of this account. 'Primitivist' critics, such as Lord Monboddo, Alexander Gerard, William Duff, James Beattie, James MacPherson, Lord Kames, Adam Smith, Hugh Blair, Adam Ferguson and David Hume used the distinction between epic and civilised communities to provide a model of both social evolution and the development of literary form. The characteristic elements of epic writing, such as the figurative language, the simplicity of style, and the legislative function, were used to illuminate the distinction between the past and the present, rather than to display the superiority of the former to the latter. These writers constructed histories of human society which connected the succession of artistic styles with the evolution of the polity. John Ogilvie, for instance, described the different literary genres which were appropriate for different kinds of state,[25] and Richard Hurd, in his *Letters on Chivalry and Romance* argued that the similarity between Gothic and epic literature was the consequence of the similarities between the political condition of ancient Greece and that of feudal Europe.[26] Thomas Blackwell even suggested that the form of language was dependent on the social structure:

Whoever reflects upon the Rise and Fall of States will find, that along with their Manners, their *Language* too accompanies them both in their Growth and Decay. Language is the Conveyance of our Thoughts; and as they are noble, free and undisturbed, our Discourse will keep pace with them both in its Cast and Materials.[27]

The recognition of the irrelevance of epic represented not only an eschewal of the ethos of public virtue, but also a realisation that the function of literature must be to represent rather than to resist social change. Society was seen as anti-heroic, but this led to a rejection of the epic form, rather than of the social system. It was not without regret that they noted the demise of epic innocence, but they did not regret the material benefits which had speeded its passing. As Richard Hurd wrote in his *Letters on Chivalry and Romance*, 'What we have gotten by this revolution . . . is a great deal of good sense . . . What we have lost is a world of fine fabling'.[28] And in his *History of English Poetry* Thomas Warton recognised that 'Ignorance and superstition, so opposite to the real interests of human society, are the parents of the imagination.' Therefore, although the modern world has gained 'much good sense, good taste and good criticism' it is with some sorrow that he accepts that 'we have lost a set of manners, and a system of machinery, more suitable to the purposes of poetry than those which have been adopted in their place. We have parted with extravagancies that are above propriety, with incredibilities that are more acceptable than truth, and with fictions that are more valuable than reality.'[29] The primitivist writers revealed the inapplicability of epic to the modern world, but some also suggested that their society was unsuitable for representation within any literature. The social structure had become unpoetic. 'As the world advances . . . men . . . form their manners upon one uniform standard of politeness and civility. Human nature is pruned according to method and rule.'[30] Other writers looked for a different literary form which could be used to explore this civilised society, and many pointed to the novel as an eighteenth-century version of the epic. In the following section I will examine the criticism that was generated by the attempt to evaluate the nascent novel form in terms derived from the analysis of epic.

EPIC STANDARDS AND NOVEL CRITICISM

Georg Lukacs has identified a connection between the historical and economic condition of a state and the form of its dominant literary genre. He writes in *The Theory of the Novel* that,

The epic and the novel, these two major forms of great epic literature, differ from one another not by their author's fundamental intentions, but by the given historico-philosophical realities with which the authors were confronted. The novel is the epic of an age in which the extensive totality of life is no longer directly given, in which the immanence of meaning in life has become a problem, yet which still thinks in terms of totality.[31]

The novel is the appropriate form for an age which has lost the explicability of primitive society, yet which still desires to make sense of the world. Many eighteenth-century critics, however, were reluctant to embrace the disjunction between the epic and the novel, with all its implications for the nature of modern society, and attempted to interpret the novel in terms of the neoclassical standards derived from epic criticism. This departure from classical precedent was justified on the grounds that *epic* was only an adaptation of the Greek word for discourse, and so need not refer exclusively to heroic poetry. Henry James Pye, in his *Commentary Illustrating the Poetic Works of Aristotle* (1792), claimed that when Aristotle refers to the art which imitates by language alone, his term *epopoea* can be legitimately translated as referring to any work in prose or verse.[32] He therefore comments on *Tom Jones* as an example of Aristotelian formalism, and in particular points to its adherence to the unities of action and time.[33] In his essay 'On Fable and Romance' James Beattie wrote of *Amelia*:

Since the days of Homer, the world has not seen a more artful epic fable. The characters and adventures are wonderfully diversified, yet the circumstances are all so natural, and rise so easily from one another, and cooperate with so much regularity in bringing on, even while they seem to retard the catastrophe, that the curiosity of the reader is kept always awake, and instead of flagging grows more and more impatient as the story advances.[34]

There is, however, a certain irony in the persistence with which the eighteenth-century writers upheld the tenets and criteria of a literary form which had been rejected because of its manifest inapplicability to modern society. Richard Graves, in the postscript which precedes *The Spiritual Quixote*, satirised the incongruity of assessing the trivial and recreational form of the novel on the basis of the rules derived from the serious epic genre. In delineating one of a series of fictions about the origins of his text, he made a covert reference to Horace's apophthegm that even Homer nods occasionally:

Having written the following Tale for my winter-evenings amusement; when a *weakness in my eyes* would not permit me to read: and being conscious that I have transgressed, in several instances the strict rules of epopoea; I was deterred from publishing it by a sett of *censorious Christians*, lately started up, called *Reviewers*; who will not suffer a man to nod in his elbow-chair, without giving him a jog; nor to talk nonsense without contradicting or ridiculing him.[35]

The location of the incongruity of neoclassical novel criticism in the difference in status of the epic and the novel form indicates the reluctance with which the eighteenth-century writers embraced the social implications of the development of the novel. Prose fiction was identified as a low status genre, because it did not represent the heroic and masculine public virtue that was the essence of epic literature, but instead portrayed a system of morality that was private, domestic and often feminine or feminised. This is made clear in the anonymous *Critical Remarks on Sir Charles Grandison, Clarissa and Pamela* of 1754. The pamphlet is basically a damning attack on Richardson's work, and on the novel form as a whole, in which the plot and characters of *Pamela*, *Clarissa* and *Grandison* are measured against the standard of Homeric epic. Despite the generally unfavourable tone of this comparison, the author draws a striking parallel between *Clarissa* and *The Iliad*. *The Iliad* conveys the moral that 'discord among chiefs or allies engaged in a confederacy, ruins their common designs, and renders them unsuccessful' while 'concord and agreement secure them prosperity in all their undertakings'. *Clarissa*, on the other hand, shows 'the bad consequences of the cruel treatment of parents towards their children, and forcing their inclinations in marriage; and . . . the pernicious effects of a young lady's reposing confidence or engaging in correspondence with a man of profligate and debauched principles'. The author concludes that he cannot 'at present recollect any composition which, viewed in this light, can be compared with the Iliad and Clarissa. The morals of the first are of the utmost importance in public life, and those of the last in private life.'[36]

This statement does little to negate the general indictment of Richardson's work expressed within the pamphlet. *Clarissa* may be a good exposition of the nature of private morality, but this is represented as a very inferior achievement to the inculcation of 'patriotism, the love of a country, and other public and private virtues' which is the true function of literature.[37] The author suggests that the moral weakness of the novel was in part a consequence of the general degeneration of the economic and political system:

The pride of wealth in the Harlow family, and the pride of titles and descent in the Lovelace family, can no where be found, save in a monarchical and commercial state, where there is a hereditary noblesse, and a great inequality among the fortunes of the citizens. Neither can such characters as Lovelace and his associates . . . display themselves . . . any where but in a city like London, the overgrown metropolis of a powerful Empire, and an extensive commerce.[38]

The suitability of the private novel form for the representation of modern society symbolised, for many writers, the corruption of the commercial state. The maintenance of the patriarchal terms and criteria

of epic criticism in the interpretation of the novel enforced their disap-
probation of both the new literature and the new commercial morality.
As late as 1814 the novelist Mary Brunton complained to her friend Mrs
Izett of the general refusal to take novels and novel writing seriously.
'Why', she lamented,

> Should an epic or a tragedy be supposed to hold such an exalted place in
> composition, while a novel is almost a nickname for a book? Does not a novel
> admit of as noble sentiments – as lively description – as natural character – as
> perfect unity of action – and a moral as irresistable as either of them?[39]

Francis Coventry, in the dedication of *Pompey the Little*, appealed to
Henry Fielding Esquire along similar lines:

> Can one help wondering . . . at the contempt with which many people affect to
> talk of this sort of composition? They seem to think it degrades the dignity of
> their understandings, to be found with a novel in their hands, and take great
> pains to let you know that they never read them. They are people of too great
> importance, it seems, to misspend their time in so idle a manner, and much too
> wise to be amused.[40]

Such protestations almost become a convention in the eighteenth century, but they indicate the problematic status of the novel in the period,
since the novelists feel it is necessary to defend and justify the form. For
Fielding the novel was ostensibly a natural successor to the epic, yet his
concept of the 'comic Epic-poem in Prose'[41] represents at once an
acceptance and an ironic rejection of the traditional terms of critical
analysis. Fielding exploits the terminology of the hierarchy of genres in
order to describe a type of literature which, in its form as well as its
novelty, challenged the basic premises on which the hierarchy was
based. Despite the appeal in the preface to *Joseph Andrews* to the *Margites*
of Homer,[42] the comic Epic-poem in Prose, or the 'prosai-comi-epic'[43]
was not one of the forms recognised by classical and neoclassical writers
on literature. The name Fielding coins for his genre represents an
amalgam of literary terms which the critical orthodoxy defined as
essentially discrete.

   Comedy was thought to differ from epic as much as poetry from
prose, and the distinctions between these genres were identified within
critical theory as a literary corollary of social divisions within the
community. In his *Answer to Sir William Davenant's Preface before Gondibert*,
Thomas Hobbes suggested that the three types of poetry – the
Heroique, the Scommatique and the Pastoral – were based on the
divisions between the court, the city and the country, and many writers

followed Donatus in identifying the various literary genres as specific to the different strata of society. Epic and tragedy were regarded as the forms appropriate to the upper classes, comedy was for the middle classes, and as was explained in the 'Address to the Pit' of Mrs Weddell's *The City Farce* (1737), farce was the form appropriate to the tradesmen and artisans who were below the genteel merchants and squires who formed the audience for comedy. In Pope's *Dunciad* the emergence of the Empire of Dullness is heralded by a collapse of traditional genre distinctions, wherein 'Tragedy and Comedy embrace' and 'Farce and Epic get a jumbled race'.[44]

In representing the novel as just such a generic jumble, Fielding satirised the taxonomic obsession of a critical tradition which had tended to be hostile to the development of prose fiction, and emphasised the inapplicability of neoclassical terms to the analysis of the novel. But to a readership familiar with the eighteenth-century debates over the form and function of epic poetry, his ludicrous nomenclature may also have implied something more. Given the tendency of the neoclassical critics to associate the generic and social hierarchy, the portrayal of the novel as a form destructive of conventional distinctions may have had social as well as literary connotations. In identifying his work as a comic Epic-poem in Prose, Fielding suggests that its scope will be broader than that of the various poetic genres, 'its Action being more extended and comprehensive; containing a much larger Circle of Incidents, and introducing a greater Variety of Characters' including 'Persons of inferior Rank'.[45] As such, it will address a much wider range of readers than the limited social groups addressed in poetry, encompassing 'readers of the lowest class' but also the 'upper graduates in criticism'.[46] The prosai-comi-epic therefore represented a considerable challenge to those neoclassical writers who identified literary genre as a means of reinforcing the hierarchical structure of society, and saw the collapse of the traditional distinctions in literary form as evidence of social degeneration. In the minds of many of the neoclassical critics, as in the bizarre world of *The Dunciad*, moral, political and literary decline were inextricably linked.

The prioritisation of epic by many of the critics of the eighteenth century has therefore had a crucial impact on the role and status of the novel. The association of prose fiction with the portrayal of a private and thus low-status system of morality led to a widespread denigration of the form. So that although the novel was in many ways ideally suited for the exploration of the commercial ethic and the complex society, many writers were extremely anxious to emphasise that the genre was not concerned with purely private virtue. They sought to legitimate their works through an invocation of the epic tradition, and instead of stressing the flexibility of the novel as a vehicle for the analysis of the moral complexity of commercial society, they presented the genre as a form which could be used to convey a rather inflexible system of precepts, derived from a simple model of the function of fictional didacticism. The theories of fiction that emerged in the eighteenth century were not purely generated from the experience of fashioning the new literary form, but rather resulted from the assimilation of this experience into a pre-existent model of the working, aspirations and social role of literature.

THEORIES OF FICTION

Richard Graves' novel, *The Spiritual Quixote*, opens with a 'Prefatory Anecdote by the Editor' which typifies the prefatory claims of eighteenth-century fiction. The editor describes how he went into an upholsterer's shop near Grub Street, and found the shopkeeper examining a letter-case. The man recounts how he had formerly rented a room to 'a jolly plump Gentleman, with a very serious Countenance'. Since this gentleman had a trustworthy, clerical look, he was entrusted with credit, but after six weeks decamped without paying his bill. The landlord was in hopes that the letter-case would contain something of value, but was disappointed to discover it held nothing but 'the manuscript of the following history'. The editor agreed to purchase this manuscript from the upholsterer, for the equivalent of six weeks' rent, thinking it might 'suit the taste of the present age: in which also the subject appeared by no means unseasonable'.[47]

The author distances himself from the manuscript by claiming to have acquired it from a third party, who in turn acquired it from the true writer. He can therefore imply that the novel is in fact a 'History', and simultaneously disclaim responsibility for the tale itself, and for the fiction of its truth. He is not the author but the 'Editor' of a manuscript whose true origins are uncertain. In other eighteenth-century novels the manuscripts are described as having been used to wrap candles in a chandler's shop, or as gun wadding, or just as having passed into the editor's hands by some undisclosed means. From reading the prefaces to the novels of the time, one gets the impression that it was impossible to live for long in eighteenth-century Britain without encountering the manuscript of some long-lost work of fiction or other.

Much has been made in recent criticism of the eighteenth-century novel of such claims for the reality or truth of fiction, and indeed attempts to explain the preoccupation with pseudo-verisimilitude have become something of a defining feature of the contemporary critical tradition. In Lennard Davis' *Factual Fictions*, Michael McKeon's *Origins of the Novel* and William Ray's *Story and History*, attempts have been made to explain why so many eighteenth-century writers devoted their prefaces to assertions that their works of fiction are actually not works of fiction at all, but accounts of real events which they, through a series of fortuitous events, have been able to present to the public after a few editorial interventions. Davis has related the claims to be both 'newe' and 'trewe' to the novel's origins in a prestructure of news-sheets and ballads. The early novel was both 'factual' and 'fictitious', and Davis suggests that this ambivalence served to mask the ideological and journalistic functions of the form.[48] McKeon sees the claims for the 'reality' of the texts as part of a process of transformation by which the romance incorporated anti-romantic elements[49] – a process which was related to concurrent literary and social transformations in the conceptualisation of the relationship between truth and fiction as society became increasingly secular. William Ray's study stresses the complexity of the relationship between 'story' and 'history' throughout the eighteenth century. He argues that

Freed from the limitations of factual fidelity, asssured of representing the biases of the culture it depicts by virtue of its own enclosure within that culture, the novel can formulate, analyse, and illustrate general paradigms of social interaction explicitly through its plot structure, at the same time that it exemplifies in its gesture of narration the conventions of communication and representation underlying such interactions. In other words, the eighteenth-century novel instantiates or stands for the culture it depicts; in this sense the novel can claim to 'be' history: it represents the system it represents.[50]

In this context, the bogus prefatory claims are interpreted as an attempt to deny the mediating role of the producer, and identify the narrative as a simple imitation of a pre-existent reality. They therefore constitute a negation of the actual complexity of the relationship between truth and fiction.[51]

In many cases, however, as in the preface to *The Spiritual Quixote*, the claims do not posit a clear historical origin and empirical validity for the text. Instead they serve to highlight and replicate the complexity of the process of narration, and of the relationship between history and fable. Graves' tale is identified as being of uncertain status. It is the work of an unknown hand, and its ultimate justification is 'that it might suit the taste of the present age'. The preface does not, therefore, make a simple claim for mimetic historicity, but rather draws attention to the complexity of the question of textual origins, and dramatises the distancing of the named author from the character of the authorial voice. This deliberate obfuscation of the narrative position reinforced the novel's occupation of a grey area between the public and the private realms. It is not given the stamp of private authenticity, because the 'Editor' cannot vouch for its validity or truth. On the other hand, while being a private tale to the extent that it is a narrative of individual experience, its circulation is legitimated not on the grounds that it represents the present age, but that it will suit the public taste. Its primary function is therefore identified as aesthetic rather than mimetic, public as well as private, and it can move between the realms of fable and history. *The Spiritual Quixote* and similar eighteenth-century novels exemplify Ray's basic thesis more distinctly than those novels which make a less equivocal claim for historical reality and which Ray seems to read straight, as genuine attempts to masquerade as history. Given the prevalence of complex and mischievous prefaces, from Defoe's claims in *Moll Flanders* onwards, I find it hard to believe that even more muted prefatory artifices are to be taken seriously. This is made clear in James Beattie's 'On Fable and Romance', of 1783, when Beattie states that 'The fabulist and novel-writer deceive nobody; because they do not even pretend that they are true; at least, what they may pretend in this way is considered only as words of course, to which nobody pays any regard.'[52] This does not preclude Ray's reading, but it suggests that what was going on assumed the participation of the reader in a game that involved exploiting the uncertain status of narrative fiction, and its location in the interstices between public and private, fable and history.

Thus in the face of the epic conception that literature was based on the portrayal of public experience and the articulation of invariable precepts, the use of a device by which fictions masqueraded as 'histories' may have provided a justification for the location of the genre in the ostensibly inferior realm of the personal. In suggesting that their material was fact rather than fiction, the novelists appealed to different – less elevated and more prosaic – critical standards from those conventionally applied to imaginative literature, and suggested that their work should be read in different terms from those derived from the classical genres, and in particular epic poetry. The 'Editor' of *The Spiritual Quixote* can justify the novel as a private history of uncertain status, and can distance the author from the desire to create a fiction, or to spread the tale of his own life, by the device of the discovery of a manuscript. But the readers are invited to be complicit in the fiction of the confusion of the forms.

These prefatory artifices tend to be a feature of the texts of male authors (Daniel Defoe, Samuel Richardson, Richard Graves, Henry Mackenzie, Henry Brooke) and are more rarely used by the female writers of the eighteenth century. Most women novelists either provide no preface at all, and get straight down to the story,[53] or they provide a preface which explicitly identifies the work as a fictional text. Mary Hays' *Memoirs of Emma Courtney* (1796), for example, is described as the 'production of an active mind, in a season of impression rather than of leisure',[54] and is located in the fictional tradition of Ann Radcliffe and William Godwin. This apparent avoidance of the convention of the playful preface may be a consequence of the female novelists' lack of interest in the kind of games with the narrative voice, and the playful exploitation of the uncertainty over the origins of the text, that were enjoyed by male writers. But it may also indicate the greater ease with which most women writers accepted the fictionality, but also the purely private status, of the narrative voice. The female novelists were prepared to let their texts stand as fictions, within a fictional tradition, or to adopt an appropriately deprecating tone, humbly recognising, while also ironically condemning, the lack of status of the novel. It is, on the whole, the male rather than the female texts of the eighteenth century which employ the repertoire of gaps, omissions and silences which have been identified in some feminist criticism with semiotic, poetic maternal discourse, while women writers adopt the more authoritative, rationalist and scientific symbolic discourse.[55]

In the prefaces of male writers, the assertions of historicity were not always consistently applied, and were often juxtaposed with rather different models of the nature of the novel form. Defoe's prefaces are often cited as examples of authorial claims for the truth of fiction, yet it is possible to discern a gradual alteration in the terms in which the role of fiction is defended. In the preface to *The Life and Strange Surprising Adventures of Robinson Crusoe* (1719) the authorial persona makes the claim that 'the editor believes the thing to be a just history of fact; neither is there any appearance of fiction in it'.[56] But in *The Farther Adventures of Robinson Crusoe*, published some months after the first part of the book,

the attacks on his veracity had led him to refine if not retract his claims
for the historical accuracy of the work:

The Just Application of every Incident, the religious and useful Inferences
drawn from every Part, are so many Testimonies to the good Design of making
it publick, and must legitimate all the Part that may be call'd Invention, or
Parable in the story.[57]

Defoe's work is no longer described as 'history', but instead is a 'parable',
the existence of which can be justified in terms of its 'good design'. In
shifting the grounds of his defence of his narrative from the assertion of
its truth to the emphasis on its moral purpose, Defoe is able to stress the
realism rather than the reality of his story. The claims are even more
complex in the preface to the *Serious Reflections During the Life and Surprising
Adventures of Robinson Crusoe* (1720). The narrative voice identifies itself as
Robinson Crusoe, stating that 'all those Parts of the Story are real Facts
in my History . . . Thus . . . the Thing rolling on my Bed, and my
jumping out in a Fright, are all Histories and real Stories'.[58] Elsewhere in
the preface, however, the narrative voice seems to diverge from the line
that the events actually happened to Crusoe, arguing that 'there is a Man
alive, and well known too, the Actions of whose Life are the just Subject
of these Volumes, and to whom all or most Part of the Story most directly
alludes'.[59] The irony of these words, ostensibly spoken by the fictional
character Crusoe, is reinforced by the assertion that 'this may be
depended upon for Truth, and to this I set my Name'.[60] So while the
fictional voice claims 'that the Story, though Allegorical, is also Historical',[61] the final justification for the text is based on its didactic rather than
simply its representational powers: 'here is the just and only good End of
all Parable or Allegorick History brought to pass, *viz*. for moral and
religious Improvement'.[62] The preface to *Colonel Jacque* (1722) asserts that
the novel form has a validity wholly independent of its historical function. Defoe claims that it is not 'of the least moment to inquire whether
the colonel hath told his own story true or not; if he has made a History
or a Parable, it will be equally useful, and capable of doing good &c.'

Defoe's concept of the prose parable represents a retreat from the
image of the novel as *vrai*, and is based on an idea of the role of
vraisemblance which emphasised the two qualities that, throughout the
eighteenth century, were regarded as the defining elements of the genre:
its moral message and its plausibility or 'truth to nature'. McKeon has
detailed how these qualities were increasingly taken to distinguish the
serious novel from the more improbable and morally misleading form of

the prose romance,[63] and although these concepts are often discussed in deceptively simple terms in eighteenth-century texts,[64] it is clear that the relationship between them was complex.[65] The fictional form was conditioned by the tension between moral and mimetic requirements, and when writers referred to 'truth to Nature', their words were often predicated on a Platonic rather than a purely realistic concept of representation. Representation could therefore be interpreted as incorporating moral elements, but as the preceding chapters have indicated, there was also considerable uncertainty over the basis for contemporary morality. There was a conflict between on the one hand a desire to explore and present the nature of the modern commercial state, and on the other an adherence to a more traditional system of anti-commercial values. The relationship between the representational and didactic roles of literature was therefore further complicated by an underlying uncertainty about what the didactic structure ought to convey. With the questioning of how literature could present moral precepts that was consequent on the failure of the epic genre, the whole issue of the relationship between literature and morality was fraught with difficulties and doubts.

For many novelists and some critics the probability of the novel was the source of its moral as well as its aesthetic power. Hugh Blair claimed that 'fictitious histories . . . furnish one of the best channels for conveying instruction, for painting human life and manners, for showing the errors into which we are betrayed by our passions, for rendering virtue amiable and vice odious'.[66] Yet this view was strongly countered by one which drew on a different image of the role of literature within modern society. Many critics argued that the realism and probability of the novel form could disrupt its didactic function, for the mimetic requirement to portray vice as well as virtue could lead to a glorification of sin which would render it attractive to impressionable readers. Particularly pernicious was the tendency of novelists to portray what became known as 'mixed characters'.

The most well-known exposition of this view was Samuel Johnson's article in *Rambler*, 4, when he expressed his anxiety that

Many writers, for the sake of following nature, so mingle good and bad qualities in their principal personages, that they are both equally conspicuous; and as we accompany them through their adventures with delight, and are led by degrees to interest ourselves in their favour, we lose the abhorrence of their faults, because they do not hinder our pleasure, or, perhaps, regard them with kindness for being united with so much merit.[67]

Johnson's suggestion that the novel should represent 'the most perfect idea of virtue, of virtue not angelical, nor above probability . . . but the highest and purest that humanity can reach',[68] was developed by Henry Mackenzie in an article in the *Lounger*:

The reproach which has been sometimes made to Novels of exhibiting 'such faultless monsters as the world ne'er saw', may be just on the score of entertainment to their readers, to whom the delineation of uniform virtue, except when it is called into striking situation, will no doubt be insipid. But in point of moral tendency, the opposite character is much more reprehensible; I mean, that character of mingled virtue and vice which is to be found in some of the best of our Novels.[69]

Mackenzie upholds Johnson's emphasis on the moral function of fiction, even while recognising that this didacticism is liable to be at the expense of aesthetic achievement. Clara Reeve[70] and James Beattie,[71] too, identified a conflict between moral and aesthetic criteria, and emphasised the need for novelists to sacrifice the latter to the former. While the originality and much of the value of the novel was located in its ability to portray complex, sophisticated and realistic characters, and thus to embody the moral dilemma of modern society, some critics believed that the novelists should reject these aspects of their form and concentrate on the portrayal of simple characters embodying ideal virtue or abhorrent vice.

This view provides an interesting insight into the way that these writers believed that narrative should function and novels should be read. For although Wolfgang Iser's reception theory has stressed the active role of the reader in many eighteenth-century novels, and we have seen above the importance of the reader's complicity in the fictions concerning the origins of the narratives, these writers and critics are clearly assuming that the reader is utterly unable to make moral and thus literary judgements. He or she cannot distinguish good from bad within a contemporary context, and is expected to be wholly receptive, passive and unquestioning. This view may in part derive from the preoccupation with the preceptual function of literature that was a feature of neoclassical theories of epic, but it is also a consequence of the image of the readership of fiction. Johnson believed that novels were chiefly for

The young, the ignorant and the idle, to whom they serve as lectures of conduct and introductions into life. They are the entertainment of minds unfurnished with ideas, and therefore easily susceptible of impressions; not fixed by principles, and therefore easily following the current of fancy; not informed by experience, and consequently open to every false suggestion and partial account.[72]

Implicit in Johnson's words is a recognition that a large part of the novel's readership was female or middle class – made up of those who had been denied access to a sound classical education, with its tendency to furnish ideas and fix principles; who had no experience of the world; and who were liable to be fanciful and easily misled. Such a readership required sound and uncomplicated moral texts, providing clear models of virtue and vice, which could be followed without discrimination.

This view is endorsed with what appears to be a tinge of irony in the preface to *Le Sopha* by Claude Prosper Jolyot de Crébillon, fils, published in English translation as *The Sofa: A Moral Tale* in 1742. The narrative voice asserts that

Even if it be true that tales adorn the understanding, and that the knowledge or notions that we glean from them are both agreeable and sublime, it is dangerous to read nothing but books of this sort. Only those who are really enlightened, above prejudice, knowing the hollowness of science, realize how useful to society such books really are; and how much one ought to esteem, and even revere, those who have genius enough to invent them, and sufficient firmness of mind to devote their lives to making them, in spite of the stigma of frivolity which pride and ignorance have fostered upon this sort of writing. The salutary lessons such fables contain, the fine flights of imagination so often to be met with in them, and the ludicrous notions they always abound in, make no appeal to the vulgar; for these commend most what they least understand, while flattering themselves that they do so perfectly.[73]

The explicit rather than implicit nature of the references to the class perspective may result from the French origins of the text, but Crébillon's address to the readers is designed to forestall the criticism of the moral purpose of fiction that was a feature of both France and England. He accepts that reading such tales may be dangerous for some, but he ensures that anyone who fails to apprehend the 'salutary lessons' inevitably defines themselves as 'the vulgar', unable to provide a correct interpretation. This is ironic in the context of the content of his work. *The Sofa* is a moral tale in that it satirises the corruption of French aristocratic society, but it does so by providing a vivid representation of decadence, viewed from the perspective of the eponymous sofa. Thus it was clearly liable to accusations not only of 'frivolity', but also of a more active tendency to corrupt and deprave. In suggesting that the moral message can only be properly read by those who are 'really enlightened', the preface challenges the concept that fiction is primarily addressed to the uneducated mass and attempts to evade accusations that the work is a piece of salacious sensationalism.

   The preface reflects the active role that was in practice demanded of eighteenth-century readers, despite the rather dim view that was often taken of their abilities in the prefatory analyses. Tristram Shandy declared in the course of his *Life and Opinions* (1759–67) that

No author, who understands the just boundaries of decorum and good-breeding, would presume to think all: The truest respect which you can pay to the reader's understanding is to halve this matter amicably, and leave him something to imagine in his turn, as well as yourself. For my own part, I am eternally paying him compliments of this kind, and do all that lies in my power to keep his imagination as busy as my own.[74]

John Cleland noted in his review of Smollett's *Peregrine Pickle* in the *Monthly Review* that

Something in all productions of this sort must be left to judgment: and if fools have not the gift, and are sometimes, in such reading, hurt by the want of it; such a consideration surely says but little against works from benefitting by which, only fools are excluded, and even that is a misfortune to which nature has made them as insensible as they are incorrigible.[75]

These writers recognised that the reader had an important role in the construction of the narrative. The novel-reading public was represented as inherently discriminatory, part of the thoughtful elite, rather than the thoughtless mass. The pleasure of fiction was therefore located in a constant process of judgement and evaluation, rather than in the absorption of an inescapable moral lesson and the acceptance of this is manifested in the prevalence of irony in the works of mid-century writers such as Fielding. Ironic discourse is predicated on the assumption that the reader is able to discern the real sentiments behind the apparent meaning, and creates a sense that the reader is part of a cultural community, with a set of shared aims and values, and is capable of making responsible moral judgements. These novelists were therefore able to present the reader with the kind of mixed characters and complex moral issues which were identified as inherently immoral by advocates of a more autocratic relationship between text and reader. Their faith in the interpretative role of the public enabled them to see didacticism and representation as congruent rather than in conflict. As 'The Apology or A Word to the Wise' preceding *The Spiritual Quixote* puts it,

I can see no more harm in a Fable of this kind (if properly conducted) than in any other either mythological or parabolical representation of the truth. Nay, I am convinced that Don Quixote or Gil Blas, Clarissa or Sir Charles Grandison, will furnish more hints for correcting the follies and regulating the morals of young persons, and impress them more forcibly on their minds, than volumes of severe precepts seriously delivered and dogmatically enforced.[76]

The individual story conveyed within fiction, Graves suggests, is not only capable of enforcing a moral lesson, but is actually more effective at doing so than a work explicitly devoted to morality or religion.

But although many eighteenth-century novels were based on an assumption of a high degree of interpretative diversity, and a belief in the evaluative role and moral autonomy of the audience, there was no simple opposition between a reactionary critical establishment and a more liberal and progressive circle of creative writers. Many critics were themselves novelists, and many of the novels which in practice exploited the moral discrimination and integrity of their readership also contained either explicit authorial statements, or didactic structures, which indicated an overt adherence to an old-fashioned 'epic' concept of the exemplary and preceptual function of literature. In the uncertain moral climate of the eighteenth century, the conflict between opposing ideas of the moral role of fiction and of the nature of the reading public in the commercial state was manifested within individual narratives, as well as between different theorists.

The acknowledgement within the novel of the evaluative rather than purely receptive role of the reader was only in part a consequence of the novelists' identification of the changing nature of the reading public. In part it was the result of the location of the novel within the realm of private experience and private morality. This did more than just condition the terms of the overt ethic, for it was tied to the whole moral structure of the narrative. For the morality of the novel was not only private in the sense that it represented rather limited and personal virtues such as benevolence. It was also private in that its moral judgements were not based on the articulation of absolute and universal principles, but on the analysis of personal circumstances. Experience was the key to the moral structure of most of the novels of the eighteenth century, and this is particularly clear in those works which adapted the previous tradition of the picaresque romance.

In *Gil Blas* (1715–35, translated into English by Smollett, 1749) the hero is shown travelling about Spain and making his way by lying, tricking and cheating.[77] In the novels of Sarah Fielding, Henry Fielding and

Tobias Smollett, however, the picaresque hero is transformed. Instead of being active he becomes a largely passive character, who is continually cheated, tricked and deceived. It is knowledge of the world that is gained by the heroes of the novel in the course of their travels and adventures, rather than the wealth or power that is sought by their picaresque counterparts. This knowledge enables them to refine those private virtues which are clearly represented as the only morality possible for the essentially powerless individuals within the complex state. These at once picaresque and anti-picaresque novels indicate the importance of experience within the novel, but also illustrate the private nature of this experience.

At the end of most eighteenth-century novels the heroes are loaded with blessings – they marry the heroine and are usually awarded an immense fortune and/or a beautiful country estate. These benefits serve, however, only to supplement what is portrayed as the real reward of their sufferings – the sense of private virtue which has been gained through experience. The characters are represented as having learned from their adventures, so that at the end of their novels they can be shown to have become virtuous, even if they were vitiated at the start. Peregrine Pickle, on succeeding to his father's fortune,

Found himself immediately a man of vast consequence among his country neighbours, who visited him with compliments of congratulation, and treated him with such respect as would have effectually spoiled any young man of his disposition, who had not the same advantages of experience as he had already purchased at a very extravagant price.[78]

By the end of Fielding's novel, Tom Jones 'hath', we are informed, 'by Reflexion on his past Follies, acquired a Discretion and Prudence very uncommon in one of his lively Parts'.[79] The assertions of the novel writers that their form was essentially moral were therefore dependent on the role of experience in the inculcation of virtue, while the assertions that morality can only be inculcated by the representation of characters who are virtuous throughout indicates that the critical rejection of the interpretative abilities of the reader was tied to a refusal to embrace the didactic potential of the portrayal of experience. Indeed, this antipathy to experiential as opposed to preceptual ethics may explain some of the hostility to the model of morality presented in David Hume's *Treatise on Human Nature*, with its heavy emphasis on the importance of experience in moral choice.

The emphasis on experience, and on the personal circumstances which reveal moral truth, symbolised the purely private nature of the code of behaviour advocated within the novel, and as such challenged the traditional idea of literary didacticism based on patterns and precepts. The morality of the novel was not only inherently private but also had the experiential, *ex-post-facto* and exculpatory form which was at the heart of the system of individual behaviour propagated within economic analysis. Thus although the identification of a conflict between the representative and didactic functions of fiction was in part a manifestation of a general anxiety over the moral structure of complex society, it also represented a dramatisation of the contention between the progressive and reactionary impulses within the critical elite. The morality, the form and the relationship with its readers of the eighteenth-century novel were crucially dependent on the fact that the genre was dedicated to the portrayal of private feminised virtue and private experience. The refusal to recognise this didactic strategy resulted from the widespread rejection of the social role of private virtue, and of the cultural function of the economic rather than the moral terms of interpretation. The production of a novel form based around a moral and social perspective derived from economics, within a culture still highly prejudiced against the articulation of that perspective within elite discourse, ensured that there was no clear and systematic interpretation of the structure, mimetic methods, and complex moral function of the form, but also that many of the novels themselves embodied the contradictory attitude to the role of didacticism and experience.

PART TWO

Texts

CHAPTER 4

The mid-eighteenth-century novel

Daniel Defoe's *Robinson Crusoe* can be read as a classic study of individualistic, economic man. Isolated on his island, cut off from the 'cash nexus', Crusoe's activities reveal what man is able to achieve through labour, but also the extent to which the lives of Defoe's contemporaries depended on a complex interdependent system. As Crusoe works away at his pots and pans, his table, his bread and so on, he becomes increasingly proud of his small but self-sufficient economy. We are told that 'it was a great pleasure to me to see all my Goods in such Order, and especially to find my stock of all Necessaries so great'.[1] Yet at the same time the bizarre nature of the figure that Crusoe cuts, in his goatskin cap and floppy shoes, reinforces the distance between this primitive economy and the complex economic system. Crusoe can provide for his wants, but the extreme difficulty of doing so continually leads him to reflect on the advantages of the modern interdependent state:

'tis a little wonderful, and what I believe few People have thought much upon, (*viz.*) the strange multitude of little Things necessary in the Providing, Producing, Curing, Dressing, Making and Finishing this one Article of Bread.

I that was reduced to a meer State of Nature, found this to my daily Discouragement.[2]

Moreover, Crusoe is not actually in a state of nature. He is himself a capitalist to the extent that he recognises the importance of his 'stock' – the goods that he salvaged from the wrecked ship: 'I spent whole Hours, I may say whole Days, in representing to myself in the most lively Colours, how I must have acted, if I had got nothing out of the Ship.'[3] The complexity of Defoe's fiction is such that Crusoe is simultaneously a figure cut off from the cash nexus, and a paradigm of capitalist man.

Maximillian E. Novak has emphasised the importance of economic ideas in Defoe's work in his study *Economics and the Fiction of Daniel Defoe,*

but he argues against the interpretation of Crusoe as Homo Econ-
omicus. Novak suggests that far from being in favour of economic
individualism, Defoe attacks the concept, and particularly the desire for
extraordinary upward mobility and excessive profit:

> If any economic moral can be drawn from Crusoe's narrative, it is a conserva-
> tive warning that Englishmen about to embark on the economic disaster of the
> South Sea Bubble should mind their callings and stick to the sure road of trade.[4]

> By reminding his audience of Crusoe's failure to follow his calling, Defoe was
> directly attacking the economic mores of a society that was abandoning the
> trade ideas of mercantilism for those of *laisser-faire* and economic individual-
> ism.[5]

There is much in *Robinson Crusoe* and Defoe's other novels to substantiate
this reading, yet there is much that does not fit quite so neatly. Crusoe
condemns the economic system, but he is also a triumphant and upwardly mobile individual. His success, like that of Moll Flanders, is
ultimately measured in economic as much as spiritual terms in that his
material wealth both sanctions and facilitates his return to the community of society. He has defied his father and not minded his calling, and
he frequently repents of this action in the course of his 'sojourn' on the
island, yet at the end of the novel he is rewarded with precisely that
worldly prosperity which his spiritual experiences are supposed to have
taught him to despise. 'Oh money, thou drug' he exclaims, adapting the
biblical image. He nonetheless carefully hoards away the stores of gold,
even as he discourses on the fact that they have no value-in-use on the
island. Once he returns to the complex community of commercial
society, he can exploit their renewed value-in-exchange and use his
wealth to establish himself within the moral and economic system.

Perhaps in part because of these disjunctions, Defoe's writings have
always tended to generate critical conflict and while Maximillian Novak
has read the economic philosophy of *Robinson Crusoe* as an endorsement
of conservatism, Michael McKeon has identified the spiritual philosophy as a manifestation of progressive ideology. He has suggested that

> It is Defoe's remarkable achievement not simply to have provided ...
> psychological access to spiritual crisis but to have specified it, with the medi-
> ating guidance of Puritan casuistry and soteriology, to the concrete dimension
> of material and social ambition.[6]

Crusoe's physical mobility, his rambling disposition, is seen as having
stimulated spiritual reflection, which can ultimately justify social mobil-

ity. For William Ray, on the other hand, the conflict within *Robinson Crusoe* is between narrative strategies:

In his reconstitution of a system of authority and program of human endeavor to replace the culture he rejects, and then loses, Crusoe's story provides an allegory of how individualism that is essentially historical in its reliance on narrative strategies of self-representation can displace the paternalistic authority of the established order by internalizing the divine authority of providence, which that order claims to represent.[7]

Ray suggests that Crusoe seeks divine sanction for his own will, having offended the providential order through the assimilation of divine and paternal authority. The creation of his calendar and journal are crucial elements of this process, for they enable him to historicise himself, and construct a narrative which is able to bring out the providential design that is working within his life:

In that sense *Robinson Crusoe* can be read not just as an allegory of economic individualism and freedom, as Watt would have it, or as an allegory of suffering and salvation, as Defoe would later argue, but also as an allegory of the transition from a providential to an historical framework.[8]

The coexistence of Ray's, McKeon's and Novak's readings indicates that Defoe's fictions can carry a range of ideological constructions and defy simple categorisation. They do not present a single coherent spiritual, economic or philosophical message, but incorporate elements of commercial and anti-commercial morality, conservative and *laisser-faire* ideology, as well as the elements of spiritual biography which George Starr highlighted, and which McKeon has shown to be challenged and mediated by the text.[9] It is this juxtaposition of conflicting ideas that is most striking to readers of the novels, and while many critics have sought to provide a single coherent reading, the diversity of the resultant versions is a testament to the validity of the reader's initial response.

Grahame Smith in *The Novel in Society* has suggested that the conflict of ideas within Defoe's fiction is a consequence of his mimetic method:

Defoe the novelist – as distinct from Defoe the man, the essayist, the quasi-economist – has no considered view of human life because his novels are themselves disordered and internally inconsistent; form and vision are indissoluble ... the formal imperfections of Defoe and earlier Smollett are clear signs that their assimilation of the world is largely unconscious.[10]

Defoe and Smollett construct disordered novels, Smith suggests, because their works provide a simple reflection of a disordered world. Yet the source of the conflict and disorder appears to be generic as much as 'real', and a consequence of the eclecticism of the novel form rather than simply its mimetic nature, or the nature of the modern world. As writers such as John Richetti, Lennard Davis, Michael McKeon and J. Paul Hunter have shown, the novel drew on diverse and disparate forms of popular literature. Each of these presented a particular vision of the economic and social structure, and tensions existed between those which emphasised a code of morality based on the negation of materialism, and those which celebrated economic and individual progress – between, for example, the spiritual biography and the travel narrative. With the development of the novel at the start of the eighteenth century, and in particular in the work of Defoe, this conflict began to be articulated within, as well as between, literary genres. Defoe analyses the nature of the complex commercial state, and the kind of behaviour that is liable to ensure the success of the acquisitive individual within it, while at the same time presenting a religious philosophy which, despite Ian Watt's assimilation of Calvinism and capitalism,[11] is in many respects in conflict with the way his characters behave. In Defoe's terms, the novel's role as 'parable' clashes with its role as 'history'.

The representation of the workings of contemporary society implies one code of behaviour, while it is the novel's explicit didactic function to enforce another. This does not mean that one set of values undermines the other, and that we should privilege either the moral or the economic aspects of the texts. I think we should see Defoe's novels as embodiments of the terms and extent of the discursive divide of his time.[12] He represented the practical acceptance of the dominance of material interests in determining individual actions, but the theoretical adherence to a rather different set of values. He portrayed within fiction the moral disjunction which Mandeville displayed in *The Fable of the Bees*. But while Mandeville identified the conflict of values as a problem that should be resolved, Defoe merely presents it, without any moral or philosophical anxiety. The protean Defoe was well aware of the extent of the generic and disciplinary boundaries within literature and, as his varied writings show, embraced the philosophy that different forms demanded different terms of social analysis.

By the middle of the eighteenth century, however, the novel did not display such a relaxed attitude to the discursive disjunction. Charlotte Lennox's novel, *The Female Quixote* (1752), recognises the challenge posed to literary representation by the decline from heroic values, and indicates the ways in which the novel must adapt, in order to meet this challenge. In the following sections I will consider Samuel Richardson's *Clarissa*, Henry Fielding's *Tom Jones*, Charlotte Lennox's *Female Quixote* and Richardson's *Sir Charles Grandison* in order to assess how far these novels succeeded in bridging the gap between public and private, heroic and economic values, in order to provide a literature and a code of personal morality which was appropriate to a complex modern age.

CLARISSA

Samuel Richardson's massive *Clarissa: Or, The History of A Young Lady* is an epistolary novel largely based on the exchange of letters between two pairs of correspondents, Clarissa Harlowe and her friend Anna Howe, and Robert Lovelace and his friend John Belford. The deployment of this 'double yet separate correspondence'[13] helped obviate the narrative problems that Richardson had experienced with the construction of his earlier largely univocal epistolary text *Pamela: Or, Virtue Rewarded*, yet the gender balance that was to characterise the novel was not obvious at its first publication. When the first two volumes appeared on 1 December 1747, 91 of the 94 letters were between the female correspondents, the vast majority being from Clarissa to Anna. This exclusion of the male perspective ensured that the female view of Robert Lovelace was firmly established before readers were exposed to his own letters. Yet the effect of this refraction of Lovelace through girlish eyes was not quite what might have been anticipated. For all her opposition to loveless marriages, and her willingness to run away with unsuitable men, Clarissa is shown to be exceptionally prudent, and her presentation of Lovelace in the first two volumes is largely based on the prioritisation of the financial information that was likely to hold sway with her materialistic family.

Leslie Fiedler has identified the mythos of class struggle within *Clarissa*, with Lovelace embodying the aristocracy, in conflict with Clarissa, who is 'disconcertingly sexless in her bourgeois form'.[14] Yet in practice the class system presented in *Clarissa* is rather more complex than this kind of schematic model would suggest. While Lovelace is clearly an aristocrat, he is also endowed with the economic knowledge and financial acumen that are more usually associated with the bourgeoisie. Clarissa conveys the information

That he was a generous landlord; that he spared nothing for solid and lasting improvement upon his estate; and that he looked into his own affairs and understood them; that he had, when abroad, been very extensive and contracted a large debt ... yet he chose to limit himself to an annual sum and to decline equipage in order to avoid being obliged to his uncle and aunts ... His estate was never mortgaged, as my brother had heard it was; his credit was always high; and, he believed, he was by this time near upon, if not quite, clear of the world.[15]

Robert Lovelace is a man of pleasure, endowed with cavalier sexual mores and an aristocratic haughtiness of temper, yet he is not the reckless spendthrift that James Harlowe has represented him to be. He is an improving landlord, with an interest in economic matters, although his activities are portrayed as being primarily connected with agriculture and land rather than with finance and commerce. Moreover, even in relation to agricultural matters, Lovelace's mercenary motivation is moderated by a sense of paternalistic responsibility. Clarissa tells Anna Howe that

When ... my uncle had represented to him that he might, if he pleased ... make three or four hundred pounds a year of his paternal estate more than he did; he answered, 'that his tenants paid their rents well; that it was a maxim with his family, from which he would by no means depart, never to rack-rent old tenants or their descendants, and that it was a pleasure for him, to see all his tenants look fat, sleek and contented.' (pp. 78–9)

The values of Lovelace are clearly set up to form a contrast with the merciless acquisitiveness of the upwardly mobile Harlowes, ever anxious to extend their estates and consolidate their political interest. Lovelace remarks to his friend Belford 'Everybody knows Harlow Place – for, like Versailles, it is sprung from a dunghill within every elderly person's remembrance' (letter 34, p. 161), and Clarissa refers to 'the darling view some of us have long had of *raising a family*, as it is called ... A view too frequently, it seems, entertained by families which having great substance, cannot be satisfied without rank and title' (letter 13, p. 77). Anna Howe's observation to Clarissa that 'You are all too rich to be happy, child' (letter 10, p. 68) is prophetic in relation to Clarissa's fate, but also a significant comment on the position of the aspiring affluent classes within a society still dominated by a landed elite.

   Lovelace is juxtaposed with the physically repellent figure of Solmes who

Has but a very ordinary share of understanding, is very illiterate, knows nothing but the value of estates and how to improve them, and what belongs to land jobbing and husbandry. (letter 8, Clarissa to Anna Howe, p. 62)

An interest in improvement is seen, in the figure of Lovelace, as a sign of aristocratic responsibility, yet in Solmes it is a manifestation of a narrow and mercenary spirit. While Lovelace has old, contented tenants, Solmes is a 'land jobber', letting his land for the maximum financial return. He exemplifies the divorcedness of the new financial systems from the culture and values of the aristocracy. Clarissa condemns him as 'The *upstart man* ... for he was not born to the immense riches he is possessed of; riches left by one niggard to another, in injury to the next heir, because that other is a niggard' (letter 13, p. 81). Solmes' wealth has not been passed down in accordance with aristocratic principles of succession and this rejection of primogeniture symbolises his alienation from the conceptual framework of the social elite. Because his obsession with the accumulation of wealth is not sanctioned by aristocratic dynastic aspirations, based on the concept of stewardship for posterity, it is identified and can be vilified as a miserly desire for riches for their own sake. The contrast between Solmes and Lovelace therefore exemplifies the dependence of aristocratic mores on patriarchal notions of property and inheritance.

The principle of primogeniture has also been challenged in the Harlowe household, but here its abandonment has been brought about as a result of the disruptive power of Clarissa's virtue. While Clarissa's uncles have refrained from marriage to concentrate the wealth of the family on her brother James, her grandfather has departed from the normal process of succession to leave his estate to 'the precious child' Clarissa (letter 4, p. 53). Clarissa's own endorsement of the patriarchal economic system is manifested in her refusal to take control of her affairs, having 'given the whole into [her] papa's power' (letter 2, Clarissa to Anna Howe, p. 42), but it is ultimately only with her death that the traditional order is properly restored. When the distorting effect of Clarissa's virtue is removed, primogeniture can be re-established. In leaving her estate to her father in her will, Clarissa indicates her acceptance of the patriarchal system of property, even as she denies the right to exert the tyranny of gender within the private affective sphere.

Lovelace knows how to accrue wealth, but like Clarissa and unlike Solmes and James Harlowe, he also knows how to dispense it and his prudential concern can be validated by appeals to posterity. His aristocracy ensures that he has a very different set of values from the grasping Harlowes and the boorish Solmes, but he does not conform to the stereotype of the dissolute and feckless noble, embodied, for example, in the portrait of Viscount Squanderfield in Hogarth's *Marriage à la Mode*

(1745). The conflict represented in *Clarissa* is not a straightforward clash between an old-fashioned, decadent, aristocratic order, and a new, commercially minded, upwardly mobile middle class. Lovelace has adjusted to the economic requirements of the new commercial order, just as the Harlowes have, but he, like them, has yet to find a system of ethics that is appropriate to the modern age. His Machiavellianism is as inappropriate as the Harlowes' ruthless materialism, or Solmes' brutish insensibility, and one of the functions of the development of the plot is to lead to the articulation of a modern code of virtue that is ultimately accepted by everyone within the text.

Yet this virtue is not developed by Lovelace, as a result of his experiences, but is embodied by Clarissa. As such it is necessarily a feminised virtue, and thus transformed into a private and affective code, which may undermine but not negate the values exposed within the masculine world. Clarissa Harlowe, like Harriet Byron in *Sir Charles Grandison*, does not wish to enter the public sphere, and as the novel develops, and we become involved in the personal struggle between Lovelace and Clarissa, the public aspects of the conflict disappear. We hear less and less about Lovelace as an embodiment of the values of a modern aristocracy, marrying paternalism and prudence. We increasingly see him, through his own letters as well as Clarissa's, in satanic terms, as a villainous embodiment of individualism. In his persecution of Clarissa he represents the patriarchalism that characterises commercial and aristocratic society alike, which is opposed to the Christian virtue with which Clarissa subverts the dominant image of masculinity. Lovelace wishes to rape Clarissa in order to show that she is an ordinary sexual woman, not a sexless angel. He wants to reduce her to mortal status because her saintly character challenges his image of individualism as necessarily selfish and acquisitive. It is ironic that it is only when Clarissa has been raped that the true extent of her virtue emerges, and only after her death that the relevance of her Christian code can be generally accepted. So while Lovelace starts the novel as a member of the progressive aristocracy, endowed with a sense of public duty, he ends the novel as a manifestation of the moral bankruptcy of the phallocentric system of exchange, which draws its validity from the denigration of domestic virtue and female sexuality.

In the prelude to the rape, Lovelace satirically invokes 'my worthy friend Mandeville's rule, *That private vices are public benefits*' (letter 246, Lovelace to John Belford, p. 847). This reference to the bad boy of moral philosophy reinforces Lovelace's construction of himself as an unprincipled and Machiavellian villain, but it also represents a significant reorientation of the Mandevillian paradox. Lovelace's vice is not luxurious consumption, but the seduction of Clarissa, which he suggests will benefit the public by providing an example to others. His words ironically prove to be true – although not in the manner he anticipates – but they also locate the centre of moral debate in the sphere of sexual rather than economic exchange.

It is perhaps because the moral and social focus is progressively sexualised that few critics have made reference to the surprising similarity of the terms in which Richardson (through his correspondents) presents Lovelace and his male hero, Sir Charles Grandison. Both are aristocrats, paternalistic and improving landlords, and energetic young men, who seek to find an ethic that is an appropriate embodiment of masculinity within the modern age. For Lovelace, the irrelevance of the martial and heroic virtue of epic tradition leads to a displacement of energy into the field of sexual rather than military conquest.

In the face of the demise of the civic humanist concept of the public, Lovelace attempts to discover the limitations of the private and feminised ethos by forcing Clarissa into a role of subservience, in which she will accede to conventional codes and request marriage, to amend the loss of 'honour' that occurred in the rape. Yet Clarissa's rejection of marriage, and assertion of moral independence, signifies the distinction between her private Christian ethos, and the manners that characterise society in general. Private virtue is feminised in the course of the text, but the feminine is not identified as inherently virtuous.

Much of the modern criticism of *Clarissa* has tended to prioritise the private plot, yet the way that we read this is complicated by the uncertainty over the relationship between text and reader that is embedded in the novel form. This has received considerable critical attention following the revival of interest in *Clarissa* in the last decades of the twentieth century, and scholars such as William Beatty Warner, Terry Castle and Terry Eagleton have opened up and explored the concealed meanings and the subtext of the work, exploring its subversive implications.[16] William Beatty Warner has highlighted the importance of Richardson's text as the locus for the conflict between the language and utterances of Clarissa and those of Lovelace:

The textual field of *Clarissa*, with its intricate history, is like a vast plain where Clarissa and Lovelace, and their respective allies, and the two ways of interpreting the world they embody, collide and contend.[17]

A similar approach, from a different perspective, is utilised by Terry Castle who, in her compelling study *Clarissa's Ciphers: Meaning and Disruption in Richardson's Clarissa*, recognises the polyphonic nature of *Clarissa*, but also the multitude of conflicting voices that are activated by the process of reading.[18] This opening up of the diverse interpretations that can be put on the text leads to an emphasis on the nature and function of narrative:

Clarissa offers no 'story' in any conventional sense, but is concerned, on some level, with a problematization of the very notion of 'story' itself.[19]

But this in turn generates an exegesis of the 'politicosexual' dimensions of narrative, through the delineation of the conflicting political and ideological meanings that coexist within it. In this context, Castle indicates the way that language is used to ensnare, entrap and reinterpret Clarissa, as those around her continually put false constructions on her words, and expose the distance between meaning and intention:

Clarissa's experience is fundamentally tragic, but ... her tragic status is inseparable from her representation, within Richardson's fiction, as an exemplary victim of hermeneutic violence. Across the text, hers is that voice which repeatedly fails to make itself heard.[20]

Yet as Tom Keymer has indicated in his book, *Richardson's Clarissa and the Eighteenth-Century Reader*,[21] it is important to bear in mind the way that contemporary readers would have approached the text, and this necessitates consideration of its exemplary and didactic functions, as well as its elements of post-Lacanian subversion. J. Paul Hunter remarks in *Before Novels: The Cultural Context of Eighteenth-Century English Fiction* that

To read Sterne or Richardson without the didacticism is to read a deformed novelist, one missing crucial parts. It is easy enough to read any eighteenth-century novelist for something else and find the text palatable in spite of the unfortunate didacticism, but such selective reading is perverse and destines writers to a short life of fashion.[22]

But while we can attempt to replace the missing parts, and reassert intentionality as at least a component, if not a determining feature of the process of production of literary meaning, this does not solve all the problems with the text. Even the 'straight' reading involves the negation of considerable complexity, and a conflict of meanings and interpretations. Clarissa's story ostensibly emphasises the moral value of experience, and presents the kind of *ex-post-facto* morality associated with economics, yet this is juxtaposed with repeated suggestions that the purpose of the novel is the portrayal of an inflexible system of values. While the epistolary structure implies a high degree of readerly autonomy, the editorial interventions, particularly in the third and subsequent editions, are predicated on an assumption of a more authoritative role for the text, and a more narrow concept of the role of fictional didacticism.[23] As Richardson wrote in the jottings which R. F. Brissenden has compiled as 'Hints of Prefaces': 'Clarissa an Example *to* the Reader: The Example not to be taken *from* the Reader.'[24] This suggests an authorial desire to present an invariant and universal text, contributing to an inescapable moral lesson, but Richardson's caution reveals an anxiety about the possibility that this will not happen. He appears to recognise that the narrative might indeed function in more complex ways, and be inscribed with a diversity of significances derived from the readership. The reader is identified as a potential locus for meaning, while Richardson stresses that this is not the way the text should be read. There is therefore an awareness of the space which the epistolary form opens up for competing interpretations, and of the tension which exists between these diverse forms of readerly exegesis and the 'Editor's' claims for the authority of the text itself.

On the one hand, the epistolary form ensures that the reader is the most authoritative figure within the text. S/he has to construct the narrative by uniting the fragmented perceptions of all the other characters, and as such is far from the passive and powerless figure that John Preston suggests in his account of Richardson's work in *The Created Self*.[25] There is none of the authorial exploitation of the dependent role of the reader which characterised the narratives of Fielding, and no exploration of moral misapprehension or doubt, for the readers are unable to enter into the mistakes and uncertainties of the characters. The structure of the text implies that the omniscient reader is in a permanent position of judgement.

On the other hand, Richardson's writings reveal a belief that the novel should educate through the portrayal of exemplary virtue – an image of fiction which assumes that the role of the reader is as the passive subject of the text. The readerly authority implicit in the epistolary structure was therefore countered by the presentation of an exemplary virtue to which the reader was assumed to be subordinate, and which Richardson believed it was impossible to misinterpret. The fragmented perceptions all contributed to reinforce a single and inescapable moral lesson. Even Richardson's bad or fallible characters were designed to serve his moral purposes and to reinforce the example which was at the centre of the work. Lovelace continually enforces the moral theme of *Clarissa*, for although he constructs a language and code of behaviour which seeks to undermine the conventional system of morality, he does so in terms which indicate his appreciation of the system which he works to subvert. Lovelace and his friends are all represented as able to recognise the immaculate virtue of Clarissa. Lovelace constantly defines his own diabolic immorality in terms of Clarissa's purity,[26] and it is his recognition of her angelic quality which stimulates his desire to destroy it.

The divided perspectives of the diverse correspondents are unified in the identification of an ideal and feminised virtue. The moral scheme of the novel is represented as inherently consensual, requiring only the passive endorsement of the reader. In constructing the text from the fragments of the various letters, the reader is put in a position not so much to judge the disparate characters as to appreciate the unifying power of virtue. Letter after letter reinforces the moral theme, and the impression of moral coherence is emphasised by the prevalence of dramatic irony. Each of the different strands of correspondence manifests an independent system of morality. Only the reader is conscious of the degree of consensus, and the power of virtue is therefore revealed far more vividly than in a text wherein the presence of an omniscient narrator gives a contrived air to the articulation of universal moral truths. The epistolary form and the exemplary function of Richardson's novels imply that there is a simple and generally acceptable moral system which fiction can embody, and which will be recognised and supported by its readers. As such, Richardson's model of the relationship between text and reader denied the uncertainty over the modern image of virtue, but also the reality of the reception of his works.

The publication of *Pamela* elicited a highly favourable response, and a Pamela industry which Terry Eagleton has compared to the modern cult of figures such as Superman.[27] Yet there was also considerable criticism of the novel. Fielding was not the only writer to parody its prurience, its suppressed eroticism, and its implicit social message that a serving-maid needs only to hold on to her virginity to marry her master.[28] The numerous 'anti-Pamelas', burlesques and critical attacks provided ample evidence that literature did not represent a simple irrefutable moral lesson which was beyond dispute or misinterpretation.[29] The octogenarian Charles Povey railed against the immorality of *Pamela* in his *The Virgin in Eden* of 1742: 'Good God! Can amorous embraces delineated in these images, tend to inculcate religion in the

minds of youth, when the blood is hot, and runs quick in every vein?'[30]
Even in *Clarissa*, where Richardson's exemplary morality was most
clearly and explicitly displayed, there were various points which aroused
critical controversy. Richardson was particularly disturbed by the tendency of his female readers to admire the character of Lovelace, and by
the discussions of the extent of Clarissa's culpability. How much was she
to blame for carrying on a secret correspondence with Lovelace? And
should she have seen through the trick which forced her to go away with
him?

It was in order to provide an irrefutable answer to these debatable
points that Richardson wrote his various prefaces and postscripts, and
the innumerable notes, revisions and additions to the text. There is
nowadays considerable confusion over which of the many editions of
Richardson's works to use, and this is a consequence of his lifelong
struggle to resist interpretative diversity. It was not purely an obsessive
perfectionism that led him to bring out revised edition after revised
edition of his novels, and continually to amend and extend and revise
them, but rather a belief that he must ensure that his readers receive a
true impression of the moral message of his work. Each didactic point
had to be clarified and emphasised in order to prevent the development
of false and immoral readings. As Terry Castle has indicated, this
inability to let the text stand represents a refusal to recognise the fatal
implications of this new fictional form for the persona of the author:

There is a posthumous quality to the editorial additions to *Clarissa* – a belated-
ness that is felt by the reader. By virtue of the epistolary form itself, Richardson
the author is dead to us, and the ghostly presence of Richardson the 'Editor'
cannot take his place.[31]

Richardson's anxiety over interpretative diversity led him to emphasise the need for fiction to portray exemplary moral lessons, and avoid
the representation of those 'mixed' characters which might be difficult
to evaluate. Yet Richardson's attempts to eliminate all scope for misinterpretation inevitably ensured that his novels prioritised the representation of exemplary virtue above the realism which he felt was necessary to
enforce the message of his story. He emphasised the importance of the
blend of realism and idealism in the author's preface to the third edition
of *Clarissa*:

The principal of these two young ladies is proposed as an exemplar of her sex.
Nor is it any objection to her being so, that she is not in all respects a perfect
character. It was not only natural, but it was necessary, that she should have

some faults, were it only to show the reader how laudably she could mistrust and blame herself, and carry to her own heart . . . the censure which arose from her own convictions.[32]

Richardson was torn over the extent to which his characters were fallible, for although he suggested that both Clarissa and Sir Charles Grandison were more rather realistic than perfect, he rushed to their defence whenever one of his correspondents ventured to offer a criticism of their behaviour. This was not merely an authorial hypersensitivity in regard to his favourite creations. It was a recognition of the challenge posed by the portrayal of realistic but fallible characters to a didacticism based on the creation of figures who can provide a model for undiscriminating imitation. The probability of Richardson's stories was therefore limited by his failure to credit his readers with any powers of moral or aesthetic judgement. The extensive revisions and additions which he appended to *Clarissa* represent his attempts to make the text conform to what he believed should be the moral role of literature, and so embody the authorial failure to recognise the true power and didactic function of his creation.

The strength of Richardson's narrative, and its influence over its readership, is located in its representation of the role of the individual within a state characterised by moral uncertainty and contradiction. In refusing to endorse the suitability of narrative fiction for the exploration of the modern state, and in framing Clarissa's story within a preceptual and exemplary moral structure, Richardson embodied the ambivalent attitude to the new codes of social analysis which characterised traditional moral discourse in the eighteenth century. This ambivalence was to be manifested even more clearly in his final novel, *Sir Charles Grandison*, where the uncertainty over commercial morality was embedded in the structure of the text, but it is also evident in Henry Fielding's *Tom Jones*, a novel which is often interpreted as the antithesis of *Clarissa*.

TOM JONES

When Tom Jones overpowers the highwayman who has attacked him on the London road,[33] he is faced with two options. He can accompany the man to the nearest magistrate, so that he can be tried and ultimately executed for his crime, or he can release, forgive and relieve the offender. He can follow the dictates of the public virtue of justice and uphold the interests of society, or he can act in accordance with a private sense of mercy and charity, and consider the interests of the individual. In a way this dilemma symbolises the options facing the novelists of the mid-eighteenth century. They could either celebrate a public moral system, or represent more private, individual virtues, which are conventionally seen to be against the long-term interests of the community.

Tom Jones chooses the path of mercy, for he not only releases the man but gives him a couple of guineas to relieve the distress that has driven him to crime (vol. II, p. 680). Yet it is clear from Fielding's non-fictional writings that, outside the world of the novel, this was not an inevitable or universally acceptable choice. Fielding's *Enquiry into the Causes of the Late Increase of Robbers* deals with the subject of the 'Remissness of Prosecutors', who fail to enforce the law out of a tender-hearted unwillingness to deprive a man of his life.[34] While the narrative voice recognises that such a disposition has its origins in virtue, and Christian virtue at that,[35] it bids those liable to such sentiments to:

Consider, that the principal Duty which every Man owes, is to his Country, for the Safety and Good of which all Laws are established; and therefore his Country requires of him to contribute all that in him lies to the Execution of those Laws. Robbery is an Offence not only against the Party robbed, but against the Public, who are therefore entitled to Prosecution; and he who prevents or stifles such a Prosecution, is no longer an innocent Man, but guilty of a high Offence against the Public Good.[36]

Private sentiments of mercy and benevolence should therefore be suppressed and subordinated to public considerations. For 'such Tenderness is indeed Barbarity, and resembles the meek Spirit of him who would not assist in blowing up his Neighbour's House, to save a whole City from the Flames'.[37]

In *Tom Jones*, however, the moral perspective is rather different from that exhibited in Fielding's non-fictional writings, even when dealing with exactly the same moral issue. The authorial voice recognises the potential diversity of moral judgements on Jones' action:

Our Readers will probably be divided in their Opinions concerning this Action; some may applaud it perhaps as an Act of extraordinary Humanity, while those of a more Saturnine Temper will consider it as a Want of Regard to that Justice which every Man owes to his Country. (vol. II, pp. 680–1)

But despite the ostensible authorial liberality of this passage, the readers are not permitted to be divided in their opinions for long. The highwayman does not just disappear out of the text in the manner of many of his picaresque predecessors. He reappears as the cousin of Jones' London

landlady, Mrs Miller. As a result, the true virtue of Jones' action can be
presented, through the portrayal of its consequences. 'O Sir' cries the
reformed highwayman when he meets Jones again:

I wish you could this Instant see my House ... My children have now a Bed to
lie on, – and they have – they have – eternal Blessings reward you for it, – they
have Bread to eat. My little Boy is recovered; my Wife is out of Danger, and I
am happy. All, all is owing to you, Sir, and to my Cousin here. (vol. II,
pp. 727–8)

Jones' decision to exercise the private virtue of mercy, rather than the
public virtue of justice, is shown to have procured a public benefit rather
than the 'Offence against the Public Good' mentioned in the *Enquiry*. It
has rescued a family from poverty and starvation but also from crime.
Jones is therefore able to exult:

In the Happiness which he had procured to this poor Family; nor could he
forbear reflecting without Horror on the dreadful consequences which must
have attended them, had he listened rather to the Voice of strict Justice, than to
that of Mercy when he was attacked on the high Road. (vol. II, pp. 728–9)

Jones embodies a private, personal, affective code of virtue, which is
seen as appropriate to the moral system of the novel. He eschews the
public concept of justice upheld in the *Enquiry*, but also the code of
self-sacrificing public virtue that is espoused in the literature on epic.
Jones is no Leonidas. He has no notion of a duty to the wider community which transcends his obligations to those around him. He sees the
need of a beggar or highwayman and he responds. His virtue is therefore a natural impulse, an open-hearted charity and benevolence, and a
freedom from that hypocrisy which is seen as prevalent in society.

   This benevolence is contrasted with the selfish and pusillanimous
prudence of Jones' companion, the barber surgeon Partridge, who
argues that 'it would be better that all Rogues were hanged out of the
way, than one honest Man should suffer' (vol. II, p. 681). The juxtaposition of Partridge's cowardly vengeance with Jones' gentlemanly and
merciful courage reinforces the identification of Jones' values as patrician, whereas Partridge expresses more populist sentiments which the
novel's readers are invited to reject. On the other hand Jones' impulsiveness is compared with the calculating caution of his devious half-
brother, Blifil. With regard to this latter virtue, we are told:

To say the Truth, there are but two Ways in which Men become possessed of
this excellent Quality. The one is from long Experience, and the other is from

Nature; which last, I presume, is often meant by Genius, or great natural Parts; and it is infinitely the better of the two, not only as we are Masters of it much earlier in Life, but as it is much more infallible and conclusive: For a Man who hath been imposed on by ever so many, may still hope to find others more honest; whereas he who received certain necessary Admonitions from within, that this is impossible, must have very little Understanding indeed, if he renders himself liable to be once deceived. (vol. i, pp. 427–8)

Blifil's persistent and inherent preoccupation with his own interest is identified as morally inferior to Jones' more open-hearted approach, and in rejecting the selfish code of behaviour as unacceptable, Fielding is able to draw on a tradition of anti-commercial discourse which represented narrow self-interest as particularly pernicious and a threat to the stability of the state.

In relation to Blifil and Partridge, therefore, Jones' behaviour is clearly celebrated, but a more significant challenge to its appropriateness as a social and moral ethic is represented in the contrast with the rather more respectable prudential doctrine upheld by Jones' uncle, Mr Allworthy. Allworthy is a magistrate and a pillar of the community, who aims to administer justice with fairness and humanity, but also with a due sense of what is in the public interest. He would probably have felt compelled to take the highwayman before the relevant authorities, had he found himself in the same position as Jones on the London road.

For Allworthy, justice is a public duty, and prudence a prerequisite for survival in the modern world. As he admonishes Jones at the end of the novel:

Prudence is indeed the Duty which we owe to ourselves; and if we will be so much our own Enemies as to neglect it, we are not to wonder if the World is deficient in discharging their Duty to us; for when a Man lays the Foundation of his own Ruin, others will, I am afraid, be too apt to build upon it. (vol. ii, p. 960)

Jones accepts Allworthy's reading that all his troubles have stemmed from a want of prudence, yet in fact Jones suffers as a result of Allworthy's failings as much as his own. Allworthy attempts to deal justly and prudently, but his actions are frequently unjust and imprudent because he works on the basis of false information. Correct moral judgements can only be derived from an accurate and impartial review of circumstances, whereas Allworthy is content to accept the partial readings of prejudiced figures. As William Ray suggests, Tom Jones is 'all motive, with little attention to circumstance and consequence', whereas Allworthy considers circumstance and consequence, but has a 'blindness to motive'.[38] Allworthy dismisses Jones from favour on the misleading and uncorroborated testimony of Blifil, and the injustice of this act is underlined by the narrator's remark that 'many Disadvantages attended poor *Jones* in making his Defence':

For as Mr *Allworthy*, in recounting the Drunkenness, &c., while he lay ill, out of Modesty sunk everything that related particularly to himself, which indeed principally constituted the Crime, *Jones* could not deny the Charge. (vol. I, p. 310)

The irony of the reference to Allworthy's modesty emphasises the egotism that underlies the injustice, and this incident is merely the last in a series of similar deeds. Allworthy's favour has been withdrawn from Black George on the basis of Blifil's falsehoods, and 'the poor Gamekeeper was condemned, without having any opportunity to defend himself' (vol. I, p. 148). When Molly Seagrim is committed to Bridewell for refusing to disclose the father of the bastard she is expecting, the narrator remarks:

A Lawyer may, perhaps, think Mr *Allworthy* exceeded his Authority a little in this Instance. And, to say the Truth, I question, as here was no regular Information before him, whether his Conduct was strictly regular. However, as his Intention was truly upright, he ought to be excused in *Foro conscientiae*, since so many arbitrary Acts are daily committed by Magistrates who have not this Excuse to plead for themselves. (vol. I, p. 192)

Allworthy is a good man, but this makes it all the more alarming that he repeatedly acts unjustly and even cruelly. His actions are as much the consequence of the limitations of human perception as they are of his personal fallibility. Tom Jones declares towards the end of the novel that 'the wisest Man might be deceived as you were, and, under such a Deception, the best must have acted just as you did' (vol. II, p. 959). There is no sure way of disentangling truth from falsehood in a world where, as William Ray suggests, 'narrational craft is systematically associated with self-promotion'[39] and the majority of characters speak in order to deceive rather than to enlighten. In this situation, the attempt to administer justice becomes potentially dangerous, and may lead to the commission of an even greater injustice than would follow a tender-hearted failure to enforce the law. The impulsive benevolence and mercy of Jones may have the consequence of rewarding the guilty, but the prudence and justice of Allworthy may punish the innocent as well. In such circumstances, where those within the social nexus cannot recognise right and wrong and good and bad with the sureness of the narrative voice which stands outside the system, it is perhaps better to stick to the less damaging policy of practising private mercy rather than the stricter public virtue of justice. Vengeance is mine, implies the narrative voice, as it hands out everybody's just deserts at the conclusion of the novel.

This adaptation of morality to the level of human fallibility is foreshadowed in the uncharacteristically descriptive passage which introduces the reader to the landscape of Allworthy's country house, Paradise Hall. We are informed that 'The *Gothick* stile of Building could produce nothing nobler than Mr *Allworthy's* House', and we are led through a Grove of old Oaks, up a fine Lawn, past a plentiful Spring which forms a constant Cascade, to a Lake, 'embellished with Groupes of Beeches and Elms', from which issued a River, which emptied itself into the sea. Elsewhere can be seen several villages, an old ruined Abbey, and Mr Allworthy's park, which is, of course, 'laid out with admirable Taste, but owing less to Art than to Nature'. Beyond this lies a 'Ridge of wild Mountains, the Tops of which were above the Clouds':

And now having sent forth Streams of Light, which ascended the blue Firmament before him as Harbingers preceding his Pomp, in the full Blaze of his Majesty, up rose the Sun; than which one Object alone in this lower Creation could be more glorious, and that Mr *Allworthy* himself presented; a human Being replete with Benevolence, meditating in what manner he might render himself most acceptable to his Creator, by doing most good to his Creatures.

Reader, take care, I have unavoidably led thee to the Top of as high a Hill as Mr *Allworthy's*, and how to get thee down without breaking thy Neck, I do not well know. However, let us e'en venture to slide down together, for Miss *Bridget* rings her Bell, and Mr Allworthy is summoned to Breakfast, where I must attend, and, if you please, shall be glad of your Company. (vol. I, pp. 43–4)

The description of the landscape may represent an encomium on Hagley Park and Prior Park, the estates of Lyttleton and Allen, but it is also a moral landscape, drawing on the traditional Augustan political and moral symbolism of the marriage of nature and art.[40] Everything in the landscape has its place, and contributes to the total effect of the scene, just as every member of the community has, and is expected to occupy, his or her place, to create social harmony out of diversity. Thus we are led through a scene in which the diverse elements are perfectly and harmoniously combined, until the favourable comparison of Allworthy walking on the terrace with the glory of the sun in his firmament leads the narrative voice to a hyperbolic height from which the only way is down. The bathos of the image of the narrator and reader sliding down the hill satirises not only the elevated tone of the previous passage, but also the sentiments it portrays. The hyperbole employed in the description of Allworthy's benevolence can no more be maintained than the high-flown language in which it is conveyed, and must be followed by a let-down. Allworthy is not in the position of the narrative voice, viewing the landscape from on high and placing everything within it with a magisterial eye. He is not above the social scene, able to discern the underlying patterns and harmony. He is part of the landscape, a little figure walking on the terrace, and his perception is therefore partial. In fact, he is not actually like the sun at all. In sliding down the hill, the narrative voice is able to return to a more prosaic, less elevated tone, but this somewhat undignified descent also prepares the reader for the fact that Mr Allworthy will prove, while worthy, to be only human, and fallible for all his benevolence. The credibility of prudence and justice as an appropriate code of behaviour within a complex society which must be judged from within is therefore seriously questioned by the importance of benevolence in the narrative, and the undermining of the moral authority of Allworthy. This has a number of significant implications: for the relationship between Fielding's fictional and non-fictional writings; for the model of public and private virtue that is presented within the text; and for the role of the authorial voice.

On the first point, the stress on the moral virtue of benevolence reinforces the difference between the moral perspective of fiction, and in particular of fictional characters, and that of discourses of social analysis. The narrative voice of *An Enquiry into the Causes of the Late Increase of Robbers* and *A Proposal for Making an Effectual Provision for the Poor* (1753) can adopt a magisterial detachment which facilitates a clear identification of the public interest, to which we are enjoined to subordinate private, affective considerations. For those enmeshed within the fictional world, however, no such detachment is possible, and the attempt to assume the magisterial perspective of characters such as Allworthy is ultimately satirised as hubristic, and a cause of public as well as private injustice. Thus in Fielding's writings, as in those of Adam Smith and David Hume, the medium dictates the message. Images of the social system that are acceptable within one form or genre or discourse are identified as distortions in another. Opinions that are acceptable for those who dominate or control the real or fictional world are dangerous for those who are only players within it.

Thus while Fielding does not describe a system of explicitly commercial behaviour, he articulates an ethic which, like the codes of the economic writers, was primarily derived from the consequences of individual actions. His characters cannot control or influence the totality of the system, they can only work to improve conditions within it. The novels therefore emphasise a much more limited concept of morality than that which was identified within writings on epic, and led to the prioritisation of private systems of virtue, and a code of behaviour based on manners and consideration for others. It is perhaps significant that Fielding's final novel was entitled *Amelia* (1751), since his fictional morality is based around the amelioratory function of the individual within the commercial state. The hero of *Amelia* eventually has to learn, from the example of his saintly and long-suffering wife, that all he can do is accept his lot, and try to make the best of things for the sake of those around him. Far from presenting an active, masculine and epic concept of public virtue, Fielding presents heroes who must acquire a limited and passive virtue from their female counterparts. Tom Jones must gain wisdom from Sophia, as Billy Booth must learn acceptance from Amelia. These characters cannot attempt to control the social structure, for they cannot occupy the position of the impartial observer, the narrator, the divinity or spectator, and perceive the true condition of the polity. Their vision is limited by their position within the social, economic and political nexus, which prevents them from discerning the true pattern of society and the motives of those around them. All they can do, therefore, is their best, within the confines of the position assigned them, and cultivate a morality of manners which does not aim to change but to ameliorate.

Finally, the emphasis on benevolence within the subtext of *Tom Jones* considerably complicates the relationship between the reader and the authorial voice. For while the bumptious narrator exploits the aura of omniscience implicit in his role, the fetichisation of control is consistently undercut. The narrative voice recurrently suggests that it has complete mastery of the text. For instance, he warns the critics not to condemn any parts of the tale as 'foreign' to the 'main Design':

This work may, indeed, be considered as a great Creation of our own; and for a little Reptile of a Critic to presume to find Fault with any of its parts, without knowing the Manner in which the Whole is connected, and before he comes to the final Catastrophe, is a most presumptuous Absurdity. (vol. II, pp. 524–5)

Many critics have stressed the significance of the omniscience of Fielding's narrator, and his role in shaping the moral message. William Ray writes that

By foregrounding his command of motive, circumstance, and consequence, and stressing his position on a plane superior to that of the characters he describes, the Author underlines the fact of his exemption from the world he details. By writing a history over which he alone had authority, he gains a command of history unavailable through other modes of social discourse.[41]

Yet the irony is that this assumption of authorial command, this assimilation of narrative and divine manipulation, is itself exposed as hubristic and ironically undermined. *Tom Jones* ostensibly presents an authoritative controlling narrator, beneath whose gaze the characters blindly stumble, but having done so it invites the reader to reach a moral verdict which is distinct from that espoused by the narrative voice. While the narrator enjoins us to prudence, the narrative points out benevolence as the most reliable code of personal conduct.

The autonomous role of the reader has been stressed by Wolfgang Iser, whose Reception Theory recognises the limitations on fictional omniscience:

The role of the reader as incorporated in the novel must be seen as something potential and not actual. His reactions are not set out for him, but he is simply offered a frame of possible decisions, and when he has made his choice, then he will fill in the pictures accordingly... Fielding was to a certain extent aware that, despite the directions given in the author–reader dialogue and the implications of the role assigned to the reader, the scope for realization could not be rigidly controlled.[42]

Yet the disparity between the message of the readerly subtext and that of the authorial text is the consequence of more than merely a failure of control. It is not that the narrator wants us to receive the message of prudence, but we perversely pick up the message of benevolence because that is what we want to hear, or because that is what fits in with our contemporary moral framework. It is rather that a benevolent subtext, derived from the reader's identification with Jones, and observation of the consequences of his actions, is juxtaposed with an explicitly prudential text, which is thereby undermined. I feel that we are supposed to regard the narrator as in many ways similar to Allworthy. Both are essentially well-meaning, both are rather full of their own importance, but they are not as firmly in control of events as they think they are. Both assume magisterial powers, one as narrator, the other as magistrate, but their verdicts are not beyond question or reproach.

This willingness to play and have fun with the role of the narrator, and satirise his own pontificating style, is revealed in *Joseph Andrews*, where the narrator is sometimes the originator of an exemplary moral tale, and sometimes the chronicler of a pre-existent reality. On the one hand we are told,

I describe not Men, but Manners; not an Individual but a Species

thus the satirical characters are intended

Not to expose one pitiful Wretch, to the small and contemptible Circle of his Acquaintance, but to hold the Glass to thousands in their Closets.[43]

On the other hand, when Joseph Andrews is recuperating in an inn, after being attacked by robbers, we are informed that he 'eat either a Rabbit or a Fowl, I never could with any tolerable Certainty discover which'.[44] Such claims for a simple mimetic function are given extra ironic piquancy from the fact that *Joseph Andrews* is itself a satire on Richardson's *Pamela*. Joseph Andrews is the virtuous brother of the virtuous Pamela Andrews, so that the novel is not just a fiction but a fiction of a fiction. Joseph Andrews ordered neither rabbit nor fowl, for he has no existence outside the knowledge of his creator. As readers, we know this perfectly well and our acceptance of the narrator's uncertainty indicates a willingness to enter into the myth of a pre-existent reality, and participate in the game of the narrative voice.

The moral structure of Fielding's fiction therefore represents a total departure from the preceptual systems and exemplary figures which characterised epic literature, and which were to some extent maintained within Richardson's narratives. For although chapter 1 of book 1 of *Joseph Andrews* opens with the claim that 'It is a trite but true Observation, that Examples work more forcibly on the Mind than Precepts',[45] both *Joseph Andrews* and *Tom Jones* utilise an experiential rather than an exemplary format. Both readers and characters use the experiences of the novel in order to acquire a sound moral code. We are not simply expected to imitate an exemplary figure, or follow a simple code of authorial advice. The ironic distancing of the author is therefore crucial to the moral structure of the narrative. We have to use our own moral experience and faculties to reach a social perspective that will be acceptable within the parameters presented through the plot and characters of the novel, but the perceptions of readers and characters alike are assimilated through the shared experience of the narrative.

The incorporation of a multiplicity of subordinate histories told by minor characters, the interpolated narrative technique, is of considerable significance to the way that the moral theme is developed in the novel, as well as to the image of society that is conveyed. This technique was derived from the picaresque tradition, and is fully exploited in le Sage's *Gil Blas*, which was translated from the French by Smollett in 1749. Smollett incorporated the 'Memoirs of a Lady of Quality' and 'Memoirs of a noted personage' into *Peregrine Pickle*, but these are only particularly lengthy examples of a convention that was virtually omnipresent in the eighteenth-century novel. Henry Mackenzie's Man of Feeling, Harley, for example, is always getting people to tell him their life stories, while the narratives of minor characters make up about a quarter of Richard Graves' *The Spiritual Quixote* (1773), and three-quarters of Sarah Scott's *Millenium Hall* (1762).

In 'The Story-Telling in *Joseph Andrews*', Bryan Burns has expressed a certain uneasiness over the prevalence of these stories-within-stories within eighteenth-century fiction,[46] and J. Paul Hunter has seen them as an important aspect of the inclusiveness of eighteenth-century narrative, and its ability to incorporate non-narrative forms.[47] Yet I would argue that the presentation of these varied histories is also a manifestation of an awareness of the significance and omnipresence of narrative within the eighteenth century. The technique implies that everyone in society has a story to tell, and that it is important to know this story in order to know the individual. The totality of these stories represents experience and this is identified by Fielding and others as the key to moral judgement. By presenting a range of stories, the novel both expands and assimilates the experience of readers and characters. We can get to know society vicariously – we do not have to become prostitutes or beggars to experience the trials of prostitution and poverty – but we are also more able to share the moral perspective of the hero or heroine. We think as they do, not because we have been told to do so by the narrative voice, but because we have heard the same tales, and gone through their experiences with them. Experience and knowledge of the world could therefore be displaced by experience and knowledge of fiction, and this was particularly appropriate given that many of the readers of the novel were women of the upper and middle classes, whose experience of the social system was necessarily limited. These readers could practise and refine the exercise of moral judgement, without going outside the sphere of respectable society and endeavour. The significance of literature within the lives of women readers, and its influence for good or evil, is recognised within some of the novels themselves. For while the novels concerned with male heroes explain their characters with reference to their early adventures and formative experiences, the novels concerned with female characters often focus on the early reading of the heroines. In Charlotte Smith's *The Old Manor House* (1793) the hero, Orlando, goes off to school before travelling to London and America, while the heroine Monimia stays at home, undertaking the course of reading prescribed by him. Charlotte Lennox's female Quixote has learned about the world through reading romances; Mary Hays' Emma Courtney has developed a taste for romance, but has also imbibed sounder principles from a programme of classical reading. And while the immoral Miss Milner in Elizabeth Inchbald's *A Simple Story* (1791) does not appear to read, her daughter, the virtuous and thoughtful Lady Matilda, is devoted to books. Reading the wrong sort of literature is a recipe for disaster that can only be corrected by long and bitter experience; but reading of the right kind is a means of absorbing and learning from experience.[48]

Experience is therefore portrayed, as it is in the moral philosophy of Hume, as essential to the formulation of individual moral judgements. Differences in personal experience, combined with variations in natural disposition or character, account for divergences in moral perspective, and thus for the wide range of moral views within commercial society. As the economic system became more complex and fragmented, individual experience became increasingly diversified. It becomes more difficult to view society from the fictitious pinnacle from which Allworthy is forced to slide, and a true perspective is impossible for those enmeshed within the interdependent community – particularly for women whose knowledge of society was severely restricted. Yet the communication and sharing of experience by means of narrative could be used as a way of counteracting the disintegrative potential of gender restrictions and the economic system. We do not all have to go round, like MacKenzie's Harley, asking passing beggars to tell us their life stories, but can gain knowledge of the social system by reading novels.

The experiential structure was crucial to the didactic strategy of Fielding's fiction, but it can also be seen as an important means of negating the collapse of social morality which was associated with the development of the economic system. Ironically, it was those advocates of traditional epic values, who inveighed against the diversity of the social system resultant from the growth of commerce, who were also most avowedly opposed to the emergence of an experiential rather than a preceptual basis for literary morality. The emphasis on experience implied a degree of interpretative autonomy on the part of the reader which was not to be found within writings based on a code of inflexible moral precepts. It is perhaps significant that Samuel Johnson, who was

an avowed opponent of the empirical philosophy of David Hume, was
also against the use of experience as part of the moral mechanism of the
novel.[49]

In Fielding's work, on the other hand, the awareness of the diversity
of interpretations and interpretative abilities within the reading public
was an important influence on the form of the novel, and the games of
the narrative voice. In the preface to his sister Sarah Fielding's novel,
David Simple (1744), Fielding comments on the problems which the
novelist encounters in interpreting human nature and human society,
but he also highlights the difficulties involved in making the resultant
observations comprehensible to the lowest and least perceptive readers:

> As the Faults of this Work want very little Excuse, so its Beauties want as little
> Recommendation: tho' I will not say but they may sometimes stand in need of
> being pointed out to the generality of Readers. For as the Merit of this Work
> consists in a vast Penetration into human Nature … and as this is the greatest,
> noblest, and rarest of all the Talents which constitute a Genius; so a much
> larger Share of this Talent is necessary, even to recognize these Discoveries,
> when they are laid before us, than falls to the share of a common Reader. Such
> Beauties therefore in an Author must be contented to pass often unobserved
> and untasted.[50]

Fielding implies that the finer points will inevitably be missed by the
majority of the audience for fiction, and throughout the narrative of *Tom
Jones* he makes reference to the range of interpretations that will be put
on his text. He is conscious not only of the differing abilities of his
readers – from the 'readers of the lowest class' to the 'upper graduates in
criticism' from whom 'much higher and harder exercises of judgement
and penetration may reasonably be expected' (vol. 1, p. 117) – but also of
the variety of moral perspectives.[51]

The recurrence of references to the disparate nature of the novel's
public underlines the impression of the complexity of the social system
conveyed by the text. By repeatedly suggesting the absence of a consensus in the interpretation of the novel, despite the presence of the
narrator, it creates an impression of the absence of a unifying ideology
within society. It is difficult and perhaps impossible to create, or assume
the existence of, a common perspective in the face of the increasing
social differences introduced by the division of labour. Yet just as the
narrative is underscored by a benevolent subtext, so the representation
of diversity is undercut by the suggestion that there is in fact a hierarchy
of readings. Not all interpretations are equally valid within the diverse
and divided commercial state. Some are seen as right, and some are

clearly identified as wrong. Fielding's narrator recognises the inescapable role of the reader in the construction of the narrative, but the repeated use of irony both reinforces the importance of this role, and emphasises the hierarchical conception of the reading public that underlies it.

The technique of irony necessitates that the reader should understand what the author really means, while appreciating what s/he could be thought to mean, and therefore what the notional 'readers of the lowest class' could take him or her to mean. The ironic voice points to a certain reading which forms an independent standpoint to which the readers must assimilate themselves. The nature of this standpoint is indicated in Fielding's novels by the identification and vilification of the archetypal wrong reader – the 'little Reptile of a Critic' (vol. II, p. 525) – and at the start of *Tom Jones* the narrator expresses his antipathy to this sector of the reading public:

Reader, I think it proper . . . to acquaint thee, that I intend to digress, through this whole History, as often as I see Occasion: Of which I am myself a better Judge than any pitiful Critic whatever; and here I must desire all these Critics to mind their own Business, and not to intermeddle with Affairs, or Works, which no ways concern them: For, till they produce the Authority by which they are constituted Judges, I shall not plead to their Jurisdiction. (vol. I, p. 37)

Fielding's attack on the critics is based on a denial of their authority. This had been a recurrent theme of his journalism[52] and in the opening chapter of book 5 of *Tom Jones* the narrator attacks the presumption which has led critics to 'assume a Dictatorial Power' (vol. I, p. 210). This criticism echoed attacks by neoclassical and non-neoclassical writers alike, who saw the critic as distinguished by his professionalism from the rest of the reading public. His criticism was motivated by private interest, rather than the free play of taste, and so it was assumed that his professionalism would inevitably lead to incorrect or prejudiced readings. There was therefore some irony in the authorial praise of 'the upper graduates in criticism', for this group was just as likely to misread the text as the 'readers of the lowest class'.

In attacking the critic, Fielding suggests that the desired audience for his work is one which is not debarred by private interest from attending the moral lessons of the text, and who can attend to the experience contained therein. In the portrayal of the hierarchy of readers, therefore, as in the use of the interpolated narrative, Fielding is able to present both the obvious diversity of society and the unifying potential of narrative within it. Yet although Fielding makes reference to the range of readers and readings of his work, it is clear that this was identified as a far more homogeneous group than the public who were the subject of his political writings. Despite its varied social and moral perspectives, the novel-reading public is neither the general public nor the limited political public of civic humanist rhetoric. It is at once a wide group of people, compared to the audience of other literary forms, and a very restricted sector of the population. As in the writings of Hume and Smith, it can be analysed as if it were the general public, because it is assumed that those outside this group, the mob, are beyond the scope of polite consideration. The mob cannot be susceptible to individual moral dilemmas because they are not conceived to be capable of moral reflection, but are motivated by the crude dictates of the economic system.

In the preface to *Evelina* (1778) Fanny Burney drew attention to the uncertain social status of the audience of the novel, for in referring to her readers as a public, she made the ironic disclaimer that '*such by novel writers, novel readers will be called*'.[53] Burney recognised that the readership of the novel was composed of a wider range of social classes and sexes than the body of male, politically active aristocrats that comprised the public interest. She therefore highlighted the pretensions of novelists in elevating their readers with the denomination 'public', but the location of this satiric reference within a passage lamenting the unjustifiably humble status of the novelist within the 'republic of letters' may suggest that the 'inferior rank' of the novel writers was in part derived from the social composition of their readership. In this context the attempt to glorify the heterogeneous audience for fiction with the title 'public' may constitute an attempt to raise the status of the fictional genre.

Although Fielding addresses himself within his fiction to a wide and socially disparate readership, this exploration of diversity is only possible because of the actual social limitations on his audience. Fielding can accept a degree of interpretative autonomy on the part of his readers, because his novels are directed to those limited sections of the community who are able to achieve a level of moral self-determination, in part through their access to the liberating forces of culture and in particular fiction. The novels are able to present a code of private virtue, and a system of permissive, exculpatory morality, because his readership was not public in any modern sense of the word. The political works, in contrast, while written for the same elite which formed the audience for Fielding's fictional works, are concerned with outlining systems of behaviour for the mass of the people who are excluded from the enlightening moral influence of literature. They do not articulate an exculpatory code of personal morality, but develop rules which will control the behaviour of the mob, and forcibly moderate the aggressive selfishness which Fielding accepts as the defining characteristic of the mass of the people within a commercial state. As Fielding explains in the *Enquiry*, since

Knaves ... form a Part, (a very considerable one, I am afraid) of every Community, who are ever lying in wait to destroy and ensnare the honest Part of Mankind, and to betray them by means of their own Goodness, it becomes the good-natured and tender-hearted Man to be watchful over his own Temper; to restrain the Impetuosity of his Benevolence, carefully to select the Objects of his Passion, and not by too unbounded and indiscriminate an Indulgence to give the Reins to a Courser, which will infallibly carry him into the Ambuscade of the Enemy.[54]

Although the moral themes and narrative structures of Fielding's novels represent a model of the private moral function of the public within the commercial polity, this model is only possible because of the tacit assumption that fiction both represents and addresses only the morally and socially enlightened few who are able to develop an autonomous moral standpoint, and are not subject to the crude dictates of economic change. Fielding can represent a system of individual morality which provides a bridge between the terms of public and private analysis of the enlightened few, and those of the mass of the people within the state. While the readers of moral philosophy and fiction are identified as, by the very process of reading, capable of fulfilling a system of private morality, the mass of the people have to be controlled by the legal and political systems of public restraint. Fielding can therefore prioritise private virtue, because he, like Adam Smith, recognised the marginal role of individual behaviour within the complex state. Tom Jones cannot embody any viable system of social morality, and so the only relevant sphere for his activity is purely private and amelioratory.

In representing the 'mixed' characters that so worried theorists of the novel, Fielding rejected the kind of didacticism advocated by those writers who identified a conflict between the moral and the realistic narrative functions. Tom Jones, Joseph Andrews and William Booth are far from being perfect characters, but they do not set out to provide models for unquestioning imitation. They are endowed with a natural predisposition to virtue, which is only converted into moral sense by means of experience. The reader and the character are intended to learn the moral responsibilities of the individual through the lessons conveyed within the narrative. It is therefore inevitable that the moral systems inculcated by Fielding's novels will be experiential, *ex-post-facto* and hence exculpatory, but also private. The public morality of civic humanist tradition was not something to be acquired by wandering about the countryside. It was divorced from, and superior to, the experience of the individual, so that adherence to this higher duty was invariably conveyed in terms of a disavowal of those personal responsibilities and perceptions which were the essence of the moral systems of Fielding's fiction.

The preoccupation with the need for preceptial didacticism in eighteenth-century writings on the novel reveals the prevalence of the expectation that the form will be used to express a public and anti-commercial system of morality. The location of Fielding's male heroes within a private moral sphere was far more controversial and significant than it appears today, and in part accounts for the condemnation of the immorality of his works. In making Tom Jones choose the path of mercy, rather than the road of justice, Fielding dramatised the direction that the novel had to take in the face of the conflict between the economic and the civic humanist models of individual behaviour, but this choice was by no means obvious. The challenge posed by commercial morality to traditional paradigms seems strong in retrospect, but in part this is because we cannot recognise and respond to the power and omnipresence of public ideology. The rhetoric and values of civic humanism dominated the discourse of political analysis in the early eighteenth century and generated a concept of the public that was still being used as an indictment of the novel at the time of the publication of *Evelina*. It is significant that the novel that developed in the mid century did not attempt to embody the terms of this social vision within its fictional and moral structure. Yet at the same time the novel was not unaffected by the prevalence of civic humanist values, in that it did not represent an unproblematic acceptance of a system of bourgeois individualism or commercial society.

THE FEMALE QUIXOTE

Charlotte Lennox's *The Female Quixote* of 1752 was one of a number of eighteenth-century novels which used the mechanism of the quixotic hero or heroine to explore the nature of modern society.[55] Lennox's heroine, Lady Arabella, is endowed with the usual female graces, but having been brought up in isolation from polite society, her knowledge of manners and mores has been largely supplied by books. From her earliest youth she has read extensively in her father's library, 'in which, unfortunately for her, were great Store of Romances, and what was still more unfortunate, not in the original *French*, but very bad Translations'.[56] Thus,

Her Ideas, from the Manner of Life, and the Objects around her, had taken a romantic Turn; and supposing Romances were real Pictures of Life, from them she drew all her Notions and Expectations. (p. 7)

The comedy of the book is derived from the disjunction between what actually happens, and Arabella's perception of events. For Arabella believes in a code of heroic virtue, and an outrageously extravagant concept of courtly love. She is immersed in stories of heroes and heroines of the ancient world, culled not from classical authors but from the fantastic and voluminous French romances of the seventeenth century, and all the events of her rather humdrum and secluded life are interpreted in these terms: when the gardener's boy is apprehended stealing carp from the pond, Arabella is convinced that he is a gentleman in disguise, about to drown himself out of hopeless passion for herself (pp. 22–6); a well-dressed young woman, who has retired to the country to give birth to an illegitimate child after a life of fashionable vice, is embraced by Arabella as a damsel in distress, who is unable to disclose her secret marriage to a powerful lord (pp. 70–9); a gentleman approaching Arabella while she is out hunting is identified as a ravisher, preparing to steal her away (pp. 154–5).

The misapprehensions of Arabella are clearly satirised in such scenes, but, as with *Don Quixote*, there is also a more elegiac strand to the novel which laments the passing of an earlier, more heroic age, and a code of heroic values, even though these values have been conveyed in the ludicrous genre of the prose romance. When Arabella's cousin and lover Glanville tells her that she should not be governed by 'such antiquated Maxims' since 'the World is quite different to what it was in those Days', Arabella makes a reply that would have had a ring of truth for an eighteenth-century audience inculcated with a belief in the superiority of heroic society and epic poetry:

I am sure, replied *Arabella*, the World is not more virtuous now than it was in their Days, and there is good Reason to believe it is not much wiser; and I don't see why the Manners of this Age are to be preferred to those of former ones, unless they are wiser and better. (p. 45)

When Glanville admits that he has not actually read the romances, Arabella declares herself amazed that he has not been able to spare the time

For the Perusal of Books from which all useful Knowledge may be drawn; which give us the most shining Examples of Generosity, Courage, Virtue, and Love; which regulate our Actions, form our Manners, and inspire us with a noble Desire of emulating those great, heroic and virtuous Actions, which made those Persons so glorious in their Age, and so worthy Imitation in ours. (p. 48)

Arabella's behaviour is bizarre, and she is unable to apprehend the nature of reality, but in many ways her values and accomplishments are seen as superior to the vanity and frivolity of fashionable life. She aspires to generosity, courage and virtue, even though she often uses rather arcane definitions of these concepts. In contrast, the other women in the book are characterised by petty jealousy and an inane dedication to the pursuit of pleasure. Their conversation revolves around card parties, clothes and the destruction of reputations. Arabella, on the other hand, 'seemed so little sensible of the Pleasure of Scandal, as to be wholly ignorant of its Nature; and not to know it when it was told her' (p. 77).

The conflict between ancient and modern values is brought out in the conflicting definitions of 'Adventure' that are used in the text. The subtitle of *The Female Quixote* is *The Adventures of Arabella*, and while Arabella consistently thinks of adventures as great and heroic actions and escapades, the rest of the world tends to interpret the word in an exclusively sexual sense. When Arabella asks the Countess of — to recount her adventures, the latter is momentarily overcome with confusion. As she explains to Arabella, 'the Word Adventures carries in it so free and licentious a Sound in the Apprehensions of People at this Period of Time, that it can hardly with propriety be apply'd to those few and natural Incidents which compose the History of a Woman of Honour' (p. 327). The recurrence of such misunderstandings reinforces the contrast between the heroic age of the past, and a modern society that is preoccupied with appearances, scandal and sexual relations.

Arabella's criticism of the effeminacy of modern men echoes the attack on the standing army of civic humanist tradition. Arabella doubts whether men with 'figures so feminine, voices so soft, such tripping steps and unmeaning gestures' could ever be capable of either courage or constancy:

Law! Cousin, reply'd Miss *Glanville*, you are always talking of Battles and Fighting. Do you expect that Persons of Quality and fine Gentlemen, will go to the Wars? What Business have they to fight? That belongs to the Officers.

Then every fine Gentleman is an Officer, said *Arabella*; and some other Title ought to be found out for Men who do nothing but Dance and Dress. (p. 279)

Miss Glanville underlines the extent to which modern society has departed from the heroic ideal, whereby the safety of the state depended on the great warrior statesmen. Nowadays the defence of the state is left to the professional soldiers, and 'gentlemen' cultivate manners and a code of politeness which emphasise their distinctness from this group. Arabella, however, echoes the classical moralists, in condemning the development of a professional soldiery and in scorning the resultant feminisation and trivialisation of male manners.

This elevation of heroic values is combined with a satire on the improbability of the form and conventions of the romance. When Arabella instructs her waiting-woman Lucy to recount her 'history' to a group of assembled guests, Lucy laments her incapacity for the task: 'it is not such simple Girls as I can tell Histories; it is only fit for Clerks, and such Sort of People, that are very learned'.

Well! exclaimed *Arabella*: I am certainly the most unfortunate Woman in the World! Every thing happens to me in a contrary manner from any other Person! Here, instead of my desiring you to soften those Parts of my History where you have greatest room to flatter, and to conceal, if possible, some of those Disorders my Beauty has occasioned, you ask me to tell you what you must say, as if it was not necessary you should know as well as myself, and be able, not only to recount all my Words and Actions, even the smallest and most inconsiderable, but also all my Thoughts, however instantaneous. (p. 121)

Janet Todd, in her account of eighteenth-century women's writing *The Sign of Angellica*, has suggested that this appeal to Lucy represents Arabella's desire to create herself as a subject of heroic romance:

Arabella knows that one tool of self-creation is literary depiction. She wishes to be the heroine of a romantic history, the subject of a narrative of which she can be the auditor.[57]

Yet the passage also functions to unravel the central narrative motif. Arabella is here used as the unconscious mouthpiece for a critique of the form she is so anxious to defend, and the transparency of the satire to some extent undermines the probability of the story – if Arabella can say all this, has it not occurred to her that the romances may not be entirely reliable? As the novel draws to a close, however, even Arabella is forced to recognise the disparity between heroic and modern society, and to accept that the values and ethics of an heroic age are not always

applicable within a contemporary context. *Don Quixote* had previously
exposed the irrelevance of the chivalric code within a complex and
interdependent community, and before that the Greek tragedies had
embodied the conflict between the *Oikos* and the *Nomos*, between the
code of values based on personal vengeance and the family and the new
systems of justice based on the power of the state. In the same way
Arabella increasingly appreciates that the conduct exalted within the
works of romance is incompatible with modern ideas of modesty and
decency, but also with Christianity and the rule of law.

It is the faithful waiting-woman, Lucy, who introduces the idea that
the Bible might be a guide to conduct, though we have previously been
assured of Arabella's sincere religious devotion (p. 67). When Arabella is
convinced that Sir George Bellmour is about to die of love for her, and
is uncertain whether she should bid him live, Lucy offers a word of
advice:

To be sure, Madam, returned Lucy, your Ladyship knows what you ought to
do better than I can advise your Ladyship, being that you are more learned
than me: But, for all that, I think it's better to save Life than to Kill, as the
Bible-Book says; and since I am sure your Ladyship is a good Christian, if the
Gentleman dies for the Want of a few kind Words, or so, I am sure you will be
troubled in Mind about it. (p. 176)

Lucy emphasises her inferiority to Arabella in the point of learning, but
the difference is, as much as anything, in the choice of text. While Lucy
has absorbed the lessons of her Bible, Arabella's superior status has
given her access to the more morally dubious form of the romance. Both
have read passively and uncritically, but Lucy's text is one which forms a
reliable guide to conduct, whereas Arabella's text requires a more active
and critical readerly response.

When Arabella is inciting her cousin, Mr Glanville, to kill those she
believes have been attempting to steal her away, in line with the
example of the romance heroes, his sister, Miss Glanville, interjects:

If those Persons you have named, said Miss *Glanville*, were Murderers, and
made a Practice of killing People, I hope my Brother will be too wise to follow
their Examples: A strange kind of Virtue and Courage indeed, to take away the
Lives of one's Fellow-Creatures! How did such Wretches escape the Gallows, I
wonder? (pp. 127–8)

Arabella interrupts her cousin with assurances that her fears for her
brother's safety are unjustified. He will not be punished for his actions
because

The Law has no Power over Heroes; they may kill as many Men as they please, without being called to any Account for it; and the more Lives they take away, the greater is their Reputation for Virtue and Glory. (p. 128)

Arabella is clearly mistaken about the workings of the legal system, but also about the nature of virtue and glory. Mass murder is not seen as virtuous in a modern commercial state, and the theological overtones of the references to 'glory' and 'being called to account' remind the reader that in a Christian state a hero such as Arabella describes can expect to be called to account at a divine as well as a legal bar.

These points are finally reinforced at the end of the book, when Arabella, lying on a sickbed (in which she has been confined following an injudicious leap into the Thames to escape an imagined ravisher), is subjected to the counsel of a 'pious and learned Doctor', supposedly a fictional embodiment of Samuel Johnson. The Doctor seeks to prove to Arabella

First, That these Histories ... are Fictions.
Next, That they are absurd.
And lastly, That they are Criminal. (p. 374)

He argues that

The immediate Tendency of these books ... is to give new Fire to the Passions of Revenge and Love; two Passions which, even without such powerful Auxiliaries, it is one of the severest Labours of Reason and Piety to suppress, and which yet must be suppressed if we hope to be approved in the Sight of the only Being whose Approbation can make us Happy. (p. 380)

Arabella is therefore brought to recognise her misconception so that she can apprehend the true nature of modern society, and follow a code of behaviour derived from a combination of Christianity, common sense and modern manners. In addition she is able to marry her cousin Mr Glanville, with whom she was 'united ... in every Virtue and laudable Affection of the Mind' (p. 383).

The doctor suggests that Arabella's misreading of romance literature was not morally culpable, but was rather almost inevitable because of her lack of experience. 'You have', he argues 'yet had little opportunity of knowing the ways of mankind, which cannot be learned but from experience, and of which the highest understanding, and the lowest, must enter the world in equal ignorance' (p. 279). Having 'lived long in a public character', the doctor can recognise the difference between human beings and heroes and heroines, but Arabella has to acquire the prerequisite experience in the course of her narrative. This is then transmitted to the readers of *The Female Quixote*, who are enabled to see the irrelevance of concepts of heroic virtue within the modern world. The experience of reading *The Female Quixote* is therefore constructed as different from Arabella's experience of reading romance. For while the latter is represented as inherently morally misleading, the former is identified as essential for the acquisition of moral discrimination.

The lesson of *The Female Quixote* is not so much the irrelevance of fiction to 'real life', but the inapplicability of certain fictional forms and preoccupations within a contemporary context. Arabella's adventures can be read in part as an indictment of the values of modern society that invokes much of the civic humanist rhetoric – the attack on the luxury and frivolity of modern manners, the decline of the martial spirit resulting from the growth of standing armies, and the collapse of a classical concept of honour. Yet in exposing these changes Arabella's adventures also provide an appeal for a different sort of fiction – a fiction that is more appropriate to the contemporary context, and relevant to the values and experiences of contemporary readers. This point is made by the learned doctor, who upholds the work of Richardson as a model of what modern fiction can do. He argues that the old romances were not intended to be taken seriously, but that the modern novel can be used to present serious moral ideas in the guise of fiction:

An admirable Writer of our own Time, has found the Way to convey the most solid Instructions, the noblest Sentiments, and the most exalted Piety in the pleasing Dress of a Novel, and to use the Words of the greatest Genius in the present Age, 'Has taught the Passions to move at the Command of Virtue'. (p. 377)

This is the point made by Richard Graves in the preface to *The Spiritual Quixote*. Fiction can be used to enforce moral lessons more strongly than preceptual works. But the learned doctor stresses that it must be the right sort of fiction, must convey the right sort of lesson, and must be read in the right sort of way. Its bounds, conventions and parameters must be established and understood, otherwise it will be liable to mislead rather than enlighten and inform. *The Female Quixote* can therefore be read as a novel about the dangers of reading the wrong sort of fiction in the wrong sort of way, rather than just an attack on the prose romance, or an indictment of fiction in general.

As the story develops, it becomes clear that Arabella's virtue is indeed in danger, from the machinations of the villainous but charming Sir

George. He exploits Arabella's foible, in a trick which is intended to make her fall into his power. Yet Arabella does not perceive the trap that is laid for her, because she is so preoccupied with imaginary dangers. She is like Catherine Moreland in Jane Austen's *Northanger Abbey*, who is so obsessed with the fictions she has culled from Gothic literature that she does not recognise the real conspiracy against her. *The Female Quixote*, like *Northanger Abbey*, can therefore be read as a novel about what novels should be about, as much as a novel about the irrelevance of earlier fictional forms. *Northanger Abbey* stresses the importance of the location of novels in what Catherine Moreland describes as those 'Midland counties of England' where

Murder was not tolerated, servants were not slaves, and neither poison nor sleeping potions to be procured, like rhubarb, from every druggist. Among the Alps and Pyrenees, perhaps, there were no mixed characters. There, such as were not as spotless as an angel, might have the dispositions of a fiend. But in England it was not so; among the English, she believed, in their hearts and habits, there was a general though unequal mixture of good and bad.[58]

The role of fiction should be to present these mixed characters, their hearts and habits, rather than the improbable and fantastic figures that may or may not exist amongst the Alps and Pyrenees. Likewise, *The Female Quixote* emphasises the importance of the inculcation of sound moral precepts and underlines the need for the emergence of a didactic fiction that is appropriate for a commercial age.

Jane Spencer, in *The Rise of the Woman Novelist*, and Janet Todd, in *The Sign of Angellica*, have both interpreted *The Female Quixote* as a variant on the 'reformed coquette tradition'[59] in which the misguided heroine is reclaimed to find her true, subordinate place within society. She must learn to resign an image of society in which women are accorded great power, and take up one in which they are not. As Todd puts it, 'Arabella wants to replace law and religion, both of which systems seem to assign lesser status to women, with heroic romance in which women have vast significance.'[60] Thus after her final conversion Arabella 'is ready to be a wife because she has learned that what romance teaches is false: men do not exist to serve women'.[61] Spencer claims that '*The Female Quixote: or, The Adventures of Arabella* is an analysis of romance as a fantasy of female power',[62] so that 'when Arabella does give up her illusions, she gives up her power'.[63]

Laurie Langbauer provides a rather different reading in her chapter on *The Female Quixote* in *Women and Romance: The Consolations of Gender in the*

English Novel. Langbauer argues that Lennox aims to deride the romance tradition, but that in drawing a contrast between the novel and romance she ultimately reveals the importance of the latter as a form that gives meaning to women as writers, readers and characters.[64] The resolution of the book, when Arabella finally abandons her fantasies of empowerment and accepts the authority of the learned doctor, represents her final submission to convention as she is subsumed within the patriarchal order.[65]

Langbauer's reading is subtle and convincing, yet Arabella's fantasy world is peopled with heroes as well as heroines. It is one in which women are accorded great sexual and emotional power, but in which they are also threatened by continual danger from powerful ravishing men. Arabella has to learn that women are no longer heroines, and men are, for the most part, neither heroes nor villains. They are mixed characters of the kind that Catherine Moreland describes, and they no longer have the scope for the kind of heroic individualistic actions that Arabella has imagined. The social roles of both women and men have become constrained and confined. Modern manners have departed from the standard of the heroic age, since the commercial system does not operate on epic principles, but emphasises the interdependence of the members of the state, and the need for each to fulfil their allotted and limited role.

As a result it is necessary to develop a new, literary form, which can present 'mixed' characters, reflect the complex nature of modern society, with its division of labour and private flexible ethics, but also embody the more sophisticated relationship between text and reader that is a feature of modern production. Langbauer has suggested that the *Female Quixote* posits a concept of a transparently referential language that can be opposed to the extravagant language of romance.[66] Yet while the language of the novel may be perceived as more passive and supine than that of romance, the role of the reader is conceived as correspondingly active and constructive. Modern readers are expected to be very different from Arabella, who takes everything literally. Indeed Arabella's univocal concept of the text is recognised as aberrant by the learned doctor. The modern reader approaches the text with more discretion and discrimination. S/he has become an autonomous agent, with an active role to play in the production of literary meaning which replicates his or her active role in the economic system. This changed relationship must be embodied within a fictional structure that can articulate a contemporary ethic. Thus by 1778, when Mary Hamilton published *Munster Village*, the Arabella figure had become a comic cameo. Hamilton described Mrs Dorothea Bingley, a maiden lady of fifty, who 'having lived all her life in the country ... derived all her ideas of love from the heroic romance':

To talk to her of love was a capital offence. Her rigour must be melted by the blood of giants, necromancers, and paynim Knights. She expected, that, for her sake, they would retire to desarts, mourn her cruelty, *subsist* on *nothing*, and make light of scampering over impassable mountains, and riding through unfordable rivers, without recollecting, that, while the imagination of the lover is linked to this *muddy vesture of decay*, she must now and then condescend to partake of the carnality of the vivres of the shambles.[67]

Mrs Bingley is a figure of fun rather than the representative of an ethos that constitutes a challenge to the dominant values of modern society, and as such is indicative of the hegemonic status that had been achieved by the novel by 1778. In the following section, however, I will look at another novel which manifests the persistence of heroic ideology – Richardson's *Sir Charles Grandison* – and will consider how far it merits the praise of Lennox's learned doctor, and managed 'to convey the most solid instructions, the noblest sentiments, and the most exalted piety in the pleasing dress of a novel'.

SIR CHARLES GRANDISON

In his third novel, *Sir Charles Grandison*, Samuel Richardson attempted to move away from the exploration of female virtue which had proved so successful in *Pamela* and *Clarissa* in order to present an image of male virtue, and 'produce into the public View the Character and Actions of a Man of TRUE HONOUR'. Yet while Richardson was confident of his ability to portray exemplary women, he doubted whether he would be able to overcome 'the Difficulty of drawing a good Man that the Ladies will not despise and the Gentlemen laugh at'. As he wrote to Lady Bradshaigh in 1751,

I own that a good woman is my favourite character; and that I can do twenty agreeable things for her, none of which would appear in a striking light in a man. Softness of heart, gentleness of manners, tears, beauty, will allow of pathetic scenes in the story of the one, which cannot have place in that of the other. Philanthropy, humanity, is all that he can properly rise to.[68]

Ever since its publication, the central problem facing readers and critics of *Sir Charles Grandison* has related to the character of this good man.[69] Sir Charles Grandison is constantly represented by his friends, relatives and acquaintances as a paragon of all virtues. He is 'in the great and yet comprehensive sense of the word, a good man',[70] who has 'an un-bounded charity, and universal benevolence, to men in all professions; and who, imitating the Divinity, regards the heart rather than the head and much more than either rank or fortune, tho' it were princely' (vol. III, p. 241). Yet despite the repeated references to his virtues, and despite the portrayal of his benevolent actions, Sir Charles comes across as a worthy and respectable but extremely pompous individual, who does not really justify the extravagant terms in which he is continually described.[71] This was not purely a result of Richardson's personal uneasiness over the nature of masculinity. It was also a consequence of a more general cultural uncertainty over the definition of male virtue, at a time when the epic concept of heroism and public endeavour was being undermined by the emergence of economic analysis, with its denial of the importance of any kind of civic humanist notion of the public, and its elevation not only of private and domestic virtue, but also of mercenary acquisitiveness.

Sir Charles Grandison is no conventional fictional hero. He does not embody traditional public virtue, but on the other hand he does not represent the acceptance of the private and amelioratory role of the fictional hero that is found in *Tom Jones*. His social position indicates Richardson's desire to assimilate the epic idea of public virtue, with an awareness of the economic forces within contemporary society. Sir Charles is a landed aristocrat, but he is also dedicated to the commercial virtues of thrift, economic prudence and careful management. Indeed so far is he from the heroic or even the romantic mode that he is not afraid of stressing the importance of money, even in relation to matters of matrimony. As he explains to the young Danby family,

We must not blame indiscriminately ... all fathers who expect a fortune to be brought into their family, in some measure equivalent to the benefit the new-comer hopes to receive from it; especially in mercantile families ... Love is a selfish Deity. He puts two persons upon preferring their own interests, nay, a gratification of their passion often *against* their interests, to those of everybody else; and reason, discretion, duty are frequently given up in competition with it. (vol. I, pp. 453–4)

This pragmatic dismissal of the value of affective relationships in part reflects Sir Charles' view of the social role of the mercantile classes. As primarily the producers of goods and money they cannot be guided by romantic or individualistic codes of behaviour. Yet his words are not exclusively confined to these groups, and in a letter to the guardian of his own future bride he reaffirmed his belief that matrimony must be seen as a financial as well as a romantic commitment (vol. III, p. 36). A similar assumption is implicit in the actions of most eighteenth-century heroes and heroines. Sophia Western and Tom Jones take for granted the fact that they will not be able to marry if the latter really is a beggarly bastard.[72] Roderick Random has to gain an independent fortune at the end of the novel to marry Narcissa.[73] The difference with Grandison is that he actually comes out and says that money is important, in the measured pompous prose that is his hallmark in the novel, and which forms such a striking contrast to the lively and emotional writing of the female supporting cast. Grandison has the self-control and careful prudence that was later to characterise Jane Austen's mature heroes, but while it takes Emma an entire novel to appreciate the charms of Mr Knightley,[74] and a similar time for Marianne Dashwood to reconsider her views on the 'exceedingly ancient' Colonel Brandon,[75] we are expected to recognise Grandison's virtues straight away. Moreover, Austen's heroes primarily serve as foils and monitors for the heroines who are the real subjects of moral concern, but in *Grandison* the hero is, nominally at least, the main focus of moral interest, and the locus of true and egregious virtue. He therefore has to combine the portrayal of the passive and prudent virtues that are appropriate within the contemporary context with a degree of activity that is incumbent on his role as hero. In *Tom Jones*, as in *Clarissa*, the heroic element of epic was maintained through the displacement of conquest from the martial to the sexual sphere, but this is clearly not appropriate for Sir Charles. His virility is instead displayed in the counting house and estate office.

We are informed how Grandison bases his system of estate management on financial acumen and suspicious caution. Dr Bartlett outlines this system to Harriet Byron, after she has become Grandison's wife. He explains that Grandison pays attention to the minutest details of estate management as well as the greatest, carrying out repairs as soon as they become necessary. This ensures that 'he is not imposed upon by incroaching or craving tenants'. As a result 'His tenants grow into circumstance under him . . . In a few years, improving only what he has in both kingdoms, he will be very rich, yet answer the generous demands of his own heart upon his benevolence' (vol. III, pp. 287–8). Sir Charles' programme of economic prudence would be admirable in an eighteenth-century aristocrat, but it is hardly the stuff of a romantic hero.

The portrayal of a benevolent but calculating landlord, attempting to evade the unreasonable demands of a grasping tenantry, through mastery of the detail of estate management, emphasises the social tensions within the world which *Grandison* sought to portray. Like the epic heroes, Grandison is tough as well as tender, but the threat which he fends off comes from within the community of the country estate – from the dominance of self-interest amongst its members. Grandison must be active in defending his own interests against the partial interests of others, and this will ultimately be of benefit to the community as a whole. Likewise, although he is often charitable and benevolent, this is presented as secondary to the primary duty of the payment of debts and obligations. Sir Charles tells his uncle, 'I will endeavour to be just; and then, if I can, I will be generous' (vol. 1, p. 380).

Instead of the impulsive liberality of Fielding's Tom Jones, or the financial indiscretion of Fanny Burney's heroines, Richardson's hero is characterised by a preoccupation with his own financial interest and a dedication to the cautious pursuit of the main chance. He is benevolent, but his is a calculating benevolence. He eschews romantic generosity (vol. III, p. 36), and his gifts are always proportioned to the moral worth as well as the needs of the recipient (vol. III, p. 240). He lives in a world which is inhabited by potential cheats and scoundrels, where the landlord must hold the line against his tenantry, and redistribution takes second place to acquisition. In such an environment benevolence must be based on the calculation of consequences, rather than motives, and you must act wisely and not just mean well. In this respect, *Grandison* has more in common with the economic vision of the social structure than most eighteenth-century novels, for the moral focus of fiction is usually the sentiments and intentions of the characters, rather than the effects of their actions.

Even Grandison's nationalism is grounded in financial calculation. In December 1753 Lady Bradshaigh wrote to Richardson complaining that in the Italian scenes of the novel Sir Charles does not show a strong enough preference for his country and religion.[76] As a result, Richardson appended an 'unlucky omission' to volume 7, which was 'restored' to the body of the text in all subsequent editions, and which could almost have been taken directly from the pages of an early economic treatise. The omission recounts how Sir Charles 'on a double Principle of Religion and Policy ... encourages the Trades-People, the Manufacturers, the Servants, of his own Country', and presents his arguments against the spread of foreign luxuries: 'Shall any one pretend to true

Patriotism, and not attempt to stem this torrent of Fashion, which impoverishes our own honest countrymen, whilst it carries Wealth and Power to those whose National Religion and Interest are directly opposite to ours!' (vol. III, pp. 263–4). The fictional hero gives voice to the bullionist ethic of the balance of trade philosophy, and while Sir Charles does not articulate the consumption-based theories of growth that were becoming accepted in economic thought, he nonetheless indicates the need to locate values such as patriotism in the calculation of the indirect consequences of individual actions.

This use of fictional characters for the articulation of rather practical and prosaic economic ideas has encouraged critical uneasiness over the novel.[77] Sir Charles has been identified as an ill-assorted blend of aristocratic status and middle-class morality. For Richardson's biographers, Duncan Eaves and Ben Kimpel, he is 'a prosperous and respectable middle class man (for his aristocracy is never very convincing)'[78] while Terry Eagleton described him as an 'impeccably middle-class aristocrat'.[79] In practice, being an eighteenth-century aristocrat involved studying rent rolls, account-books and agricultural treatises, and Grandison is probably a better example of the species than many of the more dashing heroes of eighteenth-century fiction, but while he may be a convincing landowner, he is not a convincing hero – particularly when he is discoursing on economic topics. The prose often seems to drag somewhat when Grandison is holding forth, and ennui sweeps over the reader even as the female characters within the novel are gushing with enthusiasm over their hero's astonishing prudence and virtue. The 'failure' of Grandison as a character can therefore be seen as fictional rather than social: a reflection not so much of Richardson's humble origins as of his idea of how literature worked.

For the tensions within the novel have more complex causes than merely the problem of portraying a prudent hero. The system of careful and calculating morality embodied by Sir Charles lacked a certain charm, but it was also in conflict with the model of didacticism that Richardson posited within the text. For Richardson's rejection of morally 'mixed' characters meant that Sir Charles had to function as a model of exemplary morality. He is not just an ordinary person with whom we can empathise, and with whose follies and errors we can sympathise. He is someone we should look up to, and by whom we should be inspired to virtuous actions. In this respect we, as readers, are expected to be in the same position as the numerous characters in the text who are converted from the paths of wickedness by Sir Charles.

Emily Jervois tells us 'my guardian's goodness makes every-body good' (
vol. II, p. 42), and that is supposed to include us. As John Mullan writes
in his study of *Sentiment and Sociability*, 'in the novel, as in the novelist's
correspondence, he is produced by acclamation; in the end, he *is* that
acclamation. Sir Charles remains, more than anything else, an effect of
feminine awe.'[80] This somewhat coercive didacticism, combined with
the rather priggish and prosing character of Sir Charles, may explain
why *Grandison* has remained unpopular with readers, and why, despite
the efflorescence of interest in Richardson over the last twenty years, it
has been relatively neglected by critics. Terry Castle's *Clarissa's Ciphers*,
for example, provides a thorough exegesis of the hermeneutic questions
raised by *Clarissa*, but *Grandison* merits only a footnote.

The equation of virtue with the calculation of the consequences of
individual actions is juxtaposed with the construction of Sir Charles as
an exemplary figure, and one who exemplifies a rather different model
of morality from that posited within his own economic homilies. For Sir
Charles' virtue is not only transcendent, but also essentially public. He is
not enmeshed in a complex interdependent mechanism; he is above it.
As Harriet Byron's grandmother comments: 'How know we what
[Providence] has designed for Sir Charles Grandison? *His* welfare is the
concern of hundreds, perhaps. He, compared to us, is as the public to
the private' (vol. I, p. 307).

Sir Charles is therefore like Glover's epic hero Leonidas in that his
heroism is revealed in the willingness with which he sacrifices his private
sentiments for the service of the public. It is in these terms that he
explains to General Della Poretta why he cannot accept the conditions
proposed for his marriage to Clementina:

What shall I be thought of, who, tho' I am not, nor wish to be, a public man [i.e.
a holder of an office within the state], am not of a low or inconsiderable family,
if I, against my conscience, renounce my religion and my country, for a
consideration, that, tho' the highest in private life, is a partial and selfish
consideration? (vol. II, p. 197)

This portrayal of the conflict between public and private interests, and
of the dependence of the state on the exertion of heroic public spirit, had
little connection with the image of the interdependent commercial state
which formed the background for much of *Sir Charles Grandison*. Richardson attempts to represent the workings and ethic of the modern
commercial state, but undermines this by an adherence to a didactic
and narrative strategy based on ideas of morality and mimesis that owe
much to the epic tradition.

This is evident in the terms of Richardson's presentation of Grandison's attitude to the conventional code of honour. Sir Charles sets himself up as an avowed opponent of duelling, and reiterates his condemnation of this practice as barbarous and un-Christian. Instead, he endorses the legal institutions of the state. Yet these fine words are liberally garnished with references to Sir Charles' martial abilities and physical courage. We are constantly reminded that he is an expert in the 'Science of Defence', and while proclaiming pacifism he is far from passive in his confrontation with the novel's numerous villains. Thus in using the character of 'the brave man' to reinforce the lessons of 'the *good* man', Richardson indicated the dependence of his concept of Christian virtue on the traditional epic code of heroic values.

The repeated juxtaposition of Sir Charles' speeches against 'honour' with displays of his physical prowess symbolised the novel's uncertainty over the portrayal of an autonomous commercial morality. Sir Charles is shown acting prudently and soberly, emphasising justice and mercy rather than honour, and taking account of his own economic interests while promoting the good of others. But while Richardson believed that this was the code of behaviour most suited for the complex commercial state, he was not entirely reconciled to its adequacy as a blueprint for fictional heroism, and this anxiety was inflected by concern about the issue of gender. The various competing discourses of social analysis that existed in the eighteenth century were devoted to the examination of a society that was assumed to be composed of men, and yet with the increasing recognition of the inapplicability of civic humanist man to contemporary society there was no code of behaviour that was at once relevant and clearly and unequivocally masculine. Both moral philosophy and economics stressed virtues that were essentially passive, constructing an amelioratory role for morality that was based on submergence within, rather than dominance of, the social system. This was widely perceived as an effeminate and emasculated model of male identity amongst a reading public that inherited the tradition of epic assumptions about the nature of heroism.

Richardson's doubts about his ability to represent a 'good man' have already been indicated. Throughout *Grandison* he attempted to undermine the conventional idea of heroic masculinity. Lady G. writes to Harriet Byron complaining, 'Of what violences, murders, depredations, have not the Epic poets been the occasion, by propagating false honour, false glory, and false religion?' (vol. III, pp. 197–8). When Sir Charles returns from a trip in which he has been engaged in negotiations and interventions to sort out the affairs of others, Harriet writes that

He appeared to me in a much more shining light than an hero would have done, returning in a triumphal car covered with laurels, and dragging captive princes at its wheels. How much more glorious a character is that of *The Friend of Mankind*, than that of *The Conqueror of Nations*! (vol. II, p. 70)

Yet ultimately the portrayal of Grandison as an emasculated man of commerce has to be buttressed by the evocation of his powers as a man of honour. At the same time the narrative structure emphasises the distinction between Grandison and the community of admiring females that surrounds him. It was not only Sir Charles' wealth and status, but also his sex that meant that to Harriet Byron he is 'as the public to the private', and the distinction between the male and female spheres of influence is highlighted in a letter from Harriet to her grandmother, written after her marriage to Sir Charles:

We are busied in returning the visits of our neighbours ... We have a very agreeable neighbourhood. But I want these visitings to be over. Sir Charles and his relations and mine, are the world to me. These obligations of ceremony, tho' unavoidable, are drawbacks upon the true domestic felicity. (vol. III, pp. 282–3)

While Sir Charles Grandison embraces his public role as landowner and aristocrat, the women of the novel retreat from the extensive community, and prioritise the purely private social unit. Such is the significance of familial relations that all strong affective bonds are described in these terms. Harriet Byron has only met Sir Rowland Meredith twice when she asks to be able to call him *father*, Lady D. takes on the appellation *mother*, and Harriet's denomination of the Grandison family as her siblings gives incestuous overtones to her marriage with Sir Charles.[81] In identifying all close relationships as extensions of the family system, Harriet Byron and the Grandison sisters reveal their dependence on the family as the defining unit of modern society. It is only in these terms that they can conceptualise obligations and personal ties.

Richardson's attempt to formulate an image of commercial society is continually moderated by the portrayal of the very different values of the affective community. The utilisation of the epistolary form ensured that the implications of the public commercial ethos were not fully explored, since this ethos was continually expressed through, and brought back to, the private voice of Harriet Byron. For in *Sir Charles Grandison* the actions and sententious utterances of the hero are primarily conveyed through the letters of his almost exclusively female circle of admirers – his sisters, his ward, his lover and her numerous friends and relations. The representation of the public commercial world, and the network of indirect and economic relationships, is mediated by being conveyed in a personal and female correspondence that invariably prioritised affective relations and the domestic realm.

At the same time the emphasis on preceptial morality, in *Grandison* as in *Clarissa*, suggests a reliance on a more aristocratic or epic notion of heroic virtue. The presentation of the status quo has to be legitimated by the invocation of classical, anti-commercial images of morality, and of the didactic function of literature. Thus although Richardson is often identified as a low-bourgeois writer,[82] this is a serious misinterpretation of the ideological significance of his narratives. Instead of being a triumphant advocate of the bourgeois and progressive novel form, Richardson was rather an apologist for his fictions, who was anxious to legitimate the genre by reliance on the mimetic systems of an earlier literary tradition.

It was in part this endorsement of reactionary and anti-commercial aesthetic theories, and the maintenance of ideas of the public nature of fictional morality, which ensured Richardson's popularity amongst eighteenth-century moralists, and those who were generally opposed to the novel form. For the readers of Richardson's day were far more aware of the public aspects of his work than are modern critics. While readers nowadays prioritise the subversive subtext, the construction of character, and those features of the narrative which emphasise the private bourgeois elements of the fiction, the moralists, critics and readers of Richardson's day saw these aspects of the work in the context of the explicit moral purpose and the preceptual didactic structure. They emphasised the exemplary role of Clarissa and Pamela, even if they did not feel that the characters lived up to this role. They recognised that despite his interest in money and the details of domestic economy and exchange, and despite the explicit articulation of economic values, Richardson's novels were based around a model of individual morality that was fundamentally in conflict with the idea of the form and function of ethical systems that was generated by economic analysis. It may have been for this reason that Richardson's novels were consistently represented in the eighteenth century as more moral, and of higher status, than those works of Fielding which are nowadays identified as patrician.[83]

In *Sir Charles Grandison* Richardson juxtaposed his portrayal of the feminised, commercial ethic with appeals to the concept of the masculine, epic hero. In *Clarissa* the experiential narrative structure is combined with an editorial insistence on the exemplary function of character and the preceptial nature of fictional morality. As such, Richardson's novels can be taken to embody the moral confusion of the mid-eighteenth century, and in particular the challenge presented by the emergent commercial morality to literary representation. Richardson seeks to locate the values of his narrative within the commercial world, but he cannot accept the weakening of gender distinctions, and the reorientation of the structure of morality implicit in economic analysis. His refusal to embrace the experiential morality that was the essence of the fictional form ensured that his novels internalised the conflict between didacticism and representation that had been identified in criticism of the novel.

In this chapter I have indicated the importance of the clash between private and public virtues within the novels of the mid-eighteenth century, yet despite the preoccupation with the work of Richardson and Fielding in many studies of this period, the nature and implications of this conflict have not been widely recognised. In part this is due to the distortions of the critical perspective that have been caused by the composition of the literary canon. Not only the classical corpus of the great tradition, but also the canons established more recently, particularly by feminist critics, to challenge the exclusivity of the classical approach, have tended to prioritise those novels which resolved the conflict of public and private morality by the elevation of a limited and feminised notion of virtue, and the location of the novel within a limited private sphere.[84]

F. R. Leavis emphasised the importance of a 'complex moral economy' within the novel, and based his valuations on a desire for a combination of 'formal perfection' and a sophisticated analysis of human nature.[85] *Emma* was part of the great tradition because it embodied both these virtues, but *Tom Jones* was rejected on the grounds that it had neither. The subjective nature of these judgements has been exploded on numerous occasions, and the canon has been both reconstructed and rejected. Nonetheless, many of the critics who have rewritten the literary history of the eighteenth century have perpetuated a predisposition towards novels that have a moral and formal coherence similar to that which was emphasised by Leavis. Fielding, Richardson and Smollett have been admitted into the canon, along with a host of female writers, but this has only partially been achieved by a reorientation of the entrance qualifications. The critical acknowledgement of these writers has been to a large extent dependent on demonstrations that they conform to a set of humanist and in many ways Leavisite criteria after all. Critics have emphasised the narrative coherence and psychological depth of eighteenth-century novels, and these have been identified as peculiarly feminine characteristics.[86] Those works or passages which lack a clear and unified narrative structure, and are not based around the exploration of individual character, have tended to be suppressed or ignored. As a result there has been a considerable interest in recent years in the more explicitly private novels of the eighteenth century. Richardson's *Pamela* and *Clarissa* have once more come into vogue, while his more public *Sir Charles Grandison* is still treated with some suspicion. Smollett's expansive and cumbersome *Peregrine Pickle* has tended to be sidelined, in favour of the more tightly structured *Humphry Clinker*. Those novels which represent a spectrum of society have often been neglected, since they do not have the narrative coherence of works which are centred on the actions and experiences of a single individual or a limited social group. The novel has been identified as a form that is primarily devoted to the exploration of personal relationships, with love and marriage as dominant themes, and even some of the critics who have focussed on the women writers of the period have not given extensive consideration to works such as Sarah Scott's *Millenium Hall* or Mary Hamilton's *Munster Village*, which prioritised communitarian rather than affective values, and sought in collectivity a form of public virtue which could constitute a challenge to the individualism of private ideology.[87]

Despite, therefore, the tendency of recent criticism to extend the canon of eighteenth-century narrative fiction, and to popularise formerly little-known writers such as Mary Hays, Charlotte Smith, Charlotte Lennox, Sarah Fielding, Frances Brooke, Fanny Burney, Elizabeth Inchbald and others, the emphasis on the representation of private experience has ensured that many critics have failed to appreciate the range of structures and fluidity of form which characterised the novel in the eighteenth century. J. Paul Hunter has attempted to draw attention to this diversity in his *Before Novels*, but this kind of approach has not yet percolated through to affect the terms of the general discussion of the canon, and has not yet brought about a reorientation of the criteria for the selection of works for inclusion within the popular reprint series, such as Penguin Classics and Oxford University Press's World's Classics series. Many of the more neglected novels combine the unfolding of their fictional narrative with a more general discursive function. Discussions of morality, politics and constitutional history, economics and literature are juxtaposed with the sentimental plot, and this use of the prose narrative to convey a range of political and philosophical arguments and information reveals that in the eighteenth century the novel form was identified as a vehicle for the conveyance of more diverse and general didacticism than is indicated by the canonical texts. Writers such as Henry Brooke and Charles Johnstone saw the novel as a flexible discursive genre which could be adapted for polite philosophical speculations. Indeed, these writers attempted to use the novel in a similar way to that in which Pope had exploited the poetic form in the *Epistles to Several Persons* and the *Essay on Man*. The existence of these discursive, analytical and to some extent public texts serves to highlight many of those aspects of the more canonical works which have tended to be suppressed by the predominant critical emphasis on narrative coherence and individual experience. There is nothing surprising in the interpolated narratives which characterise eighteenth-century fiction when they are seen in the context of the very loose novel structures which are quite deliberately utilised in many of the lesser-known novels. Moreover, the explicit discussions of the nature of public and private virtue, and of the impact of economic change and economic analysis within the more discursive and philosophical texts, illuminate the implicit conflict that has conditioned the works of the literary canon.

The second half of the eighteenth century saw novels used to fulfil a range of functions and explore a range of experiences. As the popularity of novels, and the number of novels produced, steadily grew, the genre began to form into a range of distinct sub-genres, with their own conventions, their own advocates, and their own demarcation of the areas of experience that were appropriate for portrayal within fiction. By the end of the century the monolithic and all-embracing fiction of Fielding and Smollett had gone, to be replaced by a plethora of forms – the Gothic novel, the sentimental novel, the jacobin novel, the anti-jacobin novel, the novel of manners, and so on. In the following chapters I will look at some of the kinds of fiction that developed in the second half of the eighteenth century, to assess how far they managed to bridge the divide between the terms of public and private morality, to provide an ethic and an image of society that was appropriate to the commercial state.

CHAPTER 5

The novel of circulation

One type of novel that has tended to be sidelined as a consequence of the critical emphasis on narrative coherence is found in a group of works which I have termed the 'novels of circulation'.[1] These were novels based neither on the adventures of an individual, nor on the correspondence of a group of friends, but on the exchange of an inanimate object. The central character – a penny, a bank-note, a dog, a cat, a peg, a hackney carriage or whatever – is passed from person to person, sold, exchanged, lost, found, swapped and so on, and recounts its adventures, its thoughts, and the characters it encounters in the course of its life. This form was utilised by Charles Gildon with the publication in 1709–10 of *The Golden Spy*, roughly based on Alain René Le Sage's *Le Diable Boiteux*, which had been translated in 1708 as *The Devil Upon Two Sticks*. In Le Sage's work the devil flies about the city taking the roofs off houses to expose what is going on below. In *The Golden Spy* the scandalous element of Le Sage is incorporated into a circulation format, as a *louis d'or* narrates a tale composed of a series of loosely connected scenes, containing political comment and satire, social satire, scandal and sexual intrigue. Crébillon's *The Sofa*, translated in 1742, rapidly achieved considerable notoriety in eighteenth-century Britain, and epitomised the importance of the *roman à clef* or *chronique scandaleuse* tradition within the novels of circulation, particularly in the early works, which were influenced by, or derived from, French originals.[2]

It was really only from the mid-century, with the publication in 1751 of Francis Coventry's story of a Bologna lapdog, *Pompey the Little*, that the novel of circulation became established as an autonomous narrative form within Britain. Amongst the numerous novels published in the second half of the century were: Susan Smythies, *The Stage-Coach* (1753); *The Sedan* (1757); Charles Johnstone's extremely popular *Chrysal: or, The Adventures of a Guinea* (1760–5); Thomas Bridges, *The Adventures of a Bank Note* (1770–1); [William Guthrie?], *The Life and Adventures of a Cat* (1760);

[Dorothy Kilner?], *The Adventures of a Hackney Coach* (1781); Dorothy Kilner, *The Life and Perambulations of a Mouse* (*c.* 1785); *The Adventures of a Watch* (1788); *The Adventures of a Silver Penny* [178?]; Helenus Scott, *The Adventures of a Rupee* (1792); and Mary Ann Kilner, *The Adventures of a Pincushion* [1790], and *Memoirs of a Peg-Top* [179?]. The form even survived into the nineteenth century with the publication in 1849 of *The Adventures of a £1000 Note*.

The use of an inhuman or inanimate narrator in these works ensures that they have a wholly different structure from either the linear narratives derived from the picaresque tradition, or the epistolary novel form. Like Tom Jones or Peregrine Pickle, the guinea, bank-note, lapdog, etc., pass through society, encountering a range of characters and experiences. But unlike the picaroons of Fielding and Smollett, the inhuman characters are devoid of volition. They do not find their own way between the various locations of the novels, but are passed from owner to owner. Even Francis Coventry's Pompey, though a dog and theoretically possessed of volition and the power of movement, is an extremely small dog. He tends to be carried about like an object, and although he gets lost on one occasion, he rarely runs away from his owners or moves of his own accord. He, like the guinea, etc., is lost, found, given, but above all exchanged, moving between individuals who otherwise have no connection with one another. As a result, the narrative structure is based around an accumulation of discrete episodes, for whereas the sentience of Fielding and Smollett's characters enables them to form relationships with the individuals they fortuitously encounter, providing a mechanism for binding the narrative into a coherent whole, in the novels of circulation the objects are unable to control events, and cannot unite the diverse scenes and diverse characters. These novels therefore lack the interactive dimension of more canonical fiction. At a time when many novels were developing signs of sentimentalism, emphasising within fiction the affective links that are perceived as at once essential to, but often absent from, relations within the commercial state, the novel of circulation provides a paradigm of the alienation but also the interdependence that is identified as characteristic of society.

In *The Adventures of a Bank Note* the bank note passes in rapid succession from a poet, to a grocer, to a doctor, to a young girl, to a silk mercer, to a stock-broker's wife, to a jeweller, to a diamond merchant's wife, to a banker's bill man, to a gentleman, to a wine merchant, to a clergyman, to a butcher and so on.[3] Charles Johnstone's *Chrysal* is a little more complicated, since a few prominent political figures, such as the Duchess of Newcastle, are made to re-encounter the guinea in the course of the narrative, but for the most part its structure, like the majority of novels of circulation, is entirely episodic. Pompey the Little passes from a Bologna courtesan, to an English fop, to Lady Tempest, a widowed countess, to a *nouveau riche* family, to a religious old maid, to a man of fashion, to a wealthy Methodist, to an alehouse-keeper's daughter, to a 'nymph of Billingsgate', to a coffeehouse-keeper, to a watchman, to a blind beggar, to an innkeeper, to a young lady of taste, to a milliner, to a nobleman, to an impoverished poet, to a hypochondriac, to a student at Cambridge, to a Cambridge fellow, to an aging beauty, before being returned to Lady Tempest, in whose possession he dies. The novels can therefore incorporate a wide range of different scenes and characters, and the full spectrum of social class and wealth. These scenes are joined together within a fairly loose, discursive form. Robert Adams Day writes in the introduction of the Oxford edition of *Pompey the Little*:

Coventry does not attempt to create a unified fiction, and throughout most of the book the 'character' of Pompey serves merely as a string on which the satiric episodes can be threaded . . . *Pompey* is not a novel, if by 'novel' one means anything more than a fictional prose narrative of a certain length.[4]

Day's assertion that *Pompey* is not a novel is, however, predicated on a particular concept of the structure of narrative fiction, which perhaps owes something to the continuing strength of the Leavisite notion of the 'marked moral intensity' of fiction.[5] It is not so much that *Pompey* is not a novel, but rather that it is a novel with a structure which embodies a different image of society from that presented within more canonical works.

These fictional prose narrations had a considerable appeal for contemporary readers, particularly since their loose form enabled them to combine general social satire and social comment with elements of the *roman à clef* or *chronique scandaleuse* tradition, presenting real characters in a satirical light. In Charles Johnstone's *Chrysal* the spirit of gold that is embodied within the guinea encounters George II, his mistress the Countess of Yarmouth, Frederick the Great, Lord Chesterfield, and, in the revised and extended edition of 1765, Sir Francis Dashwood and the members of the Hell Fire Club. Lady Mary Wortley Montagu identified the satire of *Pompey* as simultaneously universal and particular. It portrayed the manners that were characteristic of metropolitan society in general, as well as representing specific individuals. As she wrote to her daughter, Lady Bute:

Pompey the Little . . . is a real and exact representation of life as it is now acted in London, as it was in my time, and as it will be (I do not doubt) a Hundred years hence, with some little Variation of Dress, and perhaps Government. I found there many of my Acquaintance. Lady T[ownshend] and Lady O[rford] are so well painted, I fancy I heard them talk, and have heard them say the very things here repeated.[6]

The looseness and inclusiveness of this flexible narrative structure is, in part, made possible by the use of an inhuman hero. In *Pompey the Little* Pompey can serve as a symbol and embodiment of the vices of the age in which he lives. The characters he encounters may either satirise real figures in contemporary society, or represent traditional comic stereotypes, satirising particular occupations and professions – medicine, law, mendicancy, etc. At the same time the narrative voice can be used to articulate more general social criticism. In the account of Pompey's life with Lady Tempest the author presents a canine version of the vanity and vacuousness of human existence. We are told that

As [Pompey] attended his mistress to all Routs, Drums, Hurricanes, Hurly-burlys and Earthquakes, he soon established an Acquaintance and Friendship with all the Dogs of Quality, and of course affected a most hearty Contempt for all of inferior Station, whom he would never vouchsafe to play with, or pay them the least Regard. He pretended to know at first sight, whether a Dog had received a good Education, by his Manner of coming into a Room, and was extremely proud to shew *his Collar at Court*, in which he resembled certain other Dogs, who are equally vain of their Finery, and happy to be distinguished in their *respective Orders*.[7]

Pompey's pretensions and snobbery satirise the behaviour of human courtiers, but his pride is frequently deflated. Swiftian scatology high-lights the extent to which the bestial nature can be disguised but not removed by the trappings of culture. This is exemplified, for instance, in the scene in which Pompey is imprisoned in a closet containing a volume of Mr Whitefield's sermons. Pompey 'made various attempts to open the door; but not having the good fortune to succeed, he leaped upon the table, and wantonly did his occasions on the field-preachers memoirs, which lay open upon it'.[8] In part, this scene reflects the theological perspective of the orthodox Anglican Coventry and fits in with the satirical tone of anti-Methodist works such as Richard Graves'

The Spiritual Quixote, but it also develops the attack on vanity and pretension within the text. Pompey's philosophical and social aspirations are undermined by such dramatic indications that he is a mere animal, and the satire reflects on the human aspirations which he has symbolised. The fine clothes and refined manners of the courtier can disguise but not avoid the common physicality of the yahoo that is lurking underneath.

Elsewhere the social satire derives from the characters Pompey encounters, rather than from the hero himself. The atheistical Lady Sophister, after discoursing on the immortality of the soul,

Ran into much common-place raillery at the Expence only of Christianity and the Gospel; till Lady Tempest cut her short, and desired her to be Silent on that Head; for this good Lady believed all the Doctrines of Religion, and was contented, like many others, with the trifling privilege only of disobeying all its precepts.[9]

In describing the *nouveau riche* family who later take possession of Pompey, the narrator provides a satire on upward mobility and wealthy decadence that owes much to the Tory rhetoric of civic humanist tradition. The husband inherited a vast fortune from his miserly merchant father, and having been persuaded by his wife to 'quit the dirty scene of Business', the couple gave themselves up to pleasure. But

As neither of them had been used to the Company they were now to keep, and both utterly unacquainted with all the Arts of Taste, their Appearance in the Polite World plainly manifested their Original, and shewed how unworthy they were of those Riches they so awkwardly enjoy'd.[10]

The narrative voice attacks the self-made man and the pretensions of his family – their extravagance, their want of taste, their lack of manners and education. But he also despises 'polite' society for their servile acceptance of such interlopers and the acquisitive materialism which it represents:

It may be imagined that such awkward Pretenders to High-Life, were treated with Ridicule by all the People of Genius and Spirit; but immoderate Wealth, and a Coach and Six, opened them a Way into Company, and few refused their Visits, tho' all laughed at their Appearance. For to tell the Reader a Secret, Money will procure its Owners Admittance any where; and however People may pride themselves on the Antiquity of their Families, if they have not Money to preserve a Splendor in Life, they may go a begging with their Pedigrees in their Hands.[11]

This is the anti-commercial rhetoric of Tory tradition, which identified the new commercial system as a source of social instability, and a challenge to the values of the old nobility. *Pompey the Little* indicates that the emergence of new money has eroded the probity of the aristocracy, which has become decadent and corrupt. Thus when Pompey is confined in the watch house he witnesses the unmannerly and dissolute behaviour of two young lords, who have been taken in after a night on the town. 'The next Morning', we are told, 'they returned Home in Chairs, new-dressed themselves, and then took their Seats in Parliament, to enact Laws for the Good of their Country'.[12]

Likewise the bank-note who narrates his life story in Thomas Bridges' *Adventures of a Bank Note* reaches a height of indignation in his account of 'A scoundrel baronet, who had run into every body's debt, and being a member of parliament, the poor tradesmen that he had robb'd and half-ruined, had no remedy against the thief.'[13]

The actions of this 'villain' are unfavourably compared with those of a highwayman, who at least risks his life when he robs you, and the general tolerance of the situation is condemned as 'the most absurd management a wise nation could fall into'.[14] Clearly bad debt and bad credit are looked on as very serious matters by the bank-note, whose value relies on the maintenance of collective faith. Elsewhere the bank-note draws attention to the diverse satirical sources for the genre, by adopting a tone that is between the Swiftian and Sternean, in an elaborate invocation of learned authority in justification of his argument:

Hugo Grotius, in his Treatise de Jure Belli ac Pacis says – hold, I believe I am wrong, it could not be Hugo Grotius, he was too grave a writer for such an expression; and yet if it was not him, it must be somebody else, for I could never invent it myself; however, whether it was him or Pufendorf, or Heliodorus, or Theocritus, or Homer, or Virgil, or Horace, or Ovid, or Claudian, or Lucretius, or Tasso, or Spinone Speroni, or Demosthenes, or Juvenal, or Catullus, or Aristotle, or Quintilian, or Petronius, or Longinus, or Democritus, or Pythagoras, or Heraclitus, or Plato, or Epicurus, or Panaethius, or Polybius, or Thomas Aquinas, or one of ten thousand more, whose names I cannot recollect (though I have carefully perused them all) I cannot positively assert.[15]

The bank-note provides a classically Augustan mockery of the appeal to classical authority, by lumping together writers from a whole range of genres, moving from the authorities on natural jurisprudence, Grotius and Pufendorf, through poets and philosophers, including the Latin love poet Catullus. The satire is given added poignancy by being put into the mouth of a bank-note, who can assure us that he has read this assembly of writers with as much assurance, it is implied, as many of the hacks of Bridges' day.

The diffuse structure of the novel of circulation, incorporating elements of social satire, political comment, literary and economic observations, is reminiscent of the periodical journalism of the early eighteenth century, the *Spectator*, the *Tatler* and so on, and indeed *Adventurer* 5 of 1752 recounted the adventures of a transmigrated soul which was lodged in a flea.

The contrast between these narratives of objects or animals and the histories of human protagonists emphasises the extent to which the narratives of Fielding and Smollett are, as a number of critics such as Martin Battestin, Ronald Paulson, and Paul-Gabriel Boucé have shown, carefully plotted and elaborately constructed.[16] But on the other hand they also indicate that an elaborate plot and unified structure were not invariably regarded as necessary by the novel-reading public of the eighteenth century. Charles Gildon in *The Golden Spy*, Tobias Smollett in his *Adventures of an Atom*, and Charles Johnstone in his *Chrysal* utilised the freedom provided by a looser, less unified narrative structure to explore the political potential of the novel, and provided a satirical analysis of the social system which is more explicit and unequivocally political than that found in authors such as Richardson and Fielding. These aspects of the fictional genre tended, within the canonical works, to be subsumed by the abstract aesthetic demands of a unified form, and to become marginalised.

The fortuitous basis of the narrative structure of the novels of circulation, and their dependence on exchange as a plot mechanism, not only necessitated an abrogation of unity of form, but encouraged a far more extensive analysis of the economic and social basis of the commercial state than was possible within more anthropocentric works. The interpolated narratives of the linear novel form helped to broaden the range of characters and experiences portrayed, but they often provided a counterpoint to the main themes and incidents of the story. They are, in structural terms, ultimately subordinate to the narrative of the eponymous hero, whose life, loves and adventures give unity to the plot.[17] The concentration on the personal relationships of the central characters, and particularly the love story that was integral to the majority of picaresque fictions with a human protagonist, inevitably encouraged an emphasis on affective relations and the limited private community, while the structure of the epistolary novel ensured that these works were almost entirely confined to the portrayal of the confidences of a close circle of friends. In the novel of circulation, however, the use of the simple plot mechanism of exchange made possible the portrayal of an extremely wide variety of individuals and social situations, but also prioritised the indirect relations of the commercial state, rather than the direct relations of the affective community.

The fictional form of the novel of circulation was therefore peculiarly appropriate for the presentation of a Tory analysis of the social and economic system, and a satiric portrayal of the nature of the modern world. The importance of market relations and exchange mechanisms could be emphasised, and society could be portrayed as a series of atomised and alienated individuals, bound together by chance or the act of exchange, rather than by affective links. The circulation mechanism meant that the full spectrum of society could be portrayed, from the highest to the lowest in the land, but these characters did not have to know one another. The fishwife, the Cambridge fellow and the nobleman can all be included in the story of Pompey the Little through their connection with the dog, but they do not ever have to meet. Thus the novel of circulation provides an image of the links that bind society together, without having to foster an image of an organic community. The novel of circulation implies that the world of the harmonious country estate, where a common interest unites the squire and the poorest of his tenants, and all are bound together by ties of obligation and dependence, should be relegated to the mythological realm. Paradise Hall does not exist. The characters of the novel of circulation are almost invariably selfish and self seeking, the products of a fragmented society unrestrained by effective ethical codes.

Francis Coventry invokes the traditional, country party rhetoric in his description of 'The City' in his sub-Fieldingesque 'Dissertation upon Nothing' that opens book 2 of *Pompey*:

There we see Avarice, Usury, Extortion, Back-biting, Fraud, Hypocrisy, Stock-jobbing, and every Evil that can arise from the Circulation of Money. Thousands were there ruined Yesterday, thousands are ruining Today, and thousands will be ruined To-morrow: Yet all this is *Nothing*.[18]

Money circulates through society in the same arbitrary way that Pompey passes from owner to owner. The exchange process is portrayed as a lottery, devoid of rationale, principle, or justification, and whether individuals gain or lose, acquire great wealth or dissipate it, the outcome is perceived to be negative. Poverty and riches are equally bad in a society that is based on a system of commercial exchange where the possession of wealth is not necessarily allied to the ability to dispense it wisely.

This rather jaundiced approach to contemporary society is also manifested in the portrayal of charity within the novel. When Pompey is given by the watchman to a blind beggar, he breaks out into lamentations at his misfortune, yet he soon discovers that the lot of the beggar is not as bad as might have been supposed:

For tho' he was condemned to travel thro' dirty streets all Day long in quest of Charity, yet at Night, both he and his Master fared sumptuously enough on their Gains . . . He seldom failed to collect four Shillings a Day, and used to sit down to his hot Meals with as much Stateliness as a Peer could do to a regular Entertainment and Dessert.[19]

The implication of this passage is that begging is a lucrative trade, and that charitable giving must therefore be a sign of gullibility. At the same time, however, the refusal to give charitably is represented in the novel as a manifestation of the depravity of the manners of modern society, and the decay of traditional virtues of compassion and benevolence. This is demonstrated in the scene in which the beggar encounters his son Jack, a highwayman in the guise of a gentleman, in the company of two fine ladies. The youngest of the ladies, Miss Newcome, is filled with compassion, but the more jaundiced Lady Marmozet dismisses this charitable urge as 'ridiculous', asking 'Who gives any money to charity now a-days?' This argument is developed by Jack who, having recognised his own father, proclaims that 'nothing can be more idle, I think, than throwing one's money away upon a set of thievish tatterdemallion wretches, who are the burthen of the nation, and ought to be exterminated from the face of the earth'.[20]

Miss Newcome is the ingénue, as yet uncorrupted by fashionable society, and she is undeterred by the mockery of her companions. Lady Marmozet's views are given an ironic twist when they are endorsed by Jack. We know that he had good reason to identify this particular beggar, at least, as a 'thievish, tatterdemallion wretch', and yet we still condemn the values of a society that will determine whether or not to give charity on the basis of the dictates of fashion, and this satire on the absence of charity is emphasised in Jack's draconian proposal for the extermination of beggars. This is a more extreme formulation of Fielding's arguments in the *Enquiry*,[21] and within the context of a novel, where individual affective virtues are given greater prominence than they are in discourses of social analysis, such sentiments are clearly unacceptable, and a manifestation of the decay of values that is everywhere to be observed in society in *Pompey the Little*.

The use of an inhuman protagonist ensures that while the central character may be able to learn from its experiences, it cannot share these experiences with others. The bank note and guinea can accumulate knowledge of society, which can be contrasted with the ignorance and naivety of the human beings they encounter. Thus while the monetary heroes in particular are able to reflect on the economic links that bind society, the human characters remain unaware of these ties, and consider themselves endowed with an entirely illusory autonomy. The novel of circulation therefore presents an image of society bound by economic relationships, which in practice unite everybody in a complex commercial system. But these connections are not recognised by those within the nexus, because they do not carry with them any moral or social obligations. The economic mechanism is predicated on the assumption that individuals will behave selfishly, and act under the dictates of their own desires, and thus they consider themselves as autonomous units. The novel of circulation simultaneously exposes the economic links and the selfishness within modern society, while the condemnation of this system is implicit in the predominant satirical tone.

The novels of circulation demonstrate the ways in which narrative fiction could be used to explore the nature of the commercial state, and to analyse the systems of exchange without the mediation of a private system of morality. But the fact that these works did not lead to the development of a significant trend within the novel, and to further exploration of alienation rather than community (at least until the mid-nineteenth century, with the publication of Dickens' *Bleak House*, *Hard Times* and *Our Mutual Friend*), indicates the extent to which the novelists of the second half of the eighteenth century were increasingly embracing the private functions of the unified and what is now the canonical novel. Yet as the form and structure of the novel embodied the preoccupation with private rather than public virtue, a number of novels juxtaposed this system of fictional values with evocation of the nature of the commercial state.

CHAPTER 6

The sentimental novel

Since the publication in 1974 of R. F. Brissenden's *Virtue in Distress: Studies in the Novel of Sentiment from Richardson to Sade*, there has been considerable interest in sentimental philosophy and authors. Critics have analysed Sterne and Richardson in terms of their sentimentalism, and recent years have seen numerous full-length studies of the genre.[1] Janet Todd has located the rise of sentimentalism in a European cultural tradition, while John Mullan's study of *Sentiment and Sociability: The Language of Feeling in the Eighteenth Century* deploys a critical approach that could be described as 'New Biographicalism'. In tracing the efforts of David Hume, Samuel Richardson and Laurence Sterne to 'live out models of social being', Mullan posits a dynamic and reciprocal relationship between the lives and narratives of sentimental writers.[2] The philosophical origins of sentimentalism are located in John Locke, David Hume and Francis Hutcheson, while the physiological roots are also stressed, with an analysis of the work of physicians such as Richard Blackmore and George Cheyne.[3] This emphasis on the scientific basis of sentimentalism has been developed by Ann Van Sant, who has interpreted fictional representations of the body in the context of the rhetoric of physiology, psychology and the epistemology of touch. In this study, however, the focus will not be on the sentimental philosophy or physiology, which have been admirably covered in the aforementioned works, but rather on the relationship between the sentimental individual and a world which is portrayed as devoid of, or opposed to, sentimental values. For it is perhaps ironic that the novel of sentiment, with all its prioritisation of individual feeling and emotion and its feminisation of virtue, contains some of the most sustained accounts of the economic system and commercial morality that are to be found in eighteenth-century fiction. In the sentimental evocation of the complex and heteroglossic culture of the modern commercial state, the language of economic analysis looms large, challenging the language of sentiment which is constructed in opposition to it. Thus Markman Ellis, in his fascinating study of *The Politics of Sensibility*, has identified 'two modes in the senti-mental novel: on the one hand its efficiency in moulding the emotions and feelings of readers, and on the other its insertion of matters of political controversy into the text of the novel itself'.[4]

The novel of the second half of the century in some ways can be seen as having retreated from the more public, preceptual functions of the mid-century novel, to embrace a more private role, based on a preoccu-pation with individual sensations and moral decisions. But while the sentimental novels of Sarah Fielding, Oliver Goldsmith and Henry Mackenzie manifest this retreat they also dramatise it, and in doing so delineate the values of the contemporary system which are being rejec-ted. They present an image and an analysis of the social system, at the same time as they construct an alternative set of values and relationships which are identified as morally superior.

This is not to say that the sentimental novelists necessarily drew on the tradition of economic analysis that was outlined at the start of this book. Ellis has indicated their location within a spectrum of areas of intellectual history based around a discourse on virtue,[5] but the terms of the portrayal of commerce may derive from popular journalistic repre-sentations as much as from economic tracts and treatises or more high status writings on civic humanism. In the writings of Fielding and Goldsmith in particular, the economic system is not analysed in the abstract, but presented through the creation of fictional characters who epitomise the values of a commercial society. These values can then be contrasted with those of a representative of the traditional landed interest, as well as with the sentimental philosophy of the central characters. The *Spectator* juxtaposed the figures of Sir Andrew Freeport and Sir Roger de Coverley, satirising the commercial ethos of the one and the country values of the other.[6] Each of these characters can be connected with the comic archetypes of satiric tradition – the avaricious merchant and the foolish and impecunious landlord – that trace a distinguished pedigree in prose and verse back to Juvenal and Horace. Yet the deployment of these archetypes in the *Spectator* is adapted to the specific context of the early eighteenth century. In the same way, the sentimental novels utilise the traditional stereotypes to castigate both commerce and the landed elite, but these figures are reinvested with specific and contemporary meanings through the elucidation of the sentimental philosophy.

The significance of the sentimental inclusion of caricatures of the commercial interest is particularly striking given the comparative absence of comparable figures within the previous fictional tradition. The merchants and shopkeepers that are a staple of seventeenth-century comic drama are few and far between in the novels of the mid-eighteenth century, and it is the sentimental novel that revivifies the archetype. The extent of the sentimental contribution to the literary portrayal of the commercial interest can be seen in the contrast between Henry Brooke's *The Fool of Quality* (1765–7), for example, or Henry Mackenzie's *The Man of Feeling* (1771), and Henry Fielding's *Tom Jones* (1749). As John McVeagh points out in his study of *Tradeful Merchants: The Portrayal of the Capitalist in Literature*, Fielding provides a cameo portrait of the avaricious merchant in the figure of Old Nightingale,[7] but what McVeagh does not note is the rather more significant absence of representatives of the commercial system in the rest of the novel. For Fielding the corruption of modern values is epitomised in the figures of Lady Bellaston, the corrupt aristocrat, and young Blifil, the self-interested, acquisitive and economically prudent child of a gentry household. These characters are used to indict the self-seeking ethos of commercialism, but they are not themselves embodiments of the commercial system. They represent the extent of the corruptive incursion of 'new values', but are also clearly members of the old order. *Tom Jones* can therefore explore the essential conflicts of contemporary life, without penetrating the new order of finance, commerce and speculation. In the same way, Oliver Goldsmith in *The Vicar of Wakefield* (1766) portrays the corruption of the decadent modern world through the figure of the aristocratic Squire Thornhill,[8] but elsewhere in sentimental fiction the values of the commercial system are presented more directly, by merchants, bankers and financiers. Henry Clinton is the merchant-as-hero in *The Fool of Quality*, while *The Man of Feeling* incorporates explicit discussions of luxury, commerce and imperialism within its loose and inclusive narrative structure.

To begin with, however, I will explore the portrayal of commerce and economic ethics within one of the earliest sentimental novels, *The Adventures of David Simple* by Sarah Fielding.

THE ADVENTURES OF DAVID SIMPLE

The hero of *David Simple* (1744) and its sequel, *Volume the Last* (1753), comes from a background which, while prosperous, has its roots in the commercial and labouring classes. David's father was 'a Mercer on *Ludgate-hill*', while his mother 'was a downright Country Woman, who originally got her Living by Plain-Work'. The couple were able to accumulate a substantial fortune in the course of 'a very honest and industrious Life', and were able to have their two sons educated at public school, 'in a manner which put them on a level with Boys of a superior Degree'.[9] David is therefore a hero from the commercial sector of the economy, but from the start of the novel he is marked out as different not only from the members of his class, but from everybody he meets. He is an ingénue, an innocent abroad, who 'had more of what *Shakespear* calls the *Milk of Human Kind*, than any other among all the Children of Men' (p. 129). David therefore comes across as a peculiarly passive and feminised hero, embodying an affective and private ethos that can be seen as appropriate for a reading public that was increasingly identified as largely female, and therefore debarred from the field of public action, but which was also seen as being under threat from the general dominance of materialistic and acquisitive values emanating from the commercial system. The sentimental novel therefore reflects two rather different consequences of the development of economic analysis. While the sphere of virtue is clearly recognised as private, the scope for private virtue is limited by the growing acceptance of self-interest as a legitimate code of behaviour. The conflict between public and private virtue, and between civic humanist and economic terms of analysis, is refined into a conflict between a masculine, competitive economic ethos and a more feminised private code, which recognised the limited role of the individual within the complex community, but sought to stress the importance of affective values of sympathy and generosity.

Fielding's use of David and his brother Daniel as the embodiments of the two conflicting concepts of morality indicates that both codes have their origins within the new commercial order. While David embraces the private virtue of the sentimental hero, Daniel 'was in reality one of those Wretches, whose only Happiness centres in themselves' and who 'had never any other View, but in some shape or other to promote his own Interest' (p. 11). It is the discovery of the extent of the divide between his brother's guiding principles and his own ethical code that leads David to take 'the oddest, most unaccountable Resolution that ever was heard of, *viz.* To travel through the whole World, rather than not meet with a real Friend' (p. 27). The resultant search provides the vehicle for a satirical portrayal of the absence of moral values within society, in which the acquisitiveness and selfishness of the world at large are highlighted by the contrast with the unworldly David.

It is perhaps a sign of David's innocence and ignorance that he chooses to begin his journey with a visit to the Royal Exchange. A cursory knowledge of the literature on commerce would have told him that this was unlikely to be the place where he would find a real friend, but David is undeterred. This visit therefore provides the occasion for what can be seen as a set piece, satirical portrayal of the debased and corrupted values of the contemporary financial system, in a style which was familar from periodicals such as Daniel Defoe's *Review* or the *Spectator*. Yet the satire hinges on an idea that was to become increasingly important in the second part of *David Simple* and was to form an underlying theme of the sentimental novel – that commercial exchange entails the exchange and thus the corruption of language. David is shocked to hear a deceitful adviser described as '*a good Man*' (p. 29), only to discover that this means that he is worth £100,000. This exposes the extent to which moral evaluation has been replaced by commercial calculation, but it also exposes the way that language has been complicit in the change. David's assumption that language, like morality, should be stable and absolute ensures that he is increasingly excluded from the currency of the commercial community, in which language has a flexible exchange value, rather than an invariable use value. It is for this reason that David has to keep defining his terms, to fix his meaning. By friendship, for example, David means,

So perfect a Union of Minds, that each should consider himself but as a Part of one entire Being; a little Community, as it were of two, to the Happiness of which All the Actions of both should tend with an absolute disregard of any selfish or separate Interest. (p. 26)

David travels through high society and low society, encountering greed, treachery and hypocrisy, until he finally discovers not one, but three friends, one of whom becomes his wife. Camilla, her brother Valentine, and Valentine's long-lost childhood sweetheart, Cynthia, have also experienced the trials of virtue within a corrupt and decadent world. David is able to rescue all three from poverty which, in Valentine's case, has almost led to starvation.

The friends pass their time in improving conversation, exchanging edifying sentiments. These include reflections on the economic system, with particular emphasis on the problems faced by impoverished gentlefolks, but often of a more general nature as well. Cynthia, for instance, considers the small proportion of goods within the exchange system which are actually necessary 'to preserve Life or Health' (p. 189), and argues that luxury goods have an important function in stimulating employment, allowing wealth to trickle down through society, and generate employment amongst the lower classes.[10] This indicates the growing recognition within contemporary morality of the economic implications of ethical decisions, and yet at the same time it is significant that the economic justification for consumption which Cynthia articulates is not ultimately acceptable as a code of moral behaviour for the heroes and heroines of the novel. The final chapter of the first part of *David Simple* does not see the four friends settling down to a life of luxury, on the grounds that this will maintain a high level of economic activity. David, Camilla, Cynthia, Valentine and David's father-in-law retreat from the economic system, as the novel locates its conclusion in the evocation of the simple-life mythology of the organic community. This is presented as somehow divorced from the complex, commercial state, and based on very different ethical principles. David and his friends eschew the acquisitiveness and self-interest that have been shown to be endemic within, and essential to, the working of the economic system, and create a community based on pure and primitive Christian morality, so that 'it is impossible for the most lively Imagination to form an Idea more pleasing than what this little Society enjoyed, in the true proofs of each other's Love' (p. 304).

This fits into the traditional novelistic pattern of resolution in rural retirement. The hero travels through the world, and finds what he wants – a wife – and then retreats with her to an idyllic country location, where they can put their morality into practice. This morality is appropriate to the private individuals that form the audience for fiction, in that it is merely based on being nice to those around you. The limited affective community constitutes a standard by which the wider world can be judged. In *David Simple: Volume the Last*, however, Fielding brings out the pessimism implicit in the earlier work, to question the plausibility of such a simple solution. For although the friends have established a community based on common property, they cannot divorce themselves from the tentacles of the complex state. Even in their rural retreat they are tied up in the cash nexus.

Volume the Last opens with a series of financial disasters which emphasise how far David and his friends are dependent on the economic decisions and integrity of others, bringing out the complexity of the economic system, and the inability of well-meaning innocence to escape the depredations of the corrupt and cunning. This initially only serves to reinforce the message that happiness is not dependent on money since the 'Mirth and Chearfulness' of the community continues unabated (p. 333), but as the novel progresses the truth of this philosophy is put to the test. Happiness may exist without riches, but it can be threatened by the trials of poverty. Necessity increasingly disrupts the peace of the household, and ultimately breaks up the little community. Valentine and Cynthia travel to Jamaica, in an attempt to make their fortunes, but Fielding rejects the traditional plot mechanism of unexpected wealth from abroad. The colonies are not represented as a repository of money that can be used to provide an unproblematic restitution of the social and moral order.[11] In Jamaica, as in Britain, commercial considerations undermine affective values, as the economic system is exposed as international in its scope. So, far from being a retreat from capitalism, a source of opportunity that can reward the virtuous, Jamaica turns out to be a colonial outpost that perpetuates domestic injustice. Valentine dies of a fever, and Cynthia returns alone, impoverished and abused.

There is therefore no happy, get-rich-quick ending. The re-establishment of material prosperity cannot, in itself, be identified as a happy resolution, given the endemic injustice and hardness of society that have been exposed in the novel. David Simple is not like Roderick Random, and cannot be made happy in this straightforward way, so that given the corruption of contemporary values, his fate must be to suffer and endure. The children – young Cynthia, Peter, little David and Joan – die from various combinations of disease and deprivation. The cottage in which David has sought sanctuary after the loss of his fortune catches fire, and ultimately Camilla and David themselves expire in scenes of considerable pathos. The only members of the community left alive at the end of the novel are Cynthia and young Camilla. They retreat to the 'Kind Protection of one whose Power assisted his Inclination to confer the highest Benefits' (p. 429), a gentleman living near Bath who has been identified as a fictional portrait of Ralph Allen. He can shield them from the stringencies of poverty, but even this portrayal of individual benevolence cannot dispel the gloom that has been created by the picture of society delineated in *Volume the Last*.

The gradual destruction of David's family in *Volume the Last* does not merely function to elicit the sympathy of a sentimental readership who can thereby prove their refinement. It emphasises the extent of the disparity between the values of David's community and the prevalent commercial mores. The former are not just quirkily out of step with the latter. They are incompatible to the extent that they cannot survive. The simple, need-based economy has no place in the modern state, and in terms of modern economic doctrine its values make no sense. As in the Exchange scene at the start of the book, differences in moral perspective are reinforced by linguistic differences. This is indicated, for example, in the scene in which David attempts to borrow money on the, as it transpires erroneous, grounds that Valentine is about to make a fortune in the colonies. David produces a letter from Valentine, announcing his apprehended success, as security for the loan. The exchange between David and Mr Nichols, the money-lender, is presented in dramatic form to emphasise the contrast between the values of the two speakers:

MR. NICHOLS: And pray, Sir, please to shew me the Bond, or Note, or what kind of Security you are possessed of, by which, if Mr. *Valentine* should have the Success he mentions, you may legally recover any Monies of him.

DAVID: I have no Bond, or Note, Sir; *Valentine* is my Brother, my Wife's Brother, and that's the same thing.

NICHOLS: All's one for that, Sir, as you observe . . . but if you have no Security, no Monies will be forthcoming. A Brother, indeed! I have sent Officers with Executions into a Man's House, whose Brothers might have prevented it, and even with very inconsiderable Loss to themselves.

DAVID: If there are any such Wretches, Sir, that's nothing to my *Valentine*. We have always lived as one Family, and considered no separate Property.

NICHOLS: But you don't live together now; and if this Mr *Valentine* is a wise Man, he may think it most prudent to keep separately what he hath separately gotten. (p. 368)

For Nichols, wisdom and prudence are equated with a pursuit of self-interest, which is abhorrent to David and his family, so that each participant in the dialogue is incapable of comprehending the position of the other. Later in the conversation David exclaims:

DAVID: You don't talk our Language, Sir.

Here Nichols sneers.

NICHOLS: Not your Language, Sir? I think I talk plain *English*; and only want to Know what Security I should have, should I advance any Monies. (p. 369)

The sentimental hero or heroine is frequently portrayed as inarticulate, as language is shown to be inadequate to convey the depths of feeling and emotion. Van Sant suggests that this is partly due to the significance of the bodily level of experience, in that 'there are some experiences too physiological for words'.[12] Here, however, David's problem is not an inability to express himself within language, but rather the distance between his language and that spoken by others. The language of sentiment, the language of David and his extended family, is not 'plain

English', because it is predicated on an entirely different emotional and ethical basis from the language of commercial exchange. For David, language is a medium for the expression of feeling. It is direct and to be taken at face value. It admits of no ambiguity. For Mr Nichols and the other 'commercial' characters in the book, language is a medium for facilitating exchange, and must itself be continually checked, evaluated and weighed to ensure that the auditor is not being short changed. A gentleman's word is no longer acceptable as his bond. David must produce written evidence of Valentine's obligations to him, before Nichols will be prepared to accept the prospect of his success as security for David's money. The absence of moral consensus between Mr Nichols and David therefore ensured that this was a conversation 'in which neither Party could well comprehend the other' (p. 368).

The harsh and uncaring Nichols is the embodiment of the 'man of the World', in contrast to whom David represents an emasculated and feminised masculinity. Sir Charles Grandison represented a retreat from the heroic, civic-humanist image of epic masculinity, but David Simple departs even from the more limited bourgeois ideal. He is unable to speak the language of commerce and exchange, unable to value people in economic terms, and capable only of love and affection. *David Simple*, and, in particular, *Volume the Last*, embodies the conflict between the values of the aggressive, acquisitive commercial world, and the values of the simple Christian community. Despite the existence of some simple, benevolent individuals – such as farmer Dunster and his wife, and the doctor who treats David's declining family – the victory, at least in this world, is on the side of the commercial ethic. David's goodness cannot withstand the power of the ethic of self-interest. In the first part of *David Simple* the conclusion was located in retreat to the rural community. The exposure of the impossibility of such a retreat in the second part of the novel ensures that *Volume the Last* can only conclude with a further retreat, into death and presumably the idyllic community of Heaven.

David Simple therefore represents a sentimental modification of the picaresque novel, despite its clear dependence on the basic picaresque structure. For David Simple does not learn from experience in the way that Tom Jones is supposed to do, in that the knowledge which David Simple acquires of the world does not lead him to modify his behaviour. David Simple steadfastly adheres to his own ethical code, even though it is repeatedly shown to be out of step with the morality of those in the world around him. He maintains the pattern of behaviour that he displayed at the start of the novel, because this behaviour is based on firm principles. In contrast the actions of the rest of the world, those outside the ethical community of the 'simple', are identified as unprincipled, changeable, and based on expediency. They adapt to the world around them, but since this world is seen as having a dubious moral base, this adaptation is rejected as itself immoral. Thus the sentimental novel rejects the role of experience and empiricism in the development of moral codes, and stresses the importance of simple Christian precepts, reinforced by natural moral feelings. As such, the sentimental novel has a very different moral and narrative structure from the picaresque fiction of the mid-eighteenth century, but also moves away from the empiricism that was crucial to the philosophy of the Enlightenment.

Yet while *David Simple* emphasises the moral superiority of preceptial morality, and invariable, emotional concepts of good and evil, to some extent it can be read as a manifestation of the practical dominance of the empirical, experiential doctrine. Ultimately, David Simple's code of values is identified as doomed – perhaps in part because of its inflexibility. David's refusal to adapt to the ways and expectations of the world ensures that while his ethical purity remains untainted, physical survival is threatened. He and his family more or less fade away, unable but also unwilling to compete in an aggressive, acquisitive society.

THE VICAR OF WAKEFIELD

The hero of Oliver Goldsmith's *The Vicar of Wakefield* is ostensibly very different from David Simple, and draws on the comic and ironised tradition of Fielding's Parson Adams. Both Dr Primrose and Adams proclaim their humility, while displaying their pride, but the irony of their representation is not located in the simple portrayal of the disparity between their words and actions. They frequently say one thing and then do another, but are not straightforward hypocrites in the manner of Fielding's Thwackum and Square. Primrose and Adams function to expose the gaps between rhetoric and reality – the discourse of Christian humanism and commercial society – and are satirised through the delineation of the contrast between the way they believe the world to be organised, and the way that it actually works. Both believe that there is a simple connection between social behaviour and social morality. They fail to appreciate the disparity between public and private morality, and assume that since there is an ostensible acceptance of the values of Christianity, some adherence to its tenets can be expected in the actions of individuals. Like David Simple, they are innocents, who may be gently mocked for their failure to understand the ways of the world and the discursive complexity of the contemporary state, but in refusing to recognise a distance between words and actions, they highlight the extent of the departure of modern society from the Christian morality on which it is ostensibly based. To some extent, therefore, they are exploring the disparity between private and public, Christian discourse and commercial morality, that formed the basis for Mandeville's *Fable of the Bees*.

At the start of *The Vicar of Wakefield*, the Primrose family is in a flourishing condition and, with a fortune of £14,000, the Vicar can afford to give the profits of his living over to 'the orphans and widows of the clergy of our diocese'.[13] His rural existence is harmoniously integrated with the commercial system, which facilitates his benevolence and self-sufficiency. This image of the economic system is soon shattered, however, for by chapter 3 the merchant handling the vicar's money has absconded, to avoid a statute of bankruptcy, and the vicar's fortune has been reduced to £400. Ronald Paulson has indicated the allegorical significance of the Vicar's trials, with the Vicar as a modern Job, tested by God in the character of Burchell/Sir William, and Satan in the guise of Squire Thornhill, but the narrative also has economic implications. It is, as Paulson suggests, 'a novel about the transference – the loss and regaining – of property'.[14] As such, it has to negotiate between the discourses of property and of morality. The opening assertion of the interdependence of public and private in the Vicar's charitable prosperity is undermined by the collapse of the commercial system on which that prosperity was based. The Vicar's narrative reinforces the literary stereotype of the financial system as inherently unstable, but it also leaves a discursive vacuum which will have to be filled by a reformulation of the relationship between the individual and the commercial state.

This reformulation is initially signalled by the Vicar's retreat from the complex economy to a rural community which is described in terms that emphasise its isolation and its symbolic function. The Vicar invokes a golden age rhetoric which identified divorcedness from the complex economy as evidence of moral purity and innocence:

The place of our retreat was in a little neighbourhood, consisting of farmers, who tilled their own grounds, and were equal strangers to opulence and poverty. As they had almost all the conveniences of life within themselves, they seldom visited towns or cities in search of superfluity. Remote from the polite, they still retained the primeval simplicity of manners; and frugal by habit, they scarce knew that temperance was a virtue. (p. 23)

Dr Primrose's rather complacent belief in the autonomy of this community is revealed in his description of his household as 'The little republic to which I gave laws' (p. 24). The development of the plot reveals the irony of this invocation of civic humanist rhetoric. Primrose views himself as a benevolent patriarch, handing out laws to his obedient subjects; his family view themselves as free citizens, able to make their own choices and decisions. Primrose upholds an image of the organic community and patriarchal power that has been displaced by the emergence of the complex commercial system. The family, and in particular the female members, recognise the irrelevance of the patriarchal model within a contemporary context, but they fail to appreciate the extent to which the values of the new society differ from, and therefore threaten, their own. They aspire to become part of a more fashionable, more comfortable society than the organic and self-sufficient household that Primrose believes it is possible to construct. But they do not appreciate that the world of material goods entails a society of materialistic values. The choice is not between an authoritarian paternalistic social system, and a more individualistic system based on feminised affective values and participation in the complex economy. The choice is between the outmoded and irrelevant social vision of Dr Primrose, and a ruthlessly aggressive and acquisitive commercial ethos. The Primrose women are increasingly drawn into the discourse of consumption, culminating in the metaphorical embodiment of the extent to which they have got above themselves when the epic and allegorical portrait of the family is discovered to be too big to display within the house. The iconography of status is ironically transformed into a symbol of humbled pride, leaning 'in a most mortifying manner, against the Kitchen wall' (p. 79).

The plot represents the gradual decline of the Primrose family, as they depart from their rural simplicity and are drawn into a system which scorns and exploits their primitive Christian poverty. Through the machinations of the villainous Squire Thornhill, the Vicar is arrested for debt, but the resultant prison scenes provide the locus for the incorporation within the text of a politicised discourse that provides an explicit challenge to social morality. On witnessing the conditions within the prison, Primrose attempts to reform his fellow inmates, through a programme of daily readings and sermons. The success of these leads to a more practical programme of reformation, as the Vicar sets the prisoners to work cutting pegs for tobacconists and shoemakers. These were then sold 'so that each earned something every day – a trifle indeed, but sufficient to maintain him' (p. 148). This can be seen as the traditional remedy of setting the poor to work, to save them from themselves, and the Vicar goes on to show how he enforced communitarian values, through the imposition of a system of discipline based on fines and rewards:

Thus in less than a fortnight I had formed them into something social and humane, and had the pleasure of regarding myself as a legislator, who had brought men from their native ferocity into friendship and obedience. (p. 148)

This portrayal of the enlightening power of civilised man presents a characteristically eighteenth-century view of the relationship between the civilising upper and the degenerate lower classes, but it also identifies production and commercial exchange as the mechanisms by which this improvement can take place. Primrose again sees himself as a patriarch, epitomising the doctrine of public virtue and spreading a civilising influence, but in doing so he recognises the potential humanity of those who are identified as having a 'native ferocity', and their productivity is used as a means of bringing them back into the economic community which is equated with society. At the same time, the representation of the need to encourage industry and communal values within the penal system is combined with an attack on the penal laws of the country which anticipates William Godwin's *Caleb Williams* in its severity.[15] The Vicar loses his idiosyncratic private voice, to adopt a more public rhetoric, as his tone rises in condemnation:

It is among the citizens of a refined community that penal laws, which are in the hands of the rich, are laid upon the poor. Government, while it grows older, seems to acquire the moroseness of age; and, as if our property were become dearer in proportion as it increased – as if the more enormous our wealth the more extensive our fears – all our possessions are paled up with new edicts every day, and hung round with gibbets to scare every invader. (pp. 149–50)

The narrative voice appeals for the restriction of the death penalty to crimes of murder alone, arguing that a more benevolent social policy will itself prevent crime, by refining and socialising the lower classes. If a less vindictive policy were implemented,

We should then find that creatures, whose souls are held as dross, only wanted the hand of a refiner; we should then find that creatures, now stuck up for long tortures, lest luxury should feel a momentary pang, might, if properly treated, serve to sinew the state in times of danger; that as their faces are like ours, their hands are so too; that few minds are so base as that perseverance cannot amend; that a man may see his last crime without dying for it; and that very little blood will serve to cement our security. (p. 150)

The language of beasts and creatures is still here, but its use may be ironic, since the import of the passage is to emphasise the lack of difference between the reading elite and the 'criminal classes'. The people are not 'dross' but ore, that with refinement can be converted into precious metal. They are presented as commodities, but ones with considerable potential value in the hands of a refining elite.   In *The Vicar of Wakefield*, therefore, the sentimental, romantic plot is juxtaposed by a more direct analysis of the political system. At the same time, the sentimental plot constitutes an allegorical exploration of those social values that are explicitly attacked in the declamatory passages. The implicit message of the private narrative is endorsed by polemical public language that emphasises the connection between the domestic community of the Vicar, and the socially disparate community that comprises the state. Both require the concern of the Vicar's Christian morality, but at the same time the changing structure of society ensures that both have more complex systems of organisation than is implied by the Vicar's patriarchal model.

The Vicar and his family attempt to construct an idyllic rural community, based on primitive Christian values, that is cut off from the vanities and economic relationships of the world. The progress of the plot reveals that any such retreat is impossible. The Primrose family are tied by links of obligations and dependence, as well as by their own wishes and aspirations, to a wider, more dangerous and corrupt world. It is the Vicar's innocence and lack of worldly knowledge that makes it impossible for him to recognise or counter the dangers that threaten his family, and his fallibility is located firstly in his belief that it is possible to construct a self-sufficient moral economy and secondly in his assumption that this economy can be based on a model of patriarchal authority. The implication of all but the two final chapters of *The Vicar of Wakefield* is similar to the message of *David Simple* and Goldsmith's *Deserted Village* – that if a moral economy is not self-sufficient it cannot survive in the modern world, and that any such self-sufficiency is impossible in an interdependent economic system. As Sophia and Olivia are aware, the pressures that have broken down the autonomy of the local communities have also eroded the controlling power of figures of authority, by increasing the choices available to the individuals within the system. Primrose may be able to set the prisoners to work making pegs, but he cannot be a 'legislator' to his family. Indeed, the dominance of irony within the text suggests that he may not have been a 'legislator' to the prisoners either, whatever he thought himself.

In the final chapters of Goldsmith's novel the use of the *deus ex machina* in the form of the benevolent landlord Sir William Thornhill provides a sudden reversal of the material decline of the Primrose family, and enforces the religious overtones of the allegorical structure. This benevolent redeemer has been in the midst of the Vicar's family for much of the book, unknown and unrecognised by them. The final revelation of his identity, and of the extent of his power, redresses the balance to ensure the defeat of the forces of corruption, tyranny and selfishness by the primitive virtues of Christianity. Happiness and tranquillity are restored to the good, while young squire Thornhill is deprived of his inheritance, and despatched to act as paid companion in the household of a relation.

Ronald Paulson has argued that the happy ending is closer to the fairytale than the sermon, and the gap that has been exposed between the idea of divine providence and the experience of reality is set into perspective by the 'fairytale discourse of the inset ballads, whose words prove to be the only authoritative ones within the "novel"'.[16] The solution to the immorality of the world, and the perceived absence of divine providence, is therefore identified in the aesthetic experience of narratives which provide a fictional restitution of order and happiness.[17] This reading stresses the implicit secularism of the text, and the inadequacy of the 'providential discourse of the sermon' is taken to represent a lack of interest in morality.[18] Yet while *The Vicar of Wakefield* cannot be seen as a moral text in the sense that it presents a clear and unequivocal system of ethics, it would appear to be a work that is highly exercised over the problems of defining morality and of formulating a moral code that is relevant within the modern state. The Vicar moves from the sermon, to civic humanism, to the politicised rhetoric of natural jurisprudence. His experiences underline the lack of relevance of each of these discourses to the condition of the individual within the modern state, yet the Vicar's search for a language of morality underlines his persistent belief in the need to construct a contemporary ethic.

As Paulson indicates, the contrived and implausible nature of the ending of the story removes it from the realist realm and gives it a fairytale quality. I would argue that this is not so much a validation of the fairytale discourse, as a narrative technique that makes possible the closure of the story, while the discursive debate is left open. The Vicar is anxious to close the gap between moral discourse and moral experience, but ultimately this is only achieved by reference to the mythic and allegorical. The text is preoccupied with morality, since it is only through this that happiness can be attained, yet it is ultimately pessimistic about the possibility of formulating an appropriate ethics, and about the prospects of the moral individual within the modern state.   There is no suggestion that the values of the Vicar will ever be able to triumph within this world, other than on an individual level, and the assumption that a worldly system of values prevails even amongst the reading public is emphasised by the ironical and gently satirical tone of the portrayal of the Vicar's character. The comic exploitation of Dr Primrose's self-delusion and unworldliness is derived from the general recognition that society does not function in the simple ways imagined by the likes of him, David Simple and Abraham Adams. Primrose cannot control events. He has no public function in either a civic humanist or a more bourgeois sense. He can only act as an individual within a community of other autonomous individuals, and events can only be controlled by unreal fairy godfathers such as Thornhill.

The ironic undertone does not mean that *The Vicar of Wakefield* is not a sentimental text. In a way this gentle irony is central to the sentimental form. The pathos of these novels is not merely derived from incidents within the narrative, and from individual instances of benevolence, but also from a pervasive recognition that society as a whole works on principles that are avowedly anti-sentimental. This philosophy is explored from a rather different perspective in Henry Brooke's *The Fool of Quality*, for in Brooke's novel the threat to the sentimental ethos is explicitly located in the values of a corrupt and luxurious aristocracy, whereas the mercantile classes are portrayed as the potential saviours of public virtue.

THE FOOL OF QUALITY

The Fool of Quality: or, The History of Henry, Earl of Moreland was published by Henry Brooke between 1765 and 1770. It tells of the early life and education of Harry Clinton, who is snatched away from a world of luxury with his aristocratic parents by a mysterious, wealthy and benevolent merchant who turns out to be his uncle. Harry Clinton senior educates his nephew along lines derived from Jean Jacques Rousseau's *Emile*, developing his physical prowess through games and sports, and encouraging the emergence of a strong moral sense through the use of improving stories and exemplars. Harry is taken to the debtors' prison, to Bedlam and to the poorest areas of London. He witnesses the sufferings that exist in the world, while he is taught to see wealth and finery as potential snares to virtue, and desirable only insofar as they can be used for doing good. He is naturally benevolent and endowed with a lively sensibility and an eye ever ready to drop a tear of sympathy for others.

In this respect, *The Fool of Quality* is a typical sentimental novel, yet the story of Harry is only one component of the text. Interspersed with the development of this central plot are discussions of politics, economics, the role of the hero within the commercial state, and the nature of public and private virtue. Some of these discussions take place between the various characters of the book; some take the form of a dialogue between the author and an imaginary friend and critic. Amongst the topics covered are the nature and significance of blushing; the 'science' of physiognomy; the nature of the character of a gentleman; the condition of the British legal system; the British constitution; numerous topics relating to religion and religious doubt; and the immorality of duelling. As E. A. Baker wrote in 1906 in his introduction to the Library of Early Novelists edition of *The Fool*:

> It is not only a novel, but also a commonplace book, containing the author's thoughts on ethics and social economy, politics, religion, aesthetics, and indeed as many multifarious topics as those dealt with in the digressions of *La Nouvelle Heloise* itself.[19]

With its loose discursive structure and its wide range of public issues, *The Fool of Quality* can be read as a rejection of the increasingly limited and private role that characterises the canonical fiction of the second half of the eighteenth century. But while recent analyses have recognised the importance of commerce as a theme within the sentimental plot, some critics have avoided consideration of the explicitly heteroglossic narrative framework.[20] It is clear, however, that the debates and digressions in *The Fool of Quality* are as important to Brooke's project as Fielding's introductory chapters were to *Tom Jones*. This is emphasised in one of the most recent accounts of Brooke's defence of commerce. Markman Ellis suggests that while the fragmentary narrative 'at times . . . works as a critical prophylactic, having the effect of blocking understanding of the wider political issues being discussed . . . it also, curiously, enables Brooke to introduce political and controversial material into the novel itself'.[21]

The juxtaposition of the private plot and the exploration of commercial morality in *The Fool of Quality* constitutes a formulation of the challenge that was posed to social morality and also fiction in the second half of the eighteenth century. The economic system seems only to demand the kind of selfish behaviour displayed by the characters within the novels of circulation or by the bad characters that drive the heroes and heroines into retreat in the other sentimental novels. Elsewhere, the feminised virtue of sentimentalism has been shown to be threatened by the dominant language of bourgeois masculinity embodied by Sarah Fielding's Mr Nichols. Consideration of the wider economic and political world therefore seems anterior or contrary to the analysis of private morality. Fiction has traditionally represented characters who retreat from the public, economic world into the realm of private morality, instead of developing a morality that is appropriate to the modern world.

While the structure of *The Fool of Quality*, and the manner in which the discursive passages are interleaved with the development of the plot, reveal the problems of locating a private, sentimental fiction within an analysis of the commercial state, the very difficulty of the project reinforces the significance of Brooke's attempt. Moreover, the image of the commercial system presented in the digressions is reinforced by the story itself. Harry Clinton is the son of the aristocratic Richard, Earl of Moreland, but he is brought up by his mercantile uncle Henry. Although scorned by his brother on account of his humble social position, Henry becomes an immensely wealthy and powerful figure, lending large sums of money to the government. When Richard is petitioned by his unrecognised brother on an issue of commerce, his high-handed treatment provokes a lecture on the subject of the benefits and utility of trade which is reminiscent of the economic discourse of the seventeenth and eighteenth centuries. Henry argues that

The wealth, prosperity, and importance of every thing upon earth, arises from the TILLER, the MANUFACTURER, and the MERCHANT . . . The tiller supplies the manufacturer, the manufacturer supplies the merchant, and the merchant supplies the world with all its wealth. It is thus that industry is promoted, arts invented and improved, commerce extended, superfluities mutually vended, wants mutually supplied; that each man becomes a useful member of society; that societies become further of advantage to each other; and that states are enabled to pay and dignify their upper servants with titles, rich revenues, principalities, and crowns. (p. 25)

The identification of the farmer (as opposed to the landowner), the manufacturer and the merchant as the backbone of the nation and the source of its wealth strikes at the heart of civic humanist rhetoric, with its emphasis on the fundamental social, political and economic role of the land-owning elite. Labour, as opposed to property, is identified as essential to wealth generation, social harmony and stability, and the reference to the governing classes as the 'upper servants' of the state, while invoking the civic humanist framework, undermines the social status of the political elite, while reinforcing their dependent rather than controlling position within the polity. In the context of the emphasis on 'country' values in most eighteenth-century fiction, it is perhaps ironic that Henry Clinton steals young Harry away from his parents because he is anxious about the kind of moral education that he will receive in his aristocratic home. The country estate is perceived not as a 'Paradise Hall', a haven in which it is possible to escape from the evils of the world, but rather as a repository of those evils, because of the failure of the landed elite to engage with the realities of the economic system. Harry Clinton is a product of aristocratic birth, but he is educated in the moral values that the novel equates with the commercial interest. One aspect of this commercial spirit is an emphasis on charity, but a careful prudent charity, not the open-handed and unquestioning benevolence of Tom Jones.

Both Henry Clinton senior and Henry Clinton junior interrogate the recipients of their bounty, to ensure that their money is not being thrown away on the idle or dissolute. Charitable giving is thus represented as an intellectual rather than an emotional response, derived from economic calculation rather than benevolent impulse. It is represented as virtuous, and pleasurable for the donor, as Hume, Smith and Hutcheson described, but it is also of economic benefit to the community at large when it is exercised with discretion and discrimination (p. 55). The cultivation of charity is therefore portrayed as ultimately being in the private interest of the individuals within the state, as well as in the public interest. This is achieved through the propagation of a systemic view of society, which emphasises the interdependence of the component parts. In this vision of the economic system, the selfishness of individuals is identified as ultimately self-defeating, and based on a narrow and partial perception. This view is upheld by the benevolent Mr Meekly, who espouses the consonance of Christian and commercial ethics:

I look upon industry, the natural parent of opulence, to be as well a blessing as a duty to man, from the time that he was appointed to 'earn his bread in the sweat of his brow' ... It makes men healthful, brave, honest, social and pacific ... Industry further incites to commerce and good neighbourhood, in order to dispose of mutual redundancies for the supply of mutual wants. And lastly, it delighteth in peace, that its time and its labours may not be interrupted, nor the fruits thereof endangered, by rapine and invasion; and all this may be said of nations as well as of men. (p. 351)

This is Hume's argument that consumption and, by extension, luxury, will be of benefit to the community and the economy, by giving men an incentive to work, and to keep on working.[22] Moreover, commerce promotes international as well as domestic harmony, and, as a result, Mr Meekly puts forward a plan to encourage trade by improving communications within Britain through the development of the canal system. Ellis has demonstrated that much of this material has been drawn verbatim from Brooke's economic tract, *The Interests of Ireland*, which outlines the benefits that will accrue to Ireland from the development of its canal system.[23] As described in *The Fool of Quality*, it acquires a sentimental, symbolic significance. The navigable channels spreading out in a network across the country and uniting its diverse parts, constitute a metaphor for the image of the commercial system that is being proposed. Trade brings wealth and prosperity and a true understanding of its operation reveals the extent to which it binds every member of the state, and even different states, together in a common cause. Private interest, public interest and the requirements of Christian charity can be assimilated, yet this vision of society is not universally acceptable. When the Earl of Moreland asks Mr Meekly whether he has mentioned his navigation project to 'any of our great ones', he explains that no one will support the project unless he can be sure of engrossing the whole of the profit (p. 355).

This constitutes a damning indictment of contemporary morality and a reorientation of the traditional moral critique. Luxury and acquisitiveness are identified as impediments to, rather than consequences of, the development of trade and commerce. They are private vices, a sign of man's unregenerate nature, but they also constitute public vices, since they impede the natural progress of investment and improvement that is essential for the development of the economic system. Although it is possible to conceptualise society as bound by ties of interdependence and mutual obligation, wherein the prosperity of those at the bottom of the system will contribute to the prosperity of all, the fact that the majority of people do not share this vision ensures that it is not realised. Commercial society does not have to be based on selfish behaviour, a collapse of public virtue is not an inevitable corollary of the progress of trade, but nonetheless the majority of people within contemporary Britain are motivated by narrow private interests.

It is for this reason that Harry has to be plucked from his home environment, and given a special education that will enable him to see the failings of the rest of society. He must learn to avoid the tyranny of selfishness and become a 'friend of mankind', but in doing so he becomes a fool in the eyes of many in the world. While at court Harry has the label 'Fool' pinned to his back, but he rejoices in the title, as a manifestation of his divorcedness from the corruption and triviality of polite society. At the same time, almost everybody he meets is bowled over by his virtue. The hem of his coat is frequently kissed, tears are shed, and he is repeatedly branded a little angel, too good for this corrupt world.

Harry is both fool and hero, in that he departs from the conventional code of polite behaviour, but adheres to an ethic which is represented as more appropriate for survival in the modern polity. In this respect he is a modern hero, and the significance of this is brought out in one of the dialogues between the author and his imaginary friend which is interpolated in the narrative. The pair discuss the nature of heroism, citing Peter the Great as a modern hero, and Lycurgus as an ancient one. The author, however, questions the very nature of heroism, and its function within the modern world, and ends up citing Don Quixote as a true modern hero:

AUTHOR: If you demand of your own memory, for what have the great heroes throughout history been renowned? it must answer, for mischief merely, for spreading desolation and calamity among men. How greatly, how gloriously, how divinely superior was our hero of the Mancha, who went about righting of wrongs, and redressing of injuries, lifting up the fallen, and pulling down those whom iniquity had exalted! In this his marvellous undertaking, what buffetings, what bruisings, what trampling of ribs, what pounding of packstaves did his bones not endure. (p. 44)

This passage utilises the arguments of the critics of epic, or of *The Female Quixote*, in recognising the irrelevance of the public, heroic model of virtue within a complex and interdependent state, and stressing the moral superiority of passive affective values to the more bloodthirsty and active ethos of epic tradition. The modern hero is born to suffer and endure, rather than to inflict calamity, and can thus be either male or female. Although Harry does not receive many buffetings, his progress through the world involves the righting of numerous wrongs. His final marriage to the princess Abenaide brings out the internationalism implicit in the novel's commercial Christianity, for although she is Harry's cousin, she is also the daughter of a Moroccan prince.

The Fool of Quality therefore portrays a society in which selfishness and corruption dominate, but the vision is not entirely bleak. People are still able to recognise true virtue, and if only they could appreciate the true nature of the commercial state they would be able to see that the practice of virtue was actually in their own interest. *The Fool of Quality* therefore represents the importance of fiction in spreading a code of sentimental morality, but also in propagating the model of the economic system that ultimately underpins that morality.

THE MAN OF FEELING

Henry Mackenzie's *Man of Feeling* of 1771 extends the looseness of narrative structure that characterised *The Fool of Quality* to provide a novel that is so fragmentary as to appear at times on the verge of disintegration. The introduction by the 'Editor' of the work explains that he came across the manuscript while out shooting with a curate. The curate was tearing out pages to use as gun wadding, and as a result the text is full of gaps and omissions, unfinished plot threads and *non sequiturs*, which embody within the narrative the fictitious history of the manuscript. From Marilyn Butler's work on sentimentalism in *Jane Austen and the War of Ideas*, this fragmented narrative has been identified as crucial to the power of the novel. It 'makes it possible to play with mood, moving swiftly between terror and pity, or laughter and tears. Reading these works demands the same kind of energy as living through the events they describe.'[24] The conspicuous flaunting of narrative and structural conventions may be read as an ironic satire on the commodification of narrative within the commercial system, but given the growing importance of these conventions from the mid-eighteenth century, it may also have a further significance. Following the loose episodic structure of *David Simple*, and the diffuse form and authorial interventions of *The Fool of Quality*, the gaps in the text of *The Man of Feeling* appear to represent a deliberate rejection of both the mimetic principles and the social vision which were increasingly coming to characterise the fictional form. The sentimental novel attempted to represent the experience of the sentimental hero within a complex state, and therefore embodied, within its structure as well as its narrative, the experience of fragmentation, diversity and the absence of an obvious or coherent plan. The editor explains that the work is 'a bundle of little Episodes, put

together without art, and of no importance on the whole, with something of nature, and little else in them'.[25]

The Man of Feeling recounts the adventures of Harley, a young landowner and member of a Welsh gentry family, but also a man of exquisite
sensibility. His gentility, but also his comparative poverty, isolate him
from his neighbours:

Great part of the property in his neighbourhood being in the hands of rich
merchants, who had got rich by their lawful calling abroad, and the sons of
stewards, who had got rich by their lawful calling at home: persons so perfectly
versed in the ceremonial of thousands, tens of thousands, and hundreds of
thousands (whose degrees of precedency are plainly demonstrable from the first
page of the Complete Accomptant, or Young Man's Pocket Companion) that a
bow at church from them to such a man as Harley – would have made the
parson look back at his sermon for some precept of christian humility. (pp. 9–10)

A clear contrast is established here between new commercial wealth and
old landed poverty, as Mackenzie concisely indicates the rapacity and
immorality of the new men (with the ironic reference to their 'lawful'
callings) and their lack of true gentility (manifested in their mistaken
equation of social and financial status and their reliance on conduct
books). Harley is surrounded by men who seek to point him in the right
direction, and fire his enthusiasm for personal prosperity, but to no
avail. He cannot work up any interest in economic progress and his envy
is invited but not excited by the accounts of wealth and luxury. It is with
the greatest reluctance that he is forced to visit London, in an attempt to
gain the lease of some lands bordering his own. His journey to the
metropolis provides the framework for a series of sentimental/picar-
esque adventures, as he encounters various characters who recount the
miserable experiences of their lives, and receive relief and, more import-
antly, sympathy from Harley. On hearing the story of the fortune-telling
beggar, for instance,

Harley had drawn a shilling from his pocket; but virtue bade him consider on
whom he was going to bestow it. – Virtue held back his arm: – but a milder
form, a younger sister of virtue's, not so severe as virtue, nor so serious as pity,
smiled upon him: His fingers lost their compression; – nor did virtue offer to
catch the money as it fell. It had no sooner reached the ground than the
watchful cur (a trick he had been taught) snapped it up; and contrary to the
most approved method of stewardship, delivered it immediately into the hands
of his master. (pp. 22–3)

Contrary to the strictures of all the moral and economic commentators
of the eighteenth century, Harley's charity is prompted by the need

rather than the worth of the recipient. It is stimulated by benevolence, a younger sister of virtue, whose actions have frequently been identified as potentially opposed to the public interest. Harley's action is the result of his sentiments and emotions, rather than his reason, and this is underlined by the punctuation of the passage. The dashes and semi-colons suggest a departure from the rational, measured order of eighteenth-century prose, creating an impression that this sentimental language is somehow more direct and less mediated than conventional writing, reflecting the impulsiveness of Harley's behaviour and the immediacy of feeling. Harley's words, like his actions, are supposed to come straight from the heart, unconstrained by the rational, ordering impulse. This idea is reinforced by the contrast between the account of Harley's charitable act, and the rather pompous reference to 'the most approved method of stewardship'. These words suggest a concept of language and a concept of property based on rules and restraint. Harley's relationship to language is identified as different from that of the readers and writers of legal or economic tracts, and this reflects their different concepts of society and morality.

John Mullan has argued that sentimental texts cannot operate as moral texts, because of the impracticality of the vision that they offer. Thus 'the sentimental novel has evolved into a terminal formula precisely because, with all its talk of virtue, it cannot reflect at all on the problems of conduct, the practices of any existing society.'[26] Yet while *The Man of Feeling* (unlike *The Fool of Quality*) does not really advocate a practical moral code, it nonetheless provides an extensive reflection on contemporary ethics by emphasising the gap between the commercial and the sentimental code. Harley's inarticulacy is evidence of the dimensions of this gap and constitutes an affective morality, albeit one whose function is primarily minatory.

Harley's behaviour is dictated by private, personal considerations, rather than public calculations, and so is out of step with the modern world. It is therefore ironic that when Harley encounters a misanthropist in the course of his visit to London, the latter includes Harley in his strictures against the modern world: '"Honour", said he, "Honour and Politeness! this is the coin of the World, and passes current with the fools of it. You have substituted the shadow Honour, instead of the substance Virtue"' (pp. 38–9). The misanthropist goes on to rail against the vanity and insincerity inculcated by the education system in men as well as women, highlighting the public as well as the private consequences of the spread of luxury and corruption (p. 41). The fact that this civic humanist rhetoric is put into the mouth of a misanthropist, and is directed towards Harley, emphasises the disparity between this language of public virtue, and the cause of private virtue that is espoused within the sentimental tradition. Harley condemns vanity and luxury within the modern world, but in rather different terms from those of the misanthropist. Wealth is identified by Harley as the enemy of the very private virtue of love, and it is for this reason that he, mirroring the misanthropist, condemns the educational system. As he explains to the honest old gentleman whom he meets in the stagecoach:

'Perhaps,' said Harley, 'we now-a-days discourage the romantic turn a little too much. Our boys are prudent too soon. Mistake me not, I do not mean to blame them for want of levity or dissipation; but their pleasures are those of hackneyed vice . . . and their desire of pleasure is warped to the desire of wealth, as the means of procuring it. The immense riches acquired by individuals have erected a standard of ambition, destructive to private morals, and of public virtue. The weaknesses of vice are left us; but the most allowable of our failings we are taught to despise. Love, the passion most natural to the sensibility of youth, has lost the plaintive dignity he once possessed, for the unmeaning simper of a dangling coxcomb.' (pp. 82–3)

Harley's elevation of passion and emotion indicates the construction of an alternative critique of the acquisitiveness of modern society. The recognition of the irrelevance of the social model underlying civic humanist rhetoric, and its inapplicability to a society of economically active and independent individuals, ensured that its image of public virtue was increasingly relegated to the status of a misanthropic diatribe. Harley can therefore appropriate the animus against commerce in the interests of a socially inclusive concept of private virtue, rather than an exclusive public virtue. Yet the virtue which Harley embodies, while potentially accessible to all within the social system, is exceptionally passive and enervated. It represents a total contrast to the active male ethic embodied in civic humanism, but also to the active acquisitiveness of the world of commerce. The emphasis on passion and feeling and sentiment is appropriate as a fictional ethic, but is simultaneously identified within fiction as irrelevant to the wider world.

Needless to say, Harley's visit to London proves unsuccessful, and he returns empty handed and broken spirited to his aunt in Wales. His return journey provides the opportunity for further sentimental reflections on the state of the modern world, as he encounters Old Edwards, a long-lost friend from his childhood, who has joined the army to save his only son from being conscripted. Edwards recounts a harrowing tale of tyranny and injustice. His family have been oppressed and ruined by the machinations of an uncaring landlord, and when Harley and Edwards go to visit the site of an old ruined schoolhouse, the words of a passing woman reinforce the relationship between this callous behaviour, and the economic and aesthetic doctrine of improvement. The woman tells Harley that the schoolhouse has been pulled down because it stood in the way of the Squire's 'prospects':

'What! how! prospects! pulled down!' cried Harley. – 'Yes, to be sure, Sir; and the green, where the children used to play, he has ploughed up, because, he said, they hurt his fence on the other side of it.' – 'Curses on his narrow heart', cried Harley, 'that could violate a right so sacred! Heaven blast the wretch!' (p. 96)

The incoherence of Harley's response, with his ejaculations of 'What! how! prospects!' reveals how he is rendered inarticulate and almost speechless in the face of the realities of the new economic system. Coherent language, like narrative structure, appears to be implicated in the rationalist, improving ethic, and is thus inappropriate for the expression of Harley's response. The disintegration of Harley's language foreshadows the essential passivity of his conduct. It embodies his inability to confront change and construct a rational answer to it.

Harley cannot do anything to stop or alter the corruption of the values of modern society, but at the same time we are encouraged to believe that he is right in his moral standpoint. This impression is ironically enforced in 'A Fragment', entitled 'The Man of Feeling talks of what he does not understand'. The passage has no obvious connection with the rest of the text, and consists of a discussion between Edwards and Harley relating to the ethics of imperialism. In its moral and internationalist perspective, it anticipates the terms of Mackenzie's account of slavery in *Julia de Roubigné*.[27] Harley does not understand in the sense that he finds it impossible to comprehend or enter into the imperialist ethos, but he does understand in the sense that we are expected to see his intuitive ethical response as morally right. 'You tell me', he says to Edwards 'of immense territories subject to the English: I cannot think of their possessions without being led to Enquire, by what right they possess them' (p. 102). Harley's use of 'they' and 'them' may be explained by the fact that his family is Welsh rather than English, but it is also indicative of the extent of his alienation from the colonial aspirations of the state:

What title have the subjects of another kingdom to establish an empire in India? to give laws to a country where the inhabitants received them on the terms of friendly commerce? You say they are happier under our regulations than the tyranny of their own petty princes. I must doubt it, from the conduct of those by whom these regulations have been made. (pp. 102–3)

Those who have taken over India were not motivated by 'fame of conquest, barbarous as that motive is', but by a simple, avaricious desire for material wealth. They are therefore, in Harley's terms, culpable on the grounds of their basic motives, as well as for the barbarity of their conduct once in a position of power.

The inapplicability of Harley's moral position to an economic system that is predicated on an entirely different ethical basis, in which the pursuit of material interest is increasingly justifiable, is emphasised in the conclusion of the novel. Harley goes into a decline and just fades away – a pathetic symbol of the inability of a passive system of private and feminised morality to counter the active masculine economic ethic. The moral and economic significance of this sad scene is brought out in Harley's death-bed words:

This world . . . was a scene in which I never much delighted. I was not formed for the bustle of the busy, nor the dissipation of the gay . . . There are some feelings which perhaps are too tender to be suffered by the world. The world is in general selfish, interested, and unthinking, and throws the imputation of romance or melancholy on every temper more susceptible than its own. I cannot think but in those regions which I contemplate, if there is any thing of mortality left about us, that these feelings will subsist; – they are called, – perhaps they are – weaknesses here; – but there may be some better modifications of them in heaven, which may deserve the name of virtues. (pp. 127–9)

The dominance of acquisitive values within the commercial world has led to the marginalisation of Harley and the dismissal of the code of virtue which he espouses. Death is his only way out, but the resolution of the plot in death emphasises the extent to which the sentimental novel widened the gap which writers like Hume and Smith had identified between the terms of moral philosophy and economic analysis. For the philosophers, moral considerations were the preserve of a refined and civilised elite, who were divorced from the realities of economic production. They were made possible by the development of an advanced commercial state, based on the division of labour, but they rendered their subjects beyond the determination of the discourses utilised for the analysis of such a state. The civilised, effeminate and cultured philosopher was able to develop more complex reactions and motives than the simple self-interest assumed by the economists. In the sentimental novel, however, these refined feelings were not identified as a characteristic of the cultured bourgeoisie in general, but instead were confined to only a few extraordinary individuals. Sarah Fielding's hero is 'simple', and Goldsmith's vicar is a figure of fun, subject to the ironically satirical subtext of his narrative. Harry Clinton is a fool, albeit one of quality, and the man of feeling is simply unable to survive in the modern world. These characters challenge the indirect relations of the capitalist system, by the construction of a feminised and private virtue that emphasises the absence of affective values within society. The language of the commercial bourgeoisie is juxtaposed with the language of feeling and shown to be inadequate as an index of the sentiments of mankind. But at the same time, the location of the affective ethos within a few quixotic and marginalised individuals constitutes a reassertion of the dominance of indirect and economic relations and the acquisitive values of the bourgeoisie.

The novel of sentiment therefore reflects the increasing interest in private feelings and passions amongst the novel-reading public of both sexes, but yet dramatises this interest as aberrant within the commercial state. We are invited to identify with, and yet distance ourselves from, the sentimental characters, recognising that while the fictional world may celebrate and prioritise emotion, the real world assuredly does not. The sentimental novel resolves the challenge to literary representation posed by the conflict of economic and moral philosophy by portraying the dominance of the economic ethic, while creating a role for fiction in espousing a very different moral code. As such it embodied contemporary uncertainty about the nature of the modern state, and the appropriateness of an aggressive bourgeois ethic for a public that was increasingly defined to include individuals who were either female or feminised. The heroic and masculine aristocratic ethic of public virtue seemed to have been displaced by an equally masculine, private, commercial ethic, and while the heroic public ethos granted a limited, albeit inferior, sphere for the exertion of private, affective, feminine virtues, the bourgeois ethos represented the incursion of masculine values into the private realm. The affective virtues were therefore displaced into fiction.

CHAPTER 7

The jacobin novel

The sentimental novel celebrated a code of conduct which it represented as culturally marginal and even cranky. As such, it could be taken as a sign that the novel had surrendered the claim, implicit in mid-century fiction, that the genre had a crucial didactic and representational function, as a form that embodied the aspirations of society. Sentimental novelists did not attempt to portray the public virtue that had been the essence of epic, and even the private virtue they conveyed was recognised as irrelevant to the economic structure of the state. Its didactic function was increasingly fulfilled through the operation of a moral subtext that was designed to appeal to the emotions of a refined elite. As John Mullan argues, it is a type of writing which 'does not so much recommend correct conduct to its readers as assume virtue in their capacity to understand the sentimental text'.[1] In the 1790s, however, the situation changed. A new form of fiction developed which attempted to reinvest the novel with a central public and political role and to reclaim some of the didactic and social functions which had been ceded with the triumph of sentimentalism. Both radical and conservative writers sought to assert the political centrality of individual morality, and to highlight the role of fiction as an important locus for ideological debate.[2] The novel therefore became polemicised and the debate over public and private morality was repoliticised.

The writers on the opposing sides of this debate have been denominated 'jacobin' and 'anti-jacobin' in most modern critical accounts. This follows Gary Kelly's seminal work which established the jacobin novel as a recognised sub-genre of fiction.[3] The terminology owes as much to the conservative reaction to the radical cause, as it does to the radicals themselves, for it was the conservatives who branded their adversaries 'jacobin', fulminating against them from the pages of *The Anti-Jacobin*, and the label sits rather uneasily on some of the more moderate advocates of political reform. It is, however, a useful shorthand for identifying a group of novelists who shared a belief that fiction had an important political role, and could be used to urge the case for social change.[4] In this chapter I will examine three of the jacobin novels that were produced during the 1790s, to indicate how the politicisation of fiction re-established the centrality of the discursive conflict between the heroic and the commercial ethos, as the relationship between public and private ethics again became a focus of concern. The three novels I have chosen, William Godwin's *Things As They Are: Or, The Adventures of Caleb Williams* (1794), Mary Hays' *The Memoirs of Emma Courtney* (1796), and Mary Wollstonecraft's *The Wrongs of Woman: Or, Maria, A Fragment* (1798) give some idea of the diversity of response of writers broadly labelled jacobin. The discussion could be developed and extended to take account of the work of other writers, such as Thomas Holcroft, Robert Bage and Elizabeth Inchbald, whose contribution to the jacobin novel can only be touched on here. But this is unfortunately beyond the scope of this book.

Before examining the individual novels, I will give some indication of the rhetorical context within which they were produced, for the 1790s saw the development of both a new radical philosophy and a new conservatism. While the former looked to republican France, the latter sought to counter the urge for change by the resurrection of ideas of aristocratic virtue and the feudal constitution which can ironically be traced to the civic humanist writings of an earlier generation of republicans.

THE NEW FEUDALISM, BURKE AND GOTHIC

The proximate cause of the politicisation of fiction has been generally identified as the outbreak of the French Revolution, and the discussion which this stimulated in Britain. The terms of this discussion were initially established by the publication of Edmund Burke's *Reflections on the Revolution in France* in 1790, which redefined and reinvigorated the debate over public virtue, putting it at the centre of the discourses of both history and economics. Burke's antagonism to the French Revolution was primarily derived from his belief that it was based on an abandonment of tradition. Instead of utilising the powers of 'conservation and correction' to reform abuses within the state,[5] the French had attempted to construct a new political system from scratch. They rejected the idea of hereditary power, and in doing so denied the patriarchal principle that was the essence of the British system of property, law and political power, and was the foundation of the family.

The French Revolution therefore represented a dramatic culmination of a process that had been going on gradually in modern Europe, as the 'age of chivalry' was replaced by 'That of sophisters, economists and calculators'.[6] Burke identified the heroic feudal system as having been instrumental in shaping the political structures, as well as the manners, which Europe had inherited, so that 'if it should ever be totally extinguished, the loss, I fear, will be great'.[7] The force that was identified as having brought about the erosion of this 'ancient chivalry' was one that was also seen as having contributed to the destructiveness of the French Revolution: the moneyed interest. This perverted natural relationships within the state, and it is significant that one of the symptoms of the desolation caused by the Revolution in France, along with 'Laws overturned . . . commerce expiring . . . a church pillaged, and a state not relieved; civil and military anarchy' was the replacement of gold and silver (the two great recognised species that represent the lasting, conventional credit of mankind) with 'discredited paper securities'.[8] *Reflections* therefore developed the position outlined by writers on the decline of epic, to indicate the social, cultural and political consequences of the retreat from feudalism and the rise of commercialism.

A system based on landed wealth and inherited power was seen as having been abandoned in favour of a system which prioritised the interests of speculators and financiers, and sought, through the appropriation of church and private property, to bring about a redistribution of land and power. This was identified as both morally and politically lamentable, for although Burke recognised that there was some role for virtuous and talented members of the lower orders within the legislature, he believed that government should be largely composed of owners of hereditary wealth and property. Picking up the Aristotelian maritime metaphor, these were 'the ballast in the vessel of the commonwealth',[9] for as Burke explained:

Nothing is a due and adequate representation of a state that does not represent its ability, as well as its property. But as ability is a vigorous and active principle, and as property is sluggish, inert and timid, it never can be safe from the invasions of ability, unless it be, out of all proportion, predominant in the representation. It must be represented too in great masses of accumulation.[10]

This passage epitomises the complexity of Burke's political vision, for it locates the justification for the maintenance of an oligarchic aristocracy in the limitations of the aristocracy itself. Landed wealth is portrayed as inherently conservative, but it is identified as conservative to such a degree that it is unable to defend its own interests against the forces of change. The implication of this is not that the landed elite are not appropriate legislators for the country, but rather that they should be entrusted with a virtual monopoly of political power, to ensure that even in their enfeebled and supine condition, they are not challenged or threatened by people of ability. Thus while Burke's defence of the political prerogative of the landed interest is unambiguous, the terms of his defence provide a metonymic indictment of the individual members of that interest, who come across as 'sluggish, inert and timid'.

This ambivalence characterises Burke's view of the role of the aristocracy within contemporary society, as if a theoretical adherence to a feudal social model is unhappily juxtaposed with a knowledge of modern aristocrats. He at times evokes an image of feudal harmony; at times he laments that this has been lost. He asserts the importance of the patriarchal structure within both the political and social system, and he sees the changes of the French Revolution as a dramatic culmination of the movement away from the patriarchal feudal order which had been stimulated by economic developments. *Reflections* revivified the old heroic ethos of power and public virtue vested in a land-owning oligarchy, and rejected the private and individualistic ethos which had been increasingly accepted within fiction as well as economic analysis.

Burke's renovation of the discourse of public virtue provided the basis for political debate, which was waged through pamphlets, books and treatises throughout the 1790s. At the same time, the novel became increasingly preoccupied with ideological concerns, and issues of political morality. The language of politics was incorporated into fiction – sometimes without the element of ironic parodying which had tended to characterise its use within the novel of the mid-century. From being a specialised discourse to be subverted by the narrative voice, political polemic became a dominant and controlling discursive mode, as fiction sought to locate itself within the realm of the public.

But while the jacobin novel in general engaged with the rhetoric of conservatism, some addressed Burke more directly, challenging his celebration of feudal values and feudal society. In Robert Bage's novel *Man As He Is* (1792) the narrative voice expresses enthusiasm for a society dominated by a clerisy and feudal nobility, as described in a recent 'sublime and beautiful' book. The narrator's ironic outpouring is interrupted by an 'Old Friend':

The muscles of his face contracted into a sort of grin – 'Ten thousand pens', said he, 'must start from their ink-stands, to punish the man who dares attempt to restore the empire of prejudice and passion. The age of chivalry, heaven be praised, is gone. The age of truth and reason has commenced, and will advance to maturity in spite of counts or bishops. Law – active, invincible, avenging law, is here the knight-errand that redresses wrongs, protects damsels, and punishes the base miscreants who oppress them.'[11]

The words parody Burke's exclamation at his account of the arrest of the queen of France: 'I thought ten thousand swords must have leaped from their scabbards to avenge even a look that threatened her with insult. But the age of chivalry is gone.'[12] For the friend of Bage's narrator, the Middle Ages was not an heroic age of public spirit. Burke had suggested that the ancient chivalry 'subdued the fierceness of pride and power', 'obliged sovereigns to submit to the soft collar of social esteem, compelled stern authority to submit to elegance, and gave a domination vanquisher of laws, to be subdued by manners',[13] but for the unnamed parodic voice the picture is rather different. In the medieval period 'A few individuals only, the exceptions of the age, assumed to themselves the arduous task of opposing violent wrong by violent right.' Far from being a time of peace and harmony, the feudal age was characterised by great upheavals consequent on the dominance of a concept of vengeance, rather than a system of law:

All this is now happily changed. Philosophy and commerce have transformed that generous loyalty to rank, into attachment to peace, to law, to the general happiness of mankind; that proud submission and dignified obedience, into an unassuming consciousness of natural equality; and that subordination of the heart into an honest veneration of superior talents conjoined with superior benevolence.[14]

The ironic admiration for Burke expressed by the narrative voice is therefore negated by the friend's account of the progress of society. Primitivist nostalgia is dismissed in an account of the values and virtues of civil society. Progress is identified as a consequence of the benevolent influence of the spread of 'philosophy and commerce', which have ensured the creation of laws which have replaced the passions as the motive forces within society, and meant that a despotic system has been replaced by a system based on an idea of natural equality. Burke's political philosophy, in contrast, constitutes a rejection of the modern economic system which is seen as a progenitor of revolutionary fervour. He provides a romantic nostalgia for a precommercial era of heroic individualism in which authority was firmly located within patriarchy.[15]

The speech of the unnamed friend represents an ironic commentary on the celebration of feudal society, but this account is itself given an ironic turn by the bathos of the line which follows the friend's lengthy harangue. The narrator remarks 'I did not invite my friend to dinner',[16] and the subject is closed. This fits in with the ironic tone of the novel as a whole, for the political 'lectures' and polemical passages are repeatedly undermined or rendered humorous by a narrative voice that appeals to the demands of a 'fair readership' to explain the movement from the polemical to the romantic narrative. In the final paragraph of the novel, however, the narrative voice undermines the ironic prioritisation of the love plot.[17] It refuses to fulfil the expectations of the gendered audience, emphasising the importance of political events and political debate, bringing the narrative back to the French Revolution and to Burke. This indicates the essential difference between the novels of the 1790s and the earlier works of the sentimental tradition. For while the novel of sentiment genderised the moral focus of fiction into a conflict between a masculine, bourgeois, acquisitive private virtue, and a more feminised affective private ethos, the resurrection by Burke and others of heroic and aristocratic values led to a renewed emphasis on the conflict between a progressive commercial and bourgeois masculine ethic, and an aristocratic heroic public virtue that was also defined as male. At the same time, however, a number of women writers were using the novel form as a means of exploring and exposing the institutions of patriarchy, and their origins in both the bourgeoisie and the aristocracy. These institutions were challenged by the construction of feminine values that were identified not as private and marginal, but as having a public and political significance. So while the aristocratic ethos was constructed by Burke and his supporters, as a response to the levelling impulses of the French Revolution, associated with the promulgation of the 'moneyed interest', the jacobin writers developed a range of social visions which could challenge the renewed emphasis on patriarchal tradition.

In the jacobin fiction of the 1790s, however, the evocation of feudal values was inevitably associated not only with Burke and the new conservatism, but also with the fictional genre of Gothic. Novelists such as Ann Radcliffe, Matthew Lewis, Mary Meek and the Minerva writers based their Gothic tales in an often unspecified period of the past. Edward Copeland has indicated how these distanced narratives are used to work through contemporary anxieties about money, and women's vulnerability within a patriarchal economic system.[18] Other critics have highlighted the psychological significance of the Gothic themes of persecution, pursuit, false imprisonment and sexual exploitation.[19] Yet the decision to analyse these themes and problems through temporally and spatially distanced communities necessitated the construction of an historical vision, at a time when history was endemically and explicitly politicised. The despotism and oppression of the Gothic world are located in a feudal order based around a powerful and patriarchal landed elite, supported by a degenerate clerisy. Far from forming a bulwark against corruption and decay, these institutions are shown to be incapable of controlling the destructive and despotic activities of their own members. They are the source of the disruption of the moral order, and the restitution of harmony at the end of the novels is ultimately brought about by individuals who are outside the feudal elite and represent the 'vigorous and active' ability that Burke identified as a threat to property.

As such the Gothic novel constitutes a critique of the conservative celebration of the European feudal order. At the same time, the location of the stories in the past and/or abroad moderates the criticism of contemporary British society. The horrors of oppression tend to be associated with countries that are not just foreign, but also Catholic. In Italy, France and Spain the rule of law is identified as subordinate to the personal code of honour, and treachery, hypocrisy and superstition are represented as facts of life. This society is clearly identified as 'other' by the invocation of a normative standard of values within the reading public, against which the morality of the fictional world can be judged. This distancing of the fictional world of horror is most clearly displayed in Ann Radcliffe's *The Italian* (1797), which opens with an elaborate framing device. In a scene which is entirely irrelevant to the plot of the novel, we are told how 'About the year 1764, some English travellers in Italy, during one of their excursions in the environs of Naples, happened to stop before the portico of the *Santa Maria del Pianto*, a church belonging to a very ancient convent of the order of the *Black Penitents*.'[20] A shadowy figure is espied, who is identified as an assassin seeking sanctuary. The Englishman expresses great surprise at this:

'Do your altars, then, protect the murderer?' said the Englishman.
'He could find shelter no where else,' answered the friar meekly.
'This is astonishing!' said the Englishman; 'of what avail are your laws, if the most atrocious criminal may thus find shelter from them? But how does he contrive to exist here! He is, at least, in danger of being starved?'

'Pardon me,' replied the friar, 'there are always people willing to assist those, who cannot assist themselves; and as the criminal may not leave the church in search of food, they bring it to him here.'

'Is this possible!' said the Englishman, turning to his Italian friend.

'Why, the poor wretch must not starve,' replied the friend; 'which he inevitably would do, if food were not brought to him! But have you never, since your arrival in Italy, happened to see a person in the situation of this man? It is by no means an uncommon one.'

'Never!' answered the Englishman, 'and I can scarcely credit what I see now!'[21]

The function of this scene is to highlight the disparity between the 'other' of a corrupt, catholic, aristocratic society, unrestrained by the rule of law, and British society, which has been shaped by a Protestant religion, a balanced constitution, a temperate climate, and a complex legal system. The invocation of national differences within this scene is reflected in the title of the book. It is by no means clear which of the characters in the story is the 'Italian' of the title – is it Schedoni, Vivaldi or one of the female characters? The lack of any certain identification reinforces the idea that the book is dealing with the whole issue of what it is to be Italian, and what makes 'The Italian', just as the figure in the passage represents the stereotyped response of 'the Englishman'.

There may be a tinge of irony in Radcliffe's portrayal of the complacency of the Englishman in the initial, framing scene, but the message conveyed is the same as that enforced by Henry Tilney in Jane Austen's *Northanger Abbey*. Such novels are not intended as representations of human nature in the Midland counties of England.[22] Henry Tilney exhorts Austen's fanciful heroine to 'Remember the country and the age in which we live. Remember that we are English, that we are Christians.' Gothic plots cannot, therefore, be carried out 'in a country like this, where social and literary intercourse is on such a footing, where every man is surrounded by a neighbourhood of voluntary spies, and where roads and newspapers lay everything open'.[23]

In the Gothic novel, therefore, the implicit critique of the new feudalism is combined with a distancing of the narrative that emphasises the extent to which modern British society has departed from the feudal model, but also identifies these departures as the source of the liberties that are portrayed as essential for the protection of the individual within the complex state. In the jacobin novel, in contrast, the Gothic motifs of persecution, pursuit and false imprisonment are deployed, but within a society that, while in many ways essentially feudal, is clearly identified as both modern and British. If the message of the Gothic novel was to attack conservative ideology, by exposing the inapplicability of the feudal model within the complex commercial state, the message of the jacobin novel was to suggest that feudalism is not something associated with foreign countries and the distant past. Patriarchal oppression and despotism are still alive and well and operating within contemporary society.

The use of the novel for the articulation of jacobin ideology was itself significant. It represented a desire to address a wider, more socially diverse audience than that which would be reached by works of moral or political philosophy, such as Godwin's *Enquiry Concerning Political Justice*.[24] Godwin argued in his essay 'Of Romance and History' that the 'Romance' was the noblest species of history:

> The historian is confined to individual incident and individual man, and must hang upon that his invention or conjecture as he can. The writer of romance collects his materials from all sources, experience, report, and the records of human affairs; then generalizes them; and finally selects from the various elements and various combinations they afford, those incidents he is best able to portray, and which he judges most calculated to impress the heart and improve the faculties of his readers.[25]

In this vision, fiction is inherently didactic, although it is interesting that Godwin utilises the word 'romance', with its fanciful and escapist connotations, rather than the more usual 'novel', which by the time of the essay was firmly established as the term for fictitious prose narratives. The 'romance' can demonstrate the nature of virtue, but it can also explore the interaction of moral ideals and individual circumstances in a way that is not possible within either history or moral philosophy, and this was crucially important to the adherents of jacobin philosophy, with its emphasis on education, experience and individual example. Moreover, the novel was based around the celebration of those dynamic individuals who were identified within conservative rhetoric as a potential threat to the political dominance of landed wealth. The theme of moral progress that was inherent in the novel's didactic empiricism confirmed the jacobin doctrine of perfectibility, and upheld the public significance of private actions. This is implicit in Thomas Holcroft's claim in the preface to *The Adventures of Hugh Trevor* that 'In my opinion, all well written books, that discuss the actions of men, are in reality so many histories of the progress of the mind.'[26]

In *Anna St Ives* (1792) Holcroft utilised the Richardsonian epistolary structure to advocate his belief in the reforming power of reason, with the Clarissa figure of Anna St Ives finally converting the Lovelace character, Coke Clifton, from the paths of passion and depravity to a life of rational virtue. His subsequent novel, *The Adventures of Hugh Trevor* (1794–7), grafted jacobin political ideology onto the linear narrative of Fielding and Smollett. Like Tom Jones or Roderick Random, Hugh Trevor learns from his experiences, and his gradual acquisition of reason and moral sense is represented as a manifestation of the human potential for improvement.

Other novelists adapted and developed the novel form, to bring out its political and social power. Elizabeth Inchbald explored the use of doubling devices to generalise the individual narrative. *A Simple Story* juxtaposes the experiences of the indulged and wilful Miss Milner with those of her deprived and slighted daughter, Matilda, to focus on the issue of female education within a repressively patriarchal society. In *Nature and Art* the contrast is between Henry and William Norwynne, embodiments of nature and art. This moral tale of private and public life is intertwined with the narratives of Rebecca Rymer and Hannah Primrose, the respective lovers of the two boys, whose gender and humble social origins highlight the extent of the privilege that underlies the lifestyle of their partners.

This chapter will analyse how some of the female writers of the 1790s developed the form of the gendered jacobin novel to focus on the impact of the institutions of patriarchy on individual consciousness. But the discussion will begin with the work which Marilyn Butler has described as 'easily the most impressive English novel of the 1790s'.[27]

CALEB WILLIAMS

William Godwin's *Things As They Are, Or, The Adventures of Caleb Williams* was one of the earliest and most notorious jacobin novels. In the preface to the original edition Godwin explains that his intention in the novel was 'to comprehend, as far as the progressive nature of a single story would allow, a general review of the modes of domestic and unrecorded despotism, by which man becomes the destroyer of man'.[28] This despotism is portrayed as taking place in the heart of England, with the sanction and aid of the very system of laws which was identified in the Gothic novel, and celebrated by the 'Old Friend' in *Man As He Is*, as a safeguard against oppression.

At the start of the novel, the foreign origins of the Gothic psychology are picked up in the references to the years spent on the Grand Tour,

and in particular in Italy, by the hero's persecutor, Ferdinando Falkland. Falkland is a devotee of the code of honour that was explored in
Richardson's *Sir Charles Grandison*, a work which Kelly has identified as
an important influence on *Caleb Williams*.[29] He has read the heroic
poets, and from them 'imbibed the love of chivalry and romance' and
'believed that nothing was so well calculated to make men delicate,
gallant and humane, as a temper perpetually alive to the sentiments of
birth and honour'. He shares Burke's admiration for the ancient chivalry and the heroic mode. But the development of the plot gradually
reveals the oppression that is inherent in this ostensibly admirable code
of manners and morality, and its inapplicability within the modern
state.

On his return to England, Falkland employs Caleb Williams to act as
his secretary. Williams is born of peasant stock, and can be seen as
representative of the dynamism of ability, as opposed to the inertia of
property. Like the females of myth, he is fired by an insatiable curiosity
and eventually uncovers the dark secret of Falkland's past – that he has
killed a man, and suffered others to be punished for the crime. Once
Williams is in possession of this knowledge, he forfeits the love of a
master whom he recognises as true and honourable.

There are overtones of Faust, the Garden of Eden and Pandora's Box
in this story. Caleb Williams must pay the price for the knowledge he
has acquired, and when he attempts to leave Falkland's service, his
oppressor becomes more active in his persecution. Williams is arrested
on a false charge and while incarcerated in a dungeon meditates on the
institutionalised injustice of the English legal system, and also on the
English belief in the fairness and efficacy of the law:

Thank God, exclaims the Englishman, we have no Bastille! Thank God, with
us no man can be punished without a crime! Unthinking wretch! Is that a
country of liberty where thousands languish in dungeons and fetters? Go, go,
ignorant fool! and visit the scenes of our prisons! Witness their unwholesome-
ness, their filth, the tyranny of their governors, the misery of their inmates! After
that show me the man shameless enough to triumph, and say, England has no
Bastille! (p. 181)

This passage develops the criticism of the British penal policy of *The
Vicar of Wakefield*, as the political rhetoric of liberty and justice is juxtaposed with the reality of conditions which Godwin drew from John
Howard's *State of the Prisons in England and Wales, 1777–80*. The result is an
appeal for improvements in prison life, but also an attack on national-

istic complacency that is seen to have led to a denial of the limitations of the existing system. Terror and injustice are not just located in the Gothic realm of the other. Godwin's novel emphatically stresses that they are to be found here, in our own society, and even in 'the midland counties of England'.[30] So while the discourse of social policy challenges the rhetoric of nationalism, the heteroglossic narrative does not under-mine the public function of the novel. Within the different voices of *Caleb Williams*, the language of protest emerges as distinct and beyond parodic subversion, as fiction is again identified as having a crucial function in the articulation and negotiation of social values and political rhetoric.

Both Marilyn Butler and Eleanor Ty have stressed the importance of the plot in raising questions about the equity of society and the power over individuals of institutions which are constituted to safeguard the interests of the wealthy and the great.[31] Caleb Williams is a poor and friendless servant, and as such it is impossible for him to obtain any kind of justice in a case in which he is opposed by a member of the wealthy aristocracy. As Eleanor Ty remarks,

The chivalric code of honour and the ideal of gentleman's conduct extolled by Burke in his *Reflections on the Revolution* are shown to be insufficient guarantees of justice for a man with obscure birth such as Caleb Williams.[32]

Williams is an embodiment of the power and potential of individual consciousness and rationality, but also of its vulnerability in the face of institutionalised tyranny.

Caleb manages to escape from his prison, but he can find no peace or refuge thereafter. Whenever he attempts to settle and find a place for himself, he is discovered by Falkland or his agents, and his character is destroyed. This bizarre chase represents a sinister version of the wan-derings of the picaresque heroes of the eighteenth-century comic tradi-tion. Like Gil Blas, Caleb Williams falls in with a gang of thieves, who constitute a microcosm of, as well as a contrast with, organised society. But whereas in the comic tradition the heroes journey to acquire knowledge, in *Caleb Williams* the pursuit of Caleb is the consequence of his attainment of knowledge. He cannot rest until he has ferreted out Falkland's secret, and once he is in possession of this secret, Falkland will not let him rest.

The novel dramatises the injustice of society through the portrayal of the relationship between two striking individuals, whose characters and ideologies clash, but who share a basic respect for one another. This illustrates the doctrine, outlined throughout *Political Justice*, of the importance of the politically conscious individual, as the embodiment of social morality. Godwin distinguishes between government and society, arguing that while the latter is beneficial, the former is pernicious. Human beings originally associated for 'mutual assistance', and it was only the 'errors and perverseness of a few' that made the restraint of government necessary.[33] So while the persecution of Caleb manifests the oppressive nature of social institutions, his suffering represents the human need to be part of society.[34] Falkland, on the other hand, indicates the destructive potential of the individual. Unlike the Gothic novel, *Caleb Williams* does not portray the thirst for vengeance as a symbol of the pride and prejudice of the Catholic religion, but instead uses it to show the corruption of any political system that is not located within the capacity and sense of justice of the individual. It was this preoccupation with the inevitably distorting impact of social institutions (as opposed to society) which led Godwin to prefer the revised ending of the novel (in which Caleb Williams has Falkland condemned for murder, and is then wholly overcome with guilt) to the earlier version in which Williams fails in his legal battle, and his narrative degenerates into incoherent ramblings, as he is poisoned by Falkland.[35]

The conflict between Falkland and Williams is perceived as a struggle between individuals – the crime, the punishment and the vengeance have all been private, so that even though in the second ending Caleb is publicly vindicated, this is perceived as a failure, since the justice should have been private as well. Individuals should be led to recognise ideas of right and wrong, instead of having them imposed from without. For Caleb Williams the triumph of truth is a sour victory, since it is only an imperfect because an external justice, achieved through a legal system which, through its institutional nature, is inevitably corrupt.

Caleb Williams is, as Godwin intended, a critique of contemporary society from the ideological perspective of *Political Justice*.[36] Like Mary Wollstonecraft's unfinished *The Wrongs of Woman: Or, Maria*, it is a powerful and frightening image of the oppression that is built into society. Both works combine fantastic and nightmarish elements with a quite specific attack on social institutions. The conclusion of *Caleb Williams* manifests Godwin's uncertainty over not only the present state of society, but also the likely consequences of political change. If Falkland is an allegorical embodiment of the *ancien régime*, based on the figure of Edmund Burke, Caleb Williams is the moderate face of the French

Revolution, of Lafayette and Dumouriez.[37] The final ending of the
novel presents the triumph of the oppressed, and the defeat of the
persecutor, but in presenting this triumph as the ultimate tragedy
Godwin manifested the disenchantment which, by 1794, was beginning
to spread through the English radicals. The verdict of *Caleb Williams*
on his own precipitance clearly invites an allegorical and political
reading:

Such has been the result of a project I formed for delivering myself from the
evils that had so long attended me. I thought that, if Falkland were dead, I
should return once again to all that makes life worth possessing. I thought that if
the guilt of Falkland were established, fortune and the world would smile upon
my efforts. Both these events are accomplished; and it is only now that I am
truly miserable.[38]

Precipitate action, even when motivated by a love of truth, is identified
as the source of even greater suffering and injustice than that experienced under traditional systems of oppression. The end of *Caleb Williams*
is haunted by images of affective relationships and private emotions
which Caleb can never enjoy, yet which he increasingly recognises as
the essential link between the individual and the community. Caleb's
final indictment of Falkland severs the bond which, while the source of
his ostracism and persecution, has also involved him in a relationship of
individuals. In ultimately allying himself with institutional power,
Williams does not open the way to his re-entry into society, but excludes
himself from it forever. The novel therefore analyses the oppression
inherent within the public institutional sphere, while its haunting evocation of individual isolation at once stresses the importance of private
affective relationships and precludes the analysis of them. In contrast,
Mary Hays' novel, *The Memoirs of Emma Courtney*, portrays the attractions
of a public sphere from which its heroine is excluded, while exploring
the restrictions of the private affective realm.

THE MEMOIRS OF EMMA COURTNEY

The Memoirs of Emma Courtney (1796) can be read as an amalgamation of
the sentimental and jacobin fictional traditions, and an example of what
can be seen as the sub-genre of gendered jacobinism. This was a form of
jacobin writing that was developed by Elizabeth Inchbald, Mary Hays
and Mary Wollstonecraft as a means of exploring political oppression
within eighteenth-century society and the position of women in public

and private life. Gary Kelly has argued in *Women, Writing and Revolution, 1790–1827* that Hays sought to interfuse the masculine discourse of philosophy and the feminine discourse of the novel, challenging what she identified as 'a dangerous separation of masculine and feminine discourse within the professional middle-class cultural revolution'.[39] She therefore used the novel form to 'generalize, politicize, theorize, and finally revolutionize her self and experience'.[40] Much of the text of *Emma Courtney* is, as Kelly has indicated, drawn directly from Hays' philosophical and sentimental correspondence with William Frend and William Godwin. The heroine is a character with an overdeveloped sensibility, fired by strong passions and emotions, and (like Thomas Holcroft's Hugh Trevor) frequently at odds with the society in which she finds herself. 'Mine, I believe, is a *solitary madness in the eighteenth century*', she declares, '*it is not on the altars of love, but of gold, that men, now, come to pay their offerings*'.[41] The materialism of the commercial ethos is thus contrasted with the affections and sensibilities of the heroine, but while these sensibilities are identified as being confined within the private sphere of female activity, their origins are located in the public rhetoric of civic humanism. They have been developed and refined by the heroine's early education, and, in particular, her reading, which develops from romances and the tales of the Arabian nights, to Plutarch's *Lives*, and a course of Greek and Roman history. This, as Pocock has indicated, formed the basis of the classical civic humanist tradition,[42] but the context of the 1790s led to a reorientation of the function and implications of this tradition. Republicanism was again constructed as a political as well as an ethical rhetoric, while the sentimental heritage led to an emphasis on the emotional appeal of public virtue and the heroic ethos as an indictment of the dominance of mercenary motivation and corruption. The perusal of Plutarch leaves Courtney's 'mind pervaded with republican ardour', her 'sentiments elevated by a high toned philosophy', and her 'bosom glowing with the virtues of patriotism' (vol. 1, p. 33). She tells us that

Accounts of the early periods of states and empires, of the Grecian and Roman republics, I pursued with pleasure and enthusiasm: but when they became more complicated, grew corrupt, luxurious, licentious, perfidious, mercenary, I turned from them fatigued, and disgusted, and sought to recreate my spirits in the fairer regions of poetry and fiction. (vol. 1, p. 40)

While the presentation of corruption and the decay of public virtue is identified as antipathetic to the sentimental individual, the evocation of public virtue within civic humanist writings is seen as a means of developing the sentimental consciousness. With polite literature, it inspires a sense and love of heroism and virtue, but this inevitably leads to censure of the manners and morals of contemporary society. As Emma's father points out, 'Aristides the just, would have made but a poor figure among our modern men of fashion!' (vol. I, p. 35).

Emma Courtney contains various scenes and passages which are devoted to exposing the political and social limitations of the modern commercial world. The reformist philosophy is espoused by Mr Francis, who emphasises the growth of reason in society, his faith in progress, and his belief that 'we may trace most of the faults, and the miseries of mankind, to, the vices and errors of political institutions' (vol. I, p. 91). As in the sentimental novel, language and its categories and discriminations are shown to embody the values and morality of the polity, and thus to be open to question by those seeking change. Emma Courtney refers to soldiers as 'murderers', while at a polite dinner party with her cousin, arguing that they are only different from 'common ruffians and housebreakers' (vol. II, p. 37) in that the latter have the excuse of 'passion, poverty, or injustice' (vol. II, p. 38), whereas the former do not. This passage has its parallel in Elizabeth Inchbald's *Nature and Art*, also published in 1796, in which the child of 'Nature', Henry Norwynne, highlights the artificial values of society by his 'childish inattention' to the 'proper signification of words': 'He would call *compliments, lies* – *Reserve*, he would call *Pride* – *stateliness, affectation* – and for the monosyllable *war*, he constantly substituted the word *massacre*.'[43] This technique effectively exposes the absence of morality within political policy, by drawing attention to the disparity between moral language and a discourse of statesmanship that is shown to be based on a euphemistic evasion of the consequences of actions.

Above all, *Emma Courtney* contains a thorough critique of the patriarchal structure of society, and the restrictions which it imposes on women. When Emma Courtney is left friendless, impoverished and dependent, she identifies the position of women in society as the true root cause of her difficulties:

Cruel prejudices! – I exclaimed – hapless woman! Why was I not educated for commerce, for a profession, for labour? Why have I been rendered feeble and delicate by bodily constraint, and fastidious by artificial refinement? Why are we bound, by the habits of society, as with an adamantine chain? Why do we suffer ourselves to be confined within a magic circle, without daring, by a magnanimous effort, to dissolve the barbarous spell? (vol. I, p. 55)

This image, of a magic circle confining women, recurs through the novel. Emma Courtney can perceive it 'without knowing how to dissolve the powerful spell' (vol. I, p. 169). Her reading of Greek and Roman history has fired her with a sense of public virtue and a love of liberty and justice, yet the restrictions of society, with its relentless denial of choices and opportunities for women, not only prevents her from using her abilities for the good of society, but even renders her incapable of helping herself. The civic humanist rhetoric therefore inspires public sentiments and aspirations which provide the basis for an attack on the patriarchal structure of the social system. As such, *Emma Courtney* challenges Edmund Burke's appeal to classical and feudal society and the ethos of public virtue. The novel suggests that the true heirs of the civic humanist tradition were not the conservative opponents of revolution, with their endorsement of the patriarchal status quo, but rather the moderate revolutionaries, who sought to extend the concept of individual liberty, to enable everyone to fulfil their public and political role. We are led to believe that Emma Courtney could have played a great role in public life, or been a force for good within society, had she been given the opportunity, but the fact that this was denied her ensured that her powerful sentiments were forced to find vent within the confines of private life: 'While men pursue interest, honor, pleasure, as accords with their several dispositions, women . . . remain insulated beings, and must be content tamely to look on, without taking any part in the great, though often absurd and tragical, drama of life' (vol. I, p. 169). As she explains to Mr Francis: 'Excluded, as it were, by the pride, luxury, and caprice of the world, from expounding my sensations, and wedding my soul to society, I was constrained to bestow the strong affections, that glowed consciously within me, upon a few' (vol. II, pp. 107–8). The result is the development of a narrative fiction that is preoccupied with the private and emotional, yet which polemicises the very process of its own retreat from the public sphere. *Emma Courtney* analyses the limited role of women within the modern state, and thus the constriction of gendered fiction based on truth to nature, but she does so in a work which adopts a politicised and public voice that is not ironically undermined by the narrative. It is therefore this engagement with public rhetoric, while complaining against the exclusion of women from the sphere of public action, that renders the narrative susceptible to accusations that it is 'preachy'. The location of the novel in the sphere of private rather than public virtue ensured that in writers such as Fielding and Lennox the incorporation of political language was always accompanied by a parodic subtext that satirised this public discourse, reinforcing the identification of fiction as a form adapted for the exploration of private sentiments and individual codes of morality. In Hays' narrative the polemical narrative voice is allowed to emerge without ironic mediation, although the reader's response may be influenced by reactions to the character of Courtney.

In the second volume of *Emma Courtney* the restrictions imposed on women lead to a further retreat from the public ideal, as the heroine develops a morbid and obsessive emotionalism. Courtney falls passionately in love with Augustus Harley, and when Harley suggests that he is not in a position to return her affection, she besieges him with requests for an explanation. She even offers to live with him without marriage, on the grounds that '*the individuality of an affection constitutes its chastity*' (vol. II, p. 65). The narrative dramatises the limited role of women in society in its own confinement within the private sphere of action, while the increasing dominance of a sentimental voice is itself a manifestation of the exclusion of women from the discourses and rhetoric of power. The attack on the 'magic circle' of patriarchal society, with the lack of educational and employment opportunities for women, and the problems of financial dependence are crystallised in the second volume of the novel into an assessment of social and sexual convention, which ultimately identifies sensibility itself as a magic circle of restriction facing women.

When Emma Courtney learns that Harley had been secretly married to another woman for some years before she met him, she is overcome with anguish at the impropriety of her conduct, yet she is also able to recognise the role of 'society' in events. In defending herself to Mr Francis, who suggests that she is the cause of her own misfortune, she argues that women cannot be blamed for their actions, since their ability to make decisions has been so severely restricted: 'Why call woman, miserable, oppressed, and impotent, woman – *crushed, and then insulted* – why call her to *independence* – which not nature, but the barbarous and accursed laws of society, have denied her? *This is mockery!*' (vol. II, p. 107). She appeals to Francis, who admires the public passion of an Alexander or a Caesar, to be more tolerant of 'a passion, though differing in nature, generated on the same principles, and by a parallel process' (vol. II, p. 115).

The development of the plot of *Emma Courtney* therefore dramatises the gendered nature of narrative in the late eighteenth century. Hays presents a character who is full of patriotism and love of public virtue, but who is trapped within a purely private sphere, constantly confronting the injustice which her education teaches her to fight against, while society prevents her from doing so. Heroic virtue is therefore simultaneously radicalised, and portrayed as irrelevant and inaccessible within the gendered jacobin novel. Patriarchal oppression is not associated with the 'other' of foreign, Catholic societies, in which confinement is physical rather than social. It is located within the modern, commercial state, and its consequence is a necessary prioritisation within the female novel of issues of private rather than public virtue. At the same time, however, the incorporation within the gendered jacobin novel of the discourse of civic humanism, with its celebration of public virtue and the juxtaposition of this language with the emotionalism of the sentimental plot, serves not to satirise the public and political but rather to politicise the retreat into the private. The constriction of female energies within the modern state, and the location of the novel within the private sphere, are identified not as inevitable but rather as lamentable consequences of a particular political system which could be susceptible to change. The narrative of *Emma Courtney* adopts a polemical tone to reappropriate the public function of literature in appealing against its location within the private realm.

THE WRONGS OF WOMAN

In her *Vindication of the Rights of Woman*, Mary Wollstonecraft analyses the position of women in modern society, and the constructions of femininity that are put upon them by the patriarchal establishment. In the context of this analysis, she outlines a model of the development of society which draws on, but redefines, the civic humanist concept of history. Wollstonecraft describes the emergence from barbarism to aristocratic and ultimately monarchical government, which is secured by the establishment of feudal tenures and a hierarchical social system. The increasing power of the people, however, 'obliges their rulers to gloss over their oppression with a show of right':

Thus, as wars, agriculture, commerce, and literature, expand the mind, despots are compelled to make covert corruption hold fast the power which was formerly snatched by open force. And this baneful lurking gangrene is most quickly spread by luxury and superstition.[44]

Wollstonecraft shares the civic humanist perception that aristocracy and monarchy are natural forms of early government, but while civic humanist rhetoric associated commerce with luxury and condemned them both as a threat to the stability of the state, Wollstonecraft saw commerce and luxury as opposing forces. Wars, agriculture, commerce and literature are identified as mechanisms to expand the minds of the common people, encouraging them to question the legitimacy of their government; whereas corruption and luxury are tools of the administration, bribing the people to support a system of government which is manifestly unsuitable to their needs.

Wollstonecraft therefore reorients the civic humanist attack on the luxury of the working people to present an attack on the luxury of the upper class in the manner of the eighteenth-century economic writers. These 'weak, artificial beings, raised above the common wants and affections of their race, in a premature unnatural manner, undermine the very foundations of virtue and spread contagion through the whole mass of society!'[45] Her focus will not be on these corrupting and corrupted creatures, but on 'the middle class, because they appear to be in the most natural state'.[46] Wollstonecraft does not justify her exclusion from consideration of the working class, but this could be seen to be implicit in her portrayal of the demoralising and degenerating influence of physical drudgery and poverty.

The identification of the middle class as the locus for moral and social improvement echoes the emphasis in fictional tradition on heroes and heroines of the middling sort, and undermines the celebration in civic humanism, endorsed by the writings of Burke, of the feudal values of the aristocratic elite. Wollstonecraft's final unfinished novel, *The Wrongs of Woman: Or, Maria*, embodies the attack on feudal society that was found within *Caleb Williams*, but develops the insights of *A Vindication* to concentrate on the mechanisms for the repression of female individuality and creativity within a system of patriarchal values.

The Wrongs of Woman recounts the story of Maria, but the preface informs us that 'the history ought rather to be considered, as of woman, than of an individual'.[47] Maria is, at the start of the narrative, separated from her baby and confined in a lunatic asylum by a husband who wishes to gain control of her independent fortune. During her confinement she forms a friendship with a fellow inmate, Henry Darnford, which gradually develops into love. The majority of the 'fragment' is made up of Maria's account of her history, interspersed with the narrative of the servant Jemima. Both women have been hounded and oppressed in society, and the common themes in these stories of women from very different social backgrounds generalise the presentation of patriarchal oppression.

Jemima, the illegitimate daughter of a servant, tells of a life that is a catalogue of brutality and neglect. She recounts: 'I was . . . born a slave, and chained by infamy to slavery during the whole of existence, without any companions to alleviate it by sympathy, or teach me how to rise above it by their example' (p. 106). Jemima suffers rape, infamy and neglect, and is forced to live by prostitution and petty theft, apart from a brief, happy period as the mistress of an educated man. Her reflections on her private suffering are, like those of Emma Courtney, explicitly polemical, emphasising the public significance of private experience within the gendered jacobin novel.

'How often have I heard', said Jemima, interrupting her narrative, 'in conversation, and read in books, that every person willing to work may find employment? It is the vague assertion of insensible indolence, when it relates to men; but with respect to women I am sure of its fallacy, unless they will submit to the most menial bodily labour; and even to be employed at hard labour is out of the reach of many, whose reputation misfortune or folly has tainted.

How writers, professing to be friends to freedom, and the improvement of morals, can assert that poverty is no evil, I cannot imagine!' (p. 114)

Jemima's words and her narrative challenge the perspective of Elizabeth Inchbald's *Nature and Art*. Inchbald's novel ends with a celebration of rural retirement and a life of simple poverty. For Jemima, as for Inchbald's fallen woman Hannah Primrose, poverty does not mean happy freedom from the temptations and corruptions of luxury, but a lack of the basic necessaries of life. Moreover, as Maria argues, the poor are not only physically deprived, but intellectually repressed and brutalised:

The mind is necessarily imprisoned in its own little tenement; and, fully occupied by keeping it in repair, has no time to rove abroad for improvement. The book of knowledge is closely clasped, against those who must fulfil their daily task of severe manual labour or die; and curiosity, rarely excited by thought or information, seldom moves on the stagnant lake of ignorance. (p. 114)

Jemima's own considerable intellectual abilities are a testament to the fact that it is opportunity rather than potential which the working classes lack, and under the benevolent influence of Maria's sympathy, Jemima blossoms into a loyal and affectionate companion.

While Jemima has experienced the brutality and oppression of the working class, Maria suffers at the hands of the gentry and the wealthy commercial classes. Oppressed at home by a tyrannical father and domineering brother, Maria is encouraged to fancy herself in love with George Venables, the son of a prosperous London merchant. As soon as they are married, Venables proves himself to be an equally brutal tyrant – a mean, selfish libertine who continually presses Maria to extort money from her uncle to fund his over-ambitious and unsuccessful commercial ventures. When Venables attempts to prostitute his wife to a friend, Maria leaves the marital home. There then follow scenes reminiscent of *Caleb Williams*, as Maria is 'hunted, like an infected beast' (p. 178) by her husband and his agents, until she is finally drugged and imprisoned in the asylum (pp. 183–5). The unfinished text of *The Wrongs of Woman* concludes with Maria, Darnford and Jemima escaping from the asylum, and setting up house in London. While Darnford travels to Paris, Maria appears in court on his behalf, defending him against an action for seduction and adultery filed by Venables. The final chapter contains Maria's reasoned appeal to the jury and the judge's summing up. Maria's paper is based on an intuitive sense of right and wrong, emphasising her belief that women should have the right to end their marriages, where the conduct of the husband renders this necessary. In this context, she argues that her relationship with Darnford should not be viewed as adulterous:

I wish my country to approve of my conduct; but, if laws exist, made by the strong to oppress the weak, I appeal to my own sense of justice, and declare that I will not live with the individual, who has violated every moral obligation which binds man to man. (p. 197)

Such an appeal to natural justice and individual rights cuts little ice with the judge, who explains to the jury that

We did not want French principles in public or private life – and, if women were allowed to plead their feelings, as an excuse or palliation of infidelity, it was opening a flood-gate for immorality. What virtuous woman thought of her feelings? – It was her duty to love and obey the man chosen by her parents and relations, who were qualified by their experience to judge better for her, than she could herself. (p. 199)

Ironically, although Maria has earlier displayed some of the excessive sensibility which in *Emma Courtney* was identified as a consequence of the constriction of the female within the private sphere, her paper to the court is not based on an appeal to feelings. Even so, the judge identifies the 'appeal to [her] own sense of justice' as an example of 'French principles' and women being 'allowed to plead their feelings'. This indicates the extent of the alienation of the patriarchal legal establishment from any concept of a system of law grounded in a sense of justice and individual rights, but it also suggests that the conservative opponents of change tended to associate the radical cause with those aspects of the female character which were emphasised within fiction. Despite the jacobin stress on rationalism, the threat to social stability is located in the dominance of private emotion and sensibility.[48] 'Feelings' and a desire to exercise personal preference in relation to marriage are represented as directly opposed to duty and obedience and against the interests of society.

Maria recognises a duty to herself and to justice which she identifies as the proper basis for the public institutions of the polity – in line with the principles of Godwin's *Political Justice*. Yet the story of Maria's confrontation with the legal institutions of the state is contained within the story of her suffering at the hands of individuals who embody the horrors of patriarchal oppression as manifested within private life. Margaret George, in a less than flattering account, claimed that in Wollstonecraft's work 'Men, all of them, were always the same, united in their freedom and power and united in their resistance to women's equality, whether they were deliberate tyrants, overbearing boors and oafs, or charming liars.'[49] This view is a little extreme. Wollstonecraft is prepared to accept that men may be decent, tender and virtuous provided they suffer from consumption.[50] But since this is invariably fatal it does little to moderate the generally critical terms in which men are portrayed. Wollstonecraft's notes suggest that Darnford was ultimately going to prove unfaithful to Maria (pp. 201–3), yet George is wrong to analyse Wollstonecraft's portrayal of men in terms of the 'psychological bases' of 'resentment, envy, and self doubt'.[51]

While Wollstonecraft shares the jacobin belief in the power and importance of the individual spirit, her portrayal of the working classes, emotionally stultified by unremitting drudgery, reveals the extent of her recognition of the importance of environment in determining character. Her novels are full of 'beastly males'[52] because this is what a social system of patriarchal oppression has fostered. Within a society founded on the commodification of women, it is hardly surprising if women are treated like commodities. Their oppression is implemented by individuals, but its cause is systemic. Eleanor Ty has emphasised Wollstonecraft's willingness to confront Burke and his ideal of the benevolent patriarch,[53] yet while Wollstonecraft clearly traces the origins of patriarchy to the feudal system, she indicates that its structures have been reinforced by the commercial economy. Despite her portrayal in *A*

Vindication of commerce as a force that has the potential to enlarge the mind of the lower class, in *The Wrongs of Woman* it is clearly seen as a mechanism for the maintenance of a status quo that is based on the systematic oppression of women. The division of labour has ensured that the working people are kept in a degraded condition that renders their brutality unsurprising. And the dominance of avarice in the values of the bourgeoisie prevents the development of affective feelings which could lead the way to a more positive attitude to women. George Venables is not a descendant of a landed family, but a failed financier who is 'considered . . . on 'Change as a swindler' (p. 160). He is a corrupt representative of the new order, yet his gender-based power is maintained by the institutions inherited from the past. He eschews sentimentalism and emotion as weaknesses to be exploited in the pursuit of financial gain, and in the absence of emotion, love is indistinguishable from libertinism.

The attitude to sentiment and feeling within *The Wrongs of Woman* is therefore complicated, for while sentimentalism is seen as a mechanism for the manipulation of women (employed by both Venables and Darnford), it is also represented as a refuge for female energy and emotion, which are denied any other outlet. This in part explains the ambivalence towards sentimentalism and romance which a number of critics have noted in the text.[54] As Laurie Langbauer writes, 'on the one hand, her novels set up romance as what they especially, as women's work, must transcend; on the other, her work redefines the romantic as what might unsettle or elude the control of the male order.'[55] The cultivation of romance and sensibility is both a challenge to, and an endorsement of, patriarchal society. It is one of the few ways in which women can express passion and creativity, but the fact that this is the case is itself testament to the oppressive nature of the social system.

In general, therefore, the gendered jacobin novel presents a much bleaker vision of contemporary society than the jacobin works in the masculine tradition of Bage and Holcroft, with their invocation of narratives of experience. Hays and Wollstonecraft question the value of sentimentalism, while they draw on the pessimism of the sentimental vision. A clear consciousness of the injustices of the patriarchal system is not combined with a sense of how these injustices can be rectified, since the portrayal of individuals as the product of a patriarchal environment undermines any sense of individual perfectibility. The commercial system is not represented, as it is in *The Fool of Quality*, as a potential engine for positive social change, containing a model of individual behaviour that reconciles the private with the public. Despite the attitude to commerce expressed in Wollstonecraft's *Vindication*, the modern economic structure is identified as an instrument of patriarchy which perpetuates the tyranny developed within the feudal system.

The novel, with its focus on private sentiments and feelings, is an appropriate medium for the exploration of the emotional consequences of this tyranny. It can articulate a feminised and affective ethic which can confront the dominant values of materialism. Yet the role of this ethic, and thus of fiction, is necessarily marginal, and within gendered jacobinism the prioritisation of feeling, and the identification of sentiment as a primarily female preserve, are themselves symbols of the exclusion of women from other, more public, realms. While the more optimistic male jacobin writers sought to emphasise the public significance of the private narrative, stressing that the story of the species was the story of individuals, the female writers recognised the constrictive potential of the privileging of the private. The sentimental novelists had identified excessive feeling as the preserve of a refined moral elite. For Wollstonecraft and Hays it is part of a system that is based on the exclusion of a gendered group from the true realms and discourses of power.

CHAPTER 8

Conclusion

This book has attempted to argue that within the novels of the eighteenth century lies an important debate about the relationship between public and private virtue, and the role and nature of each. This debate was both stimulated and fuelled by the absence within eighteenth-century society of any single discourse which could be taken to embody contemporary morality. The widespread apprehension that society was losing its social cohesion, and was becoming increasingly fragmented into economic and political interest groups, was accompanied by an anxiety that there was no single genre within which clear and unequivocal moral guidance could be sought. The conflicts between orthodox Christianity, civic humanism and the new economic code gave a particular imperative to the role of the novel as a locus for moral debate, and the form was increasingly recognised as appropriate for the expression of moral values and the formulation of a sense of national identity. Yet while the structure of the novel made it peculiarly suitable for the articulation and analysis of private morality, the maintenance of traditional epic ideas of the function of literature ensured that in the mid-century the fictional portrayal of private virtue was juxtaposed with an ostensible adherence to more public codes of behaviour. It was only with the twin processes of the growing dominance of private morality and the increasing respectability of the novel form, that adherence to public virtue and epic moral and mimetic codes were gradually abandoned. The irrelevance and yet the emotional appeal of the traditional aristocratic code of honour were emphasised in the period 1770 to 1800 by the terms of the exploration of the code within fiction. In the Gothic novels of writers like Ann Radcliffe and Matthew Lewis, honour was identified as morally ambivalent or positively dangerous, but also as 'other' – no longer applicable to the condition of the state or to the ordinary life within Britain, and it was this ordinary life that was increasingly recognised as the natural subject matter of literature. Far from being a repository of public and private virtue, the aristocracy was frequently represented as inherently depraved and corrupt, associated with the descendants of Lovelace rather than Leonidas – immoral anachronisms within modern society. While few writers went so far as Henry Brooke, in advocating the abduction of infant aristocrats to give them the advantages of a commercial education, there was a growing tendency to locate virtue and fictional heroism within the middle order of society, in the lesser gentry or the bourgeoisie whom the jacobins identified as most susceptible to moral and intellectual improvement.

At the same time, the tensions within bourgeois ideology became themselves a subject for fictional scrutiny. The novel of circulation exposed the links within the economic system, denuded of any affective gloss, and satirised the atomisation, alienation and selfishness that were taken to characterise the modern commercial state. A similar pursuit of materialism was represented in the sentimental novel, but this genre explored the contrast between the dominant economic ethos, and the values of a group of characters who embodied charity, benevolence and piety. Adherence to this feminised code was not represented as gender specific, but signalled the marginalisation of the caring individual within contemporary society. In the work of the female jacobin writers, in contrast, the maintenance of affective values and private virtue was represented as both gender specific and a confirmation of the circumscribed role of women in the economy.

Thus while in one sense the novel was consolidating its cultural position in the eighteenth century, as novel writing became an increasingly respectable and lucrative occupation, in another it was becoming more restricted, accepting a particular vision of the scope of fiction within society. By tending to embody a feminised ethic which it identified as *not* the dominant code of social morality, the novel highlighted the limited applicability of its representations. In this respect the jacobin novelists developed rather than challenged the social critique that had characterised the novels of circulation and sentimental fiction. Yet while the latter genres tended to accept the economic system with irony and melancholy resignation respectively, the jacobin writers appealed for justice and reform in the here and now rather than the hereafter, and emphasised the need for the general reformation of social consciousness and thus of the polity.

In the hands of Godwin, Holcroft and Bage, the jacobin novel sought to resurrect and redefine the notion of public virtue that had conditioned the fiction of the mid-eighteenth century. At the same time the female jacobins identified the patriarchal assumptions that were implicit within any delineation of a public sphere, and fictionalised the dependence of female consciousness on the sentimental construction of private feeling. The 1790s therefore saw the efflorescence of engaged and polemical fiction, yet it was the novel of manners that survived and came to define the form that emerged into the nineteenth century. While Fanny Burney and Jane Austen shared the jacobin preoccupation with money and the position of women within a patriarchal and commercial state, the novel form that they developed was explicitly located in the private realm. Burney's preoccupation is with manners and marriage, the processes by which the female individual can overcome her social and financial restrictions to be absorbed into the status quo. As such, her fiction constitutes a rejection of both the public and polemical role which had been sought by the jacobin writers, and the ethical and cognitive functions claimed by Richardson and Fielding. If the history of the eighteenth-century novel can be read as a struggle between public and private ideology, as the genre sought to establish its status and a clear didactic role, the end of the century seems to represent the reconciliation of the form with a private and feminised identity, in which debates over commerce were refined into anxieties over consumption and expenditure.[1]

So although the novel embodied the moral and social objections to commercial morality, first through the code of aristocratic public virtue, then through the invocation of private bourgeois individualism, its development through the eighteenth century can ironically be seen as an endorsement of the terms of economic analysis. As economic ideas became increasingly socially acceptable with the publication of the writings of Hume and Smith, and as moral philosophy retreated into the marginal cultural role of the consideration of the motivation of the educated few, the novel accepted the limited private realm which was the product of the dominance of the economic image of the state, and the separation of the public and the private.

It is perhaps in the literature of the nineteenth century, in the work of Gaskell, Dickens, Kingsley, maybe even Disraeli, that we should seek a movement towards the reformulation of the fictional conflict between high- and low-bourgeois terms of social analysis, between private and public, moral and economic perspectives. For it was only in the nineteenth century that economic writers, and with them novelists and moral philosophers, began to reconsider the nature of the public interest, and question the automatic association of the concept with economic expansion and the enrichment of the bourgeoisie. Once the working classes began to be perceived – however simplistically or patronisingly – as having needs that constituted part of the public interest, the way was open for an alteration in the concept of commercial morality, and the terms of its relation to the novel form. It was only in the course of the nineteenth century that the novel could develop from the marginal private role and attempt to reappropriate some of the social and political functions which it had striven to fulfil in the mideighteenth century.

Notes

I INTRODUCTION

1 Lennard Davis, *Factual Fictions: The Origins of the English Novel* (New York: Columbia University Press, 1983); Michael McKeon, *The Origins of the English Novel, 1600–1740* (London: Radius, 1988); William Ray, *Story and History: Narrative Authority and Social Identity in the Eighteenth-Century French and English Novel* (Oxford and Cambridge, Mass.: Basil Blackwell, 1990); J. Paul Hunter, *Before Novels: The Cultural Contexts of Eighteenth-Century English Fiction* (New York: Norton, 1990).

2 John Richetti, *Popular Fiction Before Richardson: Narrative Patterns 1700–1739* (Oxford: Clarendon Press, 1969).

3 Ian Watt, *The Rise of the Novel: Studies in Defoe, Richardson and Fielding* (London: Hogarth Press, 1987).

4 Richetti, *Popular Fiction*, p. 9.

5 Hunter, *Before Novels*, pp. ix–x.

6 Caroline Robbins, *The Eighteenth-Century Commonwealthman: Studies in the Transmission, Development and Circumstances of English Liberal Thought from the Restoration of Charles II until the War of the Thirteen Colonies* (Cambridge, Mass.: Harvard University Press, 1959); J. G. A. Pocock, *The Machiavellian Moment: Florentine Political Thought and the Atlantic Republican Tradition* (Princeton, N.J.: Princeton University Press, 1975).

7 Pocock, *Machiavellian Moment*, pp. 462–505.

8 John Barrell, *The Political Theory of Painting from Reynolds to Hazlitt* (New Haven: Yale University Press, 1986); David Solkin, *Painting for Money: The Visual Arts and the Public Sphere in Eighteenth-Century England* (New Haven: Yale University Press, 1993).

9 Stephen Copley (ed.), *Literature and the Social Order in Eighteenth-Century England* (London: Croom Helm, 1984), pp. 6–7.

10 Although see Joyce Oldham Appleby, *Economic Thought and Ideology in Seventeenth-Century England* (Princeton: Princeton University Press, 1979).

11 J. C. D. Clark, *English Society 1688–1832: Ideology, Social Structure and Political Practice during the Ancien Régime* (Cambridge: Cambridge University Press, 1985), pp. 8–14.

12 Elizabeth Bellamy, 'Private Virtues, Public Vices: Commercial Morality

and the Novel, 1740–1800' (unpublished Ph.D. thesis, Jesus College, Cambridge, 1988).

13 Gary Kelly, 'The English Jacobin Novel and its Background 1780–1805' (unpublished Ph.D. thesis, University of Oxford, 1972); Marilyn Butler, *Jane Austen and the War of Ideas* (Oxford: Clarendon Press, 1975), pp. 29–87; Gary Kelly, *The English Jacobin Novel, 1780–1805* (Oxford: Oxford University Press, 1976).

2 THE ECONOMIC CONTEXT

1 Leslie Stephen, *History of English Thought in the Eighteenth Century*, 2 vols. (London, 1876), vol. II, p. 283; Eduard Heimann, *History of Economic Doctrines: An Introduction to Economic Theory* (London: Oxford University Press, 1945), pp. 9–10; William J. Barber, *A History of Economic Thought* (Harmondsworth: Penguin, 1967), p. 17; Istvan Hont and Michael Ignatieff, 'Needs and Justice in the *Wealth of Nations*: An Introductory Essay', in *Wealth and Virtue: The Shaping of Political Economy in the Scottish Enlightenment* (Cambridge: Cambridge University Press, 1982); see also Keith Tribe, *Genealogies of Capitalism* (London: Macmillan, 1981), p. 121.

2 Samuel Fortrey, *England's Interest and Improvement* (London, 1673), reprinted in J. J. McCulloch, *Early English Tracts on Commerce*, first published by the Political Economy Club (London, 1856) and reprinted for the Economic History Society (1952 and 1954), pp. 211–50, p. 226.

3 George Berkeley, *An Essay towards Preventing the Ruin of Great Britain*, in *The Works of George Berkeley, Bishop of Cloyne*, ed. A. A. Luce and T. E. Jessop, 9 vols. (London: Thomas Nelson, 1953), vol. VI, p. 74.

4 John Brown, *Estimate of the Manners and Principles of the Times* (1757), 6th edn (London, 1757, for L. Davis and C. Reymers), p. 29.

5 John Sekora, *Luxury: The Concept in Western Thought, Eden to Smollett* (Baltimore and London: Johns Hopkins University Press, 1977) p. x.

6 *Ibid.*, pp. 18–19.

7 *Ibid.*, p. 73.

8 *Ibid.*, p. 310, note 10.

9 Anon., *Britannia Languens: Or, A Discourse on Trade* (1680), in McCulloch, *Early English Tracts*, pp. 377–81.

10 Elizabeth Lamond, preface to John Hales, *A Discourse of the Common Weal of this Realm of England* [written 1549], ed. Elizabeth Lamond (Cambridge: Cambridge University Press, 1893 and 1929), pp. xxv–xxix.

11 *Britannia Languens*, p. 373.

12 Hales, *Common Weal*, p. 63.

13 *Britannia Languens*, p. 430.

14 Sekora, *Luxury*, pp. 18–19.

15 Alexander Pope, *The Rape of the Lock*, lines 133–4.

16 Fortrey, *England's Interest and Improvement*, p. 234.

17 John Philips, *Cyder: A Poem in Two Books* (London, 1708), lines 23–30.

18 Appleby, *Economic Thought*, p. 37.
19 Thomas Mun, *England's Treasure by Forraign Trade: Or, The Ballance of our Forraign Trade is the Rule of our Treasure* (London, 1664), in McCulloch, *Early English Tracts*, p. 180.
20 Sir Dudley North, *Discourses upon Trade* (London, 1691), p. 14.
21 Jacob Vanderlint, *Money Answers All Things: Or, An Essay to Make Money Sufficiently Plentiful Amongst All Ranks of People, and Increase our Foreign and Domestic Trade* (London, 1734), p. 21.
22 Ibid., pp. 6–11 and pp. 50–74.
23 *Ibid.*, p. 103.
24 Edward Misselden, *The Circle of Commerce or the Ballance of Trade* (London, 1623), p. 17.
25 Mun, *England's Treasure*, pp. 189–90.
26 Richard Cantillon, *Essai sur la Nature du Commerce en Général, Traduit de L'Anglais* (London, 1755).
27 Alexander Pope, *Epistle to Bathurst* (1733), lines 39–40.
28 J. G. A. Pocock, *The Machiavellian Moment: Florentine Political Thought and the Atlantic Republican Tradition* (Princeton: Princeton University Press, 1975), pp. 423–61.
29 *Ibid.*, p. 426.
30 *Ibid.*, pp. 423–61.
31 *Ibid.*, p. 445.
32 Bernard Mandeville, *The Fable of the Bees: Or, Private Vices, Public Benefits* (1714), ed. F. B. Kaye, 2 vols. (Oxford: Clarendon Press, 1924).
33 Philip Pinkus, 'Mandeville's Paradox', in *Mandeville Studies: New Explorations in the Art and Thought of Dr Bernard Mandeville (1670–1733)*, ed. Irwin Primer (The Hague: Martinus Nijhoff, 1975), pp. 193–211, p. 193.
34 Bernard Mandeville, 'A Search into the Nature of Society', in *Fable*, vol. 1, pp. 323–69; see also: F. B. Kaye, introduction to *Fable*, pp. lxxii–lxxvi; Irwin Primer, 'Mandeville and Shaftesbury: Some Facts and Problems', in *Mandeville Studies*, ed. Primer, pp. 126–41; Thomas A. Horne, *The Social Thought of Bernard Mandeville: Virtue and Commerce in Early Eighteenth-Century England* (London: Macmillan, 1978), pp. 32–50; Richard I. Cook, *Bernard Mandeville* (New York: Twayne, 1974), pp. 128–31.
35 Howard Erskine-Hill, *The Social Milieu of Alexander Pope: Lives, Example and the Poetic Response* (New Haven and London: Yale University Press, 1975), pp. 174–90.
36 Sir James Steuart, *An Inquiry into the Principles of Political Oeconomy* (1767), ed. Andrew Skinner, 2 vols. (Edinburgh and London: Oliver and Boyd, 1966), vol. 1, p. 126.
37 David Hume, *A Treatise of Human Nature*, ed. L. A. Selby-Bigge, revised P. H. Nidditch (Oxford: Clarendon Press, 1978), p. xii.
38 *Ibid.*, pp. 216, 269–71; David Hume, *Enquiry Concerning Human Understanding*, in *Enquiries Concerning Human Understanding and Concerning the Principles of Morals*, ed. L. A. Selby-Bigge, revised P. H. Nidditch (Oxford: Clarendon Press, 1975).

39 David Hume, 'Of the Rise and Progress of the Arts and Sciences', in *Essays Moral, Political and Literary* (1777), ed. T. H. Green and T. H. Grose (1874–5, 1882, 1889) revised with variant readings, ed. Eugene Miller (Indianapolis: Liberty Classics, 1985), p. 112.
40 Hume, 'Arts and Sciences', in *Essays*, p. 112.
41 *Ibid.*
42 *Ibid.*, p. 113.
43 Hume, 'The Sceptic', in *Essays*, p. 170.
44 Hume, 'Of Commerce', in *Essays*, p. 255.
45 *Ibid.*, pp. 255–6.
46 Hume, 'Of Refinement in the Arts', in *Essays*, p. 269.
47 Duncan Forbes, *Hume's Philosophical Politics* (Cambridge: Cambridge University Press, 1975), pp. 87–8.
48 Thomas A. Horne, *The Social Thought of Bernard Mandeville: Virtue and Commerce in Early Eighteenth-Century England* (London: Macmillan, 1978), p. 76.
49 Hume, 'Of Refinement in the Arts', in *Essays*, p. 279.
50 Francis Hutcheson, *Reflections upon Laughter and Remarks upon the Fable of the Bees* (Glasgow, 1750), p. 56.
51 *Ibid.*
52 Hume, 'Of Refinement in the Arts', in *Essays*, p. 279.
53 Hutcheson, *Remarks*, p. 63.
54 Cook, *Bernard Mandeville*, pp. 124–8.
55 Hume, 'Of Refinement in the Arts', in *Essays*, p. 280.
56 *Ibid.*
57 Hume, 'Arts and Sciences', in *Essays*, p. 113.
58 Adam Smith, *The Theory of Moral Sentiments* (London, 1759), ed. D. D. Raphael and A. L. Macfie (Oxford: Clarendon Press, 1976), p. 9.
59 Adam Smith, *An Inquiry into the Nature and Causes of the Wealth of Nations* (1776), 2 vols., ed. R. H. Campbell and A. S. Skinner, textual editor W. B. Todd (Oxford: Clarendon Press, 1976), vol. I, pp. 26–7.
60 See A. L. Macfie, *The Individual in Society* (London: Allen and Unwin, 1967), essays 4, 5 and 6; T. D. Campbell, *Adam Smith's Science of Morals* (London: Allen and Unwin, 1971); Raphael and Macfie, introduction to *Moral Sentiments*.
61 Andrew Skinner and Thomas Wilson, *Essays on Adam Smith* (Oxford: Clarendon Press, 1975), p. 5.
62 Hont and Ignatieff, 'Needs and Justice', p. 1.
63 Smith, *Moral Sentiments*, pp. 52 ff.
64 *Ibid.*, p. 61.
65 *Ibid.*, p. 182.
66 *Ibid.*, p. 183.
67 *Ibid.*, p. 168.
68 Quoted in Stefan Collini, Donald Winch and John Burrow, *That Noble Science of Politics: A Study in Nineteenth Century Intellectual History* (Cambridge: Cambridge University Press, 1983), p. 52.
69 Hont and Ignatieff, 'Needs and Justice', p. 2.

70 Adam Ferguson, *Essay on the History of Civil Society, 1767*, ed. Duncan Forbes (Edinburgh: Edinburgh University Press, 1978), pp. 182–3.
71 Smith, *Wealth of Nations*, vol. I, p. 28.
72 Smith, *Wealth of Nations*, vol. II, p. 782.
73 *Ibid.*
74 *Ibid.*
75 *Ibid.*, p. 788.
76 Adam Smith, 'Early Draft', in *Lectures on Jurisprudence*, ed. R. L. Meek, D. D. Raphael and P. G. Stein (Oxford: Clarendon Press, 1978), pp. 562–81, p. 574.
77 Mandeville, *Fable of the Bees*, dialogue 3, paragraph 152; vol. II, p. 144.
78 Smith, 'Early Draft', p. 574.
79 Smith, *Wealth of Nations*, book 2, chapter 3.
80 Stephen Copley, 'Polite Culture in Commercial Society', in A. Benjamin, G. Cantor and J. Christie (eds.), *The Figural and the Literal: Problems of Language in the History of Science and Philosophy, 1630–1800* (Manchester: Manchester University Press, 1987), pp. 176–201, pp. 195–6.

3 THE LITERARY CONTEXT

1 John Dryden, *Of Dramatic Poesy and Other Critical Essays*, 2 vols. ed. George Watson (London and New York: Dent, Dutton, 1962), vol. II, p. 223. His words echo René Rapin that 'The *Epick* poem is that which is the greatest work that human wit is capable of', René Rapin, *Reflections on Aristotle's Treatise of Poesie, Containing the Necessary, Rational and Universal RULES for Epick, Dramatick and Other Sorts of Poetry. With Reflections on the Works of the Ancient and Modern Poets. And their Faults Noted*, trans. Thomas Rymer (London, 1674), p. 72.
2 Anthony Ashley Cooper, 3rd Earl of Shaftesbury, 'Advice to an Author', in *Characteristics of Men, Manners, Opinions, Times, etc.* (1714), ed. John M. Robertson, 2 vols. (Gloucester, Mass.: Peter Smith, 1963), vol. I, p. 145.
3 Compare, for example, the stress on rules of John Dennis, *The Critical Works of John Dennis*, 2 vols., ed. Edward Niles Hooker (Baltimore and London: Johns Hopkins University Press and Oxford University Press, 1939), vol. II, p. 282, and Dryden, *Of Dramatic Poesy*, vol. II, p. 191, with the more primitivist approach of William Hayley, *An Essay on Epic Poetry* (1782), reprinted in facsimile (Gainesville, Fl.: Scholar's Facsimiles and Reprints, 1968), pp. 125–6.
4 Richard Glover, *Leonidas: A Poem* (London, 1737), I. 225–7.
5 *Ibid.*, I. 228–36.
6 See *ibid.*, III. 528–42.
7 Dennis, *Works*, vol. II, p. 113.
8 Richard Blackmore, *Prince Arthur: An Heroick Poem in Ten Books* (1695), reprinted in facsimile (Menston, Yorks.: Scolar Press, 1971), preface.
9 Thomas Blackwell, *Enquiry into the Life and Writings of Homer* (London, 1735), reprinted in facsimile (Menston, Yorks.: Scolar Press, 1971), pp. 28–9.
10 Charles Davenant, *Preface to Gondibert, An Heroick Poem* (1650).

11 Aristotle, *Politics*, in *Works*, translated into English under the editorship of W. D. Ross, 7 vols. (Oxford: Clarendon Press, 1921, 1946, 1952), III, iii. 1–3.

12 Sir William Temple, 'An Essay upon Ancient and Modern Learning' (1690), in *The Works of Sir William Temple*, 2 vols. (London, 1720), vol. I, p. 168.

13 *Ibid.*

14 *Ibid.*

15 Blackwell, *Enquiry*, pp. 111–12.

16 John Brown, *A Dissertation on the Rise, Union, and Power, the Progressions, Separations and Corruptions, of Poetry and Music* (London, 1763), p. 196.

17 Alexander Gerard, *An Essay on Taste* (London, 1759), pp. 106–7.

18 Cf. Samuel Johnson, preface to *Dictionary*, in *Samuel Johnson*, ed. Donald Greene (Oxford: Oxford University Press, 1984), pp. 307–28.

19 Joseph Trapp, *Lectures on Poetry read in the Schools of Natural Philosophy at Oxford, translated from the Latin with additional notes* (London, 1742), p. 352.

20 Davenant, *Preface to Gondibert*.

21 William Blake, 'The Marriage of Heaven and Hell', plates 5–6, in *Blake: Complete Writings*, ed. Geoffrey Keynes (Oxford: Oxford University Press, 1972), p. 150.

22 René Wellek, *A History of Modern Criticism, 1750–1950*, 6 vols. (London: Jonathan Cape, 1955), vol. I, p. 26.

23 H. T. Swedenberg (Jr), 'Rules and English Critics of the Epic, 1650–1800', in *Studies in the Literature of the Augustan Age: Essays Collected in Honor of Arthur Ellicott Case*, ed. Richard Boys (Ann Arbor: Wahr, 1952, 1966), pp. 281–303, p. 287; *The Theory of Epic in England 1650–1800*, University of California Publications in English 15 (California, 1944; reissued New York, 1972), p. 135.

24 Terry Eagleton, *The Function of Criticism: From The Spectator to Post-Structuralism* (London: Verso, 1984), p. 11; Peter Uwe Hohendahl, *The Institution of Criticism* (Ithaca: Cornell University Press, 1982), pp. 247–8.

25 John Ogilvie, *An Essay on the Lyric Poetry of the Ancients* (London, 1762), pp. xxxiv–xxxvi.

26 Richard Hurd, *Letters on Chivalry and Romance* (1762), reprinted in facsimile edited by Hoyt Trowbridge, Augustan Reprint Society numbers 101–2 (Los Angeles: William Andrews Clark Memorial Library, 1963), p. 26.

27 Blackwell, *Life and Writings of Homer*, p. 36.

28 Hurd, *Letters*, p. 120.

29 Thomas Warton, *The History of English Poetry from the Eleventh to the Seventeenth Century* (London, 1778), vol. II, pp. 462–3.

30 Hugh Blair, *Critical Dissertation on the Poems of Ossian, the Son of Fingal*, in *Eighteenth-Century Critical Essays*, ed. Scott Elledge, 2 vols. (Ithaca: Cornell University Press, 1961), p. 849.

31 Georg Lukacs, *The Theory of the Novel* (London: Merlin, 1962), p. 56.

32 Aristotle, *Poetics*, I. 1447a 28–1447b 9.

33 Henry James Pye, *A Commentary Illustrating the Poetic Works of Aristotle* (London, 1792), pp. 182–3; 437–8.

34 James Beattie, 'On Fable and Romance', in *Dissertations Moral and Critical* (London, 1783), p. 573.

35 Richard Graves, *The Spiritual Quixote: Or, The Summer's Ramble of Mr Geoffrey Wildgoose, a Comic Romance* (1773), ed. Clarence Tracy (London: Oxford University Press, 1967), p. 5.

36 *Critical Remarks on Sir Charles Grandison, Clarissa and Pamela* (London, 1754), ed. Alan Dugald McKillop, Augustan Reprint Society number 21 (Los Angeles: William Andrews Clark Memorial Library, 1950), p. 14.

37 *Ibid.*, p. 40.

38 *Ibid.*, p. 54.

39 Alexander Brunton, 'A Memoir of Mary Brunton' (1842), in Mary Brunton, *Discipline* (London, 1842), pp. 37–8.

40 Francis Coventry, *The History of Pompey the Little: or, The Life and Adventures of a Lap-Dog* (1751), ed. Robert Adams Day (Oxford: Oxford University Press, 1974), p. xli.

41 Henry Fielding, *The History of the Adventures of Joseph Andrews and of his friend Mr Abraham Adams* (London, 1741), ed. Martin Battestin (Oxford: Oxford University Press, 1967), p. 4.

42 *Ibid.*, p. 3.

43 Henry Fielding, *The History of Tom Jones: A Foundling*, ed. Martin Battestin and Fredson Bowers, 2 vols. (Oxford: Oxford University Press, 1974), vol. 1, p. 209.

44 Pope, *The Dunciad*, 1. 67–8.

45 Fielding, *Joseph Andrews*, p. 4.

46 Fielding, *Tom Jones*, vol. 1, p. 117.

47 Graves, *Spiritual Quixote*, pp. 2–3.

48 Lennard J. Davis, *Factual Fictions: The Origins of the English Novel* (New York: Columbia University Press, 1983), p. 212.

49 Michael McKeon, *The Origins of the English Novel, 1600–1740* (London: Radius, 1988), pp. 52–64, 105–28.

50 William Ray, *Story and History: Narrative Authority and Social Identity in the Eighteenth-Century French and English Novel* (Oxford and Cambridge, Mass.: Basil Blackwell, 1990), p. 5.

51 *Ibid.*, p. 8.

52 Beattie, 'On Fable', p. 505.

53 e.g. Eliza Haywood, *The History of Miss Betsy Thoughtless* (London: Pandora, 1986); Mary Hamilton, *Munster Village* (London: Pandora, 1987); Elizabeth Inchbald, *A Simple Story* (London: Pandora, 1987) and *Nature and Art*, 2 vols. (1796), reprinted in facsimile with an introduction by Jonathan Wordsworth (Oxford and New York: Woodstock Books, 1994); Ann Radcliffe, *The Mysteries of Udolpho*, ed. Bonamy Dobrée (Oxford: Oxford University Press, 1966, 1980) (although not *The Italian*; see below pp. 163–4); Charlotte Smith, *The Old Manor House*, ed. Anne Henry Ehrenpreis (Oxford: Oxford University Press, 1969).

54 Mary Hays, *The Memoirs of Emma Courtney*, 2 vols. (1796), reprinted in facsimile with an introduction by Jonathan Wordsworth (Oxford and New

York: Woodstock Books, 1995), preface, p. 1.

55 Julia Kristeva, *Desire in Language: A Semiotic Approach to Literature and Art*, ed. Leon S. Roudiez, trans. Thomas Gora, Alice Jardine and Leon S. Roudiez (Oxford: Basil Blackwell, 1980), pp. 133–6.

56 Daniel Defoe, *The Life and Strange Surprising Adventures of Robinson Crusoe* (1719), ed. J. Donald Crowley (London: Oxford University Press, 1972), p. 1.

57 Daniel Defoe, *The Farther Adventures of Robinson Crusoe* (London, 1719), reprinted in *Daniel Defoe: Robinson Crusoe: An Authoritative Text, Backgrounds and Sources Criticism*, ed. Michael Shinagel (New York: Norton, 1975), p. 258.

58 Daniel Defoe, *Serious Reflections During the Life and Surprising Adventures of Robinson Crusoe* (London, 1720), reprinted in Shinagel (ed.), *Daniel Defoe*, p. 260.

59 *Ibid.*, pp. 259–60.

60 *Ibid.*, p. 260.

61 *Ibid.*, p. 259.

62 *Ibid.*, p. 262.

63 McKeon, *Origins*, p. 419.

64 See e.g. Clara Reeve, *The Progress of Romance Through Times, Countries, and Manners with Remarks*, 2 vols. (Dublin, 1785), vol. 1, p. 111.

65 Ray, *Story and History*, p. 6.

66 Hugh Blair, *Lectures on Rhetoric and Belles Lettres* (London, 1783), p. 442.

67 Samuel Johnson, *Rambler*, 4, Sat. 31 March 1750, in *The Works of Samuel Johnson*, ed. Arthur Sherbo, 8 vols. (New Haven and London: Yale University Press, 1963–), vol. III, p. 23.

68 *Ibid.*, p. 24.

69 Henry Mackenzie, *Lounger*, 20, Saturday 18 June 1785.

70 Reeve, *The Progress of Romance*, vol. 1, p. 139.

71 Beattie, 'On Fable'.

72 Johnson, *Rambler*, 4, in Sherbo (ed.), *Works*, vol. III, p. 21.

73 Claude Prosper Jolyot de Crebillon, fils, *The Sofa, A Moral Tale* (1742), trans. Bonamy Dobrée (London: George Routledge, 1927), pp. 15–16.

74 Lawrence Sterne, *The Life and Opinions of Tristram Shandy Gent.*, ed. Graham Petrie (Harmondsworth: Penguin, 1967), p. 127.

75 John Cleland, *Monthly Review*, 4 (March 1751), p. 357.

76 Graves, *Spiritual Quixote*, p. 3.

77 Alain René le Sage, *The Adventures of Gil Blas of Santillane*, translated from the French by Tobias Smollett (London, 1881).

78 Tobias Smollett, *The Adventures of Peregrine Pickle*, ed. James L. Clifford, rev. by Paul Gabriel Boucé (Oxford: Oxford University Press, 1983), p. 770.

79 Fielding, *Tom Jones*, vol. II, p. 981.

4 THE MID-EIGHTEENTH-CENTURY NOVEL

1 Daniel Defoe, *The Life and Strange Surprising Adventures of Robinson Crusoe* (1719), ed. J. Donald Crowley (London: Oxford University Press, 1972), p. 69.

2 *Ibid.*, p. 118.

3 *Ibid.*, p. 130.
4 Maximillian E. Novak, *Economics and the Fiction of Daniel Defoe* (Berkeley: University of California Press, 1962), p. 48.
5 *Ibid.*, p. 49.
6 Michael McKeon, *The Origins of the English Novel, 1600–1740* (London: Radius, 1988), p. 336.
7 William Ray, *Story and History* (Oxford and Cambridge, Mass.: Basil Black-well, 1990), pp. 52–3.
8 *Ibid.*, p. 57.
9 *Ibid.*, p. 332.
10 Grahame Smith, *The Novel in Society: Defoe to George Eliot* (London: Batsford, 1984) p. 66.
11 Ian Watt, *The Rise of the Novel: Studies in Defoe, Richardson and Fielding* (London: Hogarth Press, 1987) pp. 73–6.
12 Cf. Michael McKeon's related observation that 'The inescapable aura of irony that we sense in parts of Robinson's Crusoe's long passage out of sinfulness bespeaks the instability of ideas and institutions his author has tried to freeze in the midst of a secularization crisis', *Origins*, p. 332.
13 Samuel Richardson, *Clarissa: Or, The History of a Young Lady* ed. Angus Ross (Harmondsworth: Viking Penguin, 1985), preface, p. 35.
14 Leslie A. Fiedler, *Love and Death in the American Novel* (London: Jonathan Cape, 1967), pp. 62–73, p. 67.
15 Richardson, *Clarissa*, p. 50. Subsequent references will be incorporated in the text.
16 William Beatty Warner, *Reading Clarissa: The Struggles of Interpretation* (New Haven and London: Yale University Press, 1979); Terry Castle, *Clarissa's Ciphers: Meaning and Disruption in Richardson's Clarissa* (Ithaca and London: Cornell University Press, 1982); Terry Eagleton, *The Rape of Clarissa: Writing, Sexuality and Class Struggle in Samuel Richardson* (Oxford: Basil Blackwell, 1982).
17 Warner, *Reading Clarissa*, p. viii.
18 Castle, *Clarissa's Ciphers*, p. 30.
19 *Ibid.*, p. 40.
20 *Ibid.*, p. 22.
21 Tom Keymer, *Richardson's Clarissa and the Eighteenth-Century Reader* (Cambridge: Cambridge University Press, 1992).
22 J. Paul Hunter, *Before Novels: The Cultural Context of Eighteenth-Century English Fiction* (New York: Norton, 1990), p. 56.
23 For a modern text of the third edition, see the Everyman text of *Clarissa*, ed. John Butt, 4 vols. (London: Dent, 1962).
24 Samuel Richardson, *Clarissa: Preface, Hints of Prefaces and Postscript*, ed. R. F. Brissenden, Augustan Reprint Society number 103 (Los Angeles: William Andrews Clark Memorial Library, 1964), p. 5.
25 John Preston, *The Created Self: The Reader's Role in Eighteenth-Century Fiction* (London: Heinemann, 1970), p. 59.

26 Rita Goldberg, *Sex and Enlightenment: Women in Richardson and Diderot* (Cambridge: Cambridge University Press, 1984), pp. 78–85.

27 Eagleton, *Rape of Clarissa*, p. 5.

28 Henry Fielding, *An Apology for the Life of Mrs Shamela Andrews*, in *The History of the Adventures of Joseph Andrews and of his friend Mr Abraham Adams and An Apology for the Life of Mrs Shamela Andrews*, ed. Douglas Brooks-Davies (Oxford: Oxford University Press, 1980), pp. 324 and 356.

29 Bernard Kreissman, *Pamela–Shamela: A Study of the Criticisms, Burlesques, Parodies, and Adaptations of Richardson's 'Pamela'*, University of Nebraska Studies, 22 (Lincoln, Nebr.: University of Nebraska Press, 1960), pp. 23–53.

30 T. C. Duncan Eaves and Ben D. Kimpel, *Samuel Richardson: A Biography* (Oxford: Clarendon Press, 1971), p. 131.

31 Castle, *Clarissa's Ciphers*, p. 180.

32 Richardson, *Clarissa*, ed. John Butt, vol. I, p. xiv.

33 Henry Fielding, *The History of Tom Jones: A Foundling*, ed. Martin Battestin and Fredson Bowers, 2 vols. (Oxford: Oxford University Press, 1974), vol. II, pp. 678–82. Subsequent references will be included in the text.

34 Henry Fielding, *An Enquiry into the Causes of the Late Increase of Robbers and Related Writings*, ed. Malvin T. Zirker (Oxford: Oxford University Press, 1988), p. 154.

35 *Ibid.*, p. 155.

36 *Ibid.*, p. 156.

37 *Ibid.* pp. 156–7.

38 Ray, *Story and History*, p. 228.

39 *Ibid.*, p. 198.

40 Martin Battestin, *The Providence of Wit: Aspects of Form in Augustan England and the Arts* (Oxford: Clarendon Press, 1974), p. 187.

41 Ray, *Story and History*, p. 233.

42 Wolfgang Iser, *The Implied Reader: Patterns of Communication in Prose Fiction from Bunyan to Beckett* (Baltimore and London: Johns Hopkins University Press, 1974), p. 55.

43 Fielding, *Joseph Andrews*, p. 189.

44 *Ibid.*, p. 68.

45 *Ibid.*, p. 17.

46 Bryan Burns, 'The Story-telling in *Joseph Andrews*', in *Henry Fielding: Justice Observed*, ed. K. G. Simpson (London: Vision Press, 1985), pp. 119–35.

47 Hunter, *Before Novels*, pp. 47–54.

48 Charlotte Smith, *The Old Manor House* (1793), ed. Anne Henry Ehrenpreis (Oxford: Oxford University Press, 1969), p. 166; Charlotte Lennox, *The Female Quixote: Or, The Adventures of Arabella* (1752), ed. Margaret Dalziel (London: Oxford University Press, 1986), p. 7; Mary Hays, *The Memoirs of Emma Courtney*, 2 vols. (1796), reprinted in facsimile with introduction by Jonathan Wordsworth (Oxford and New York: Woodstock Books, 1995), vol. I, pp. 18, 31–3; Elizabeth Inchbald, *A Simple Story* (1791), with introduction by Jeanette Winterson (London: Pandora, 1987), p. 192.

49 Johnson, *Rambler*, 4. See also p. 59–60 above.
50 Henry Fielding's preface to Sarah Fielding, *The Adventures of David Simple* (1744), ed. Malcolm Kelsall (Oxford: Oxford University Press, 1969), pp. 5–6.
51 See, for example, Fielding, *Tom Jones*, vol. 1, p. 72; vol. 1, p. 171.
52 *Champion*, 3 and 5; *Covent Garden Journal*, 3 and 31.
53 Fanny Burney, *Evelina: Or, The History of a Young Lady's Entrance into the World*, 3 vols. (1778), ed. Edward A. Bloom (Oxford: Oxford University Press, 1968, 1982), p. 7.
54 Fielding, *Enquiry*, p. 82.
55 See also Richard Graves, *The Spiritual Quixote* (1773) and anon., *The History of Sir George Warrington: Or, The Political Quixote* (1797).
56 Lennox, *The Female Quixote*, p. 7. Subsequent references will be incorporated in the text.
57 Janet Todd, *The Sign of Angellica: Women, Writing and Fiction, 1660–1800* (London: Virago, 1989), p. 155.
58 Jane Austen, *Northanger Abbey*, in *Northanger Abbey, Lady Susan, The Watsons and Sanditon*, ed. John Davie (Oxford: Oxford University Press, 1980), p. 161.
59 Jane Spencer, *The Rise of the Woman Novelist, from Aphra Behn to Jane Austen* (Oxford: Basil Blackwell, 1986), p. 187; Todd, *Sign of Angellica*, p. 152.
60 Todd, *Sign of Angellica*, p. 156.
61 *Ibid.*, p. 160.
62 Spencer, *Rise of Woman Novelist*, p. 187.
63 *Ibid.*, p. 189.
64 Laurie Langbauer, *Women and Romance: The Consolations of Gender in the English Novel* (Ithaca and London: Cornell University Press, 1990), pp. 62–4.
65 *Ibid.*, p. 85.
66 *Ibid.*, pp. 75–6.
67 Hamilton, *Munster Village*, p. 59.
68 Samuel Richardson, 24 March 1751, in *Correspondence*, edited by Anna Laetitia Barbauld (London, 1804), pp. vi, 88.
69 Eaves and Kimpel, *Biography*, pp. 387, 391; Leslie Stephen, introduction to *The Works of Samuel Richardson* (London, 1883), vol. 1, pp. xxxix–xl; Mark Kinkead-Weekes, *Samuel Richardson: Dramatic Novelist* (Ithaca and London: Cornell University Press, 1973), p. 289; A. D. McKillop, *The Early Masters of English Fiction* (London: Constable, 1968), p. 87.
70 Samuel Richardson, *The History of Sir Charles Grandison*, 7 vols. (London, 1753–4), ed. Jocelyn Harris, 3 vols. (Oxford: Oxford University Press, 1972) vol. 1, p. 82. Subsequent references will be incorporated in the text.
71 McKillop, *Early Masters*, p. 88.
72 Fielding, *Tom Jones*, vol. 1, p. 221.
73 Tobias Smollett, *The Adventures of Roderick Random* (1748), ed. Paul-Gabriel Boucé (Oxford: Oxford University Press, 1979, 1981), p. 230.
74 Jane Austen, *Emma* (1815), ed. James Kinsley and David Lodge (Oxford: Oxford University Press, 1971, 1984), pp. 369–70.

75 Jane Austen, *Sense and Sensibility* (1811), ed. Claire Lamont and James Kinsley (Oxford: Oxford University Press, 1970), pp. 31, 333.

76 Forster Collection, Victoria and Albert Museum, pp. xi, 54–7.

77 Samuel L. Macey, *Money and the Novel: Mercenary Motivation in Defoe and his Immediate Successors* (Victoria, B.C.: Sono Nis Press, 1983), p. 102.

78 Eaves and Kimpel, *Biography*, p. 394.

79 Eagleton, *The Rape of Clarissa*, p. 99.

80 John Mullan, *Sentiment and Sociability: The Language of Feeling in the Eighteenth Century* (Oxford: Clarendon Press, 1988), p. 83.

81 Tony Tanner, *Adultery in the Novel: Contract and Transgression* (Baltimore and London: Johns Hopkins University Press, 1979), p. 178 note; Carol Flynn, *Samuel Richardson: A Man of Letters* (Princeton: Princeton University Press, 1982), p. 96.

82 Macey, *Money and the Novel*, p. 99.

83 *Ibid.*, p. 122.

84 Patricia Meyer Spacks, *Imagining A Self: Autobiography and Novel in Eighteenth-Century England* (Cambridge, Mass.: Harvard University Press, 1976), pp. 23–5; Dale Spender, *Mothers of the Novel* (London: Pandora, 1986), Spencer, *The Rise of the Woman Novelist*.

85 F. R. Leavis, *The Great Tradition: George Eliot, James and Conrad* (Harmondsworth: Peregrine, 1962, 1986), pp. 4, 8 and 16.

86 Spencer, *Rise of the Woman Novelist*, p. 22.

87 Neither Spencer, *Rise of the Woman Novelist*, nor Cheryl Turner in *Living by the Pen: Women Writers in the Eighteenth Century* (London and New York: Routledge, 1992) make more than cursory reference to these texts.

5 THE NOVEL OF CIRCULATION

1 Elizabeth Bellamy, 'Private Virtues, Public Vices: Commercial Morality and the Novel, 1740–1800' (unpublished Ph.D. thesis, Jesus College, Cambridge, 1988), pp. 258–64.

2 Charles Gildon, *The Golden Spy: Or, A Political Journal of the British Nights Entertainment*, 2 vols. (1709–10); Claude Prosper Jolyot de Crébillon, *The Sofa: A Moral Tale* (1742), trans. Bonamy Dobrée (London: George Routledge, 1927).

3 Thomas Bridges, *The Adventures of a Bank Note* (London, 1770–1).

4 Robert Adams Day, introduction to Francis Coventry, *The History of Pompey the Little: Or, The Life and Adventures of a Lap-Dog* (1751) (Oxford: Oxford University Press, 1974), p. xxi.

5 F. R. Leavis, *The Great Tradition: George Eliot, James and Conrad* (Harmondsworth: Peregrine, 1986), p. 18.

6 Lady Mary Wortley Montagu, *Complete Letters of Lady Mary Wortley Montagu*, ed. Robert Halsband and Isobel Grundy, 3 vols. (Oxford: Clarendon Press, 1967), pp. iii, 4.

7 Coventry, *Pompey the Little*, p. 30.

198 *Notes to pages 122–30*

8 *Ibid.*, p. 68.
9 *Ibid.*, pp. 38–9.
10 *Ibid.*, p. 45.
11 *Ibid.*, p. 46.
12 *Ibid.*, p. 82.
13 Bridges, *Bank Note*, p. 148.
14 *Ibid.*, p. 149.
15 *Ibid.*, pp. 110–11.
16 Martin Battestin, *The Providence of Wit: Aspects of Form in Augustan England and the Arts* (Oxford: Clarendon Press, 1974), pp. 143–4; Ronald Paulson, 'The Pilgrimage and the Family', in *Tobias Smollett: Bicentennial Essays Presented to Lewis M. Knapp*, ed. George Rousseau and Paul-Gabriel Boucé (Oxford: Oxford University Press, 1971), p. 65; Paul-Gabriel Boucé, *Les Romans de Smollett* (1971) translated by Antonia White as *The Novels of Tobias Smollett* (London and New York: Longman, 1976), p. 103.
17 See Bryan Burns, 'The Story-telling in *Joseph Andrews*' in *Henry Fielding: Justice Observed*, ed. K. G. Simpson (London: Vision Press, 1985)', pp. 119–35.
18 Coventry, *Pompey the Little*, p. 110.
19 *Ibid.*, p. 83.
20 *Ibid.*, pp. 96–7.
21 See p. 83 above.

6 THE SENTIMENTAL NOVEL

1 R. F. Brissenden, *Virtue in Distress: Studies in the Novel of Sentiment from Richardson to Sade* (London: Macmillan, 1974); Rita Goldberg, *Sex and Enlightenment: Women in Richardson and Diderot* (Cambridge: Cambridge University Press, 1984); Janet Todd, *Sensibility: An Introduction* (London: Methuen, 1986); John Mullan, *Sentiment and Sociability: The Language of Feeling in the Eighteenth Century* (Oxford: Clarendon Press, 1988); G. J. Barker-Benfield, *The Culture of Sensibility: Sex and Society in Eighteenth-Century Britain* (Chicago and London: University of Chicago Press, 1992); Ann Jessie Van Sant, *Eighteenth-Century Sensibility and the Novel: The Senses in a Social Context* (Cambridge: Cambridge University Press, 1993); Markman Ellis, *The Politics of Sensibility: Race, Gender and Commerce in the Sentimental Novel* (Cambridge: Cambridge University Press, 1996).
2 Mullan, *Sentiment and Sociability*, p. 2. Another attempt to reappropriate and rehabilitate biographical reading can be found in Roger Sales, *Jane Austen and Representations of Regency England* (London and New York: Routledge, 1994).
3 Mullan, *Sentiment and Sociability*, pp. 201–40.
4 Ellis, *Politics of Sensibility*, p. 2.
5 *Ibid.*, p. 22.
6 Joseph Addison, Richard Steele and others, The *Spectator* (1711–12) reprinted in 4 vols. ed. Gregory Smith (London: Everyman, 1979), e.g. number 2,

Friday 2 March 1711, vol. I, pp. 6–10.

7 John McVeagh, *Tradeful Merchants: The Portrayal of the Capitalist in Literature* (London: Routledge, 1981), pp. 77–9.

8 See below pp. 139–43.

9 Sarah Fielding, *The Adventures of David Simple, Containing an Account of his Travels through the Cities of London and Westminster in the Search of a Real Friend* (1744), ed. Malcolm Kelsall (Oxford: Oxford University Press, 1969), p. 9. Subsequent references will be incorporated in the text.

10 David Hume's essay 'On Luxury', subsequently renamed 'Of Refinement in the Arts', articulates a similar philosophy, (*Essays Moral, Political and Literary*, ed. T. A. Green and T. H. Groce (Indianapolis: Liberty Classics, 1985), pp. 268–80).

11 See e.g. Tobias Smollett, *The Adventures of Roderick Random*, ed. Paul-Gabriel Boucé (Oxford: Oxford University Press, 1981), pp. 409–10, 416–17.

12 Van Sant, *Eighteenth-Century Sensibility*, pp. 116–17.

13 Oliver Goldsmith, *The Vicar of Wakefield: A Tale, supposed to be written by himself*, ed. Arthur Friedman (Oxford: Oxford University Press, 1974) p. 12. Subsequent references will be incorporated in the text.

14 Ronald Paulson, *The Beautiful, Novel and Strange: Aesthetics and Heterodoxy* (Baltimore: Johns Hopkins University Press, 1996), pp. 208–9.

15 See p. 167–8 below.

16 Paulson, *The Beautiful*, p. 203.

17 *Ibid.*, pp. 203–9.

18 *Ibid.*, pp. 202–3.

19 Henry Brooke, *The Fool of Quality: or, The History of Henry, Earl of Moreland* (1765–70), ed. Ernest A. Baker (London: Routledge, 1906), p. xxviii. Subsequent references will be incorporated in the text.

20 Walter Wright, *Sensibility in English Prose Fiction, 1760–1814: A Reinterpretation* (Urbana: University of Illinois Press, 1937), pp. 30–1; Brian Downs, *Richardson* (London: Routledge, 1928), pp. 211–12; Mullan, *Sentiment and Sociability*, pp. 133–5.

21 Ellis, *Politics of Sensibility*, p. 133.

22 Hume, 'Of Commerce', in *Essays*, pp. 261–3.

23 Ellis, *Politics of Sensibility*, p. 140.

24 Marilyn Butler, *Jane Austen and the War of Ideas* (Oxford: Clarendon Press, 1975), p. 18.

25 Henry MacKenzie, *The Man of Feeling* (1771), ed. Brian Vickers (Oxford: Oxford University Press, 1967), p. 5. Subsequent references will be incorporated in the text.

26 Mullan, *Sentiment and Sociability*, pp. 118–19.

27 For an account of Mackenzie's attitude to slavery see Ellis, *Politics of Sensibility*, pp. 114–24.

7 THE JACOBIN NOVEL

1 John Mullan, *Sentiment and Sociability: The Language of Feeling in the Eighteenth Century* (Oxford: Clarendon Press, 1988), p. 119.

2 Marilyn Butler, *Jane Austen and the War of Ideas* (Oxford: Clarendon Press, 1975), p. 54.

3 Gary Kelly, 'The English Jacobin Novel and its Background, 1780–1805' (unpublished Ph.D. thesis, University of Oxford, 1972) and *The English Jacobin Novel, 1780–1805* (Oxford: Oxford University Press, 1976).

4 Kelly, *The English Jacobin Novel*, p. 8.

5 Edmund Burke, *Reflections on the Revolution in France, and on the Proceedings in Certain Societies in London, Relative to that Event: In a Letter intended to have been sent to a Gentleman in Paris* (1790) in *The Works of the Right Honourable Edmund Burke*, 16 vols. (London: Rivington, 1826), vol. v, p. 59.

6 *Ibid.*, vol. v, p. 149.

7 *Ibid.*, vol. v, p. 150.

8 *Ibid.*, vol. v, pp. 87–8.

9 *Ibid.*, vol. v, p. 109.

10 *Ibid.*, vol. v, p. 107.

11 Robert Bage, *Man As He Is*, 4 vols. (1792), reprinted in facsimile (New York: Garland, 1979), vol. iv, p. 73.

12 Burke, *Works*, vol. v, p. 149.

13 *Ibid.*, vol. v, pp. 150–1.

14 Bage, *Man As He Is*, vol. iv, pp. 74–5.

15 For an account of Burke's relationship to the female Jacobins, see Eleanor Ty, *Unsex'd Revolutionaries: Five Women Novelists of the 1790s* (Toronto and London: University of Toronto Press, 1993).

16 Bage, *Man As He Is*, vol. iv, p. 75.

17 *Ibid.*, vol. iv, pp. 271–2.

18 Edward Copeland, *Women Writing About Money: Women's Fiction in England, 1790–1820* (Cambridge: Cambridge University Press, 1995), p. 41 *et passim*.

19 E.g. Rosemary Jackson, *Fantasy: The Literature of Subversion* (London and New York: Methuen, 1981).

20 Ann Radcliffe, *The Italian: Or, The Confessional of the Black Penitents*, ed. Frederick Garber (Oxford: Oxford University Press, 1991), p. 1.

21 *Ibid.*, p. 2.

22 Jane Austen, *Northanger Abbey*, in *Northanger Abbey, Lady Susan, The Watsons and Sanditon*, ed. John Davie (Oxford: Oxford University Press, 1980), p. 160.

23 *Ibid.*, p. 159.

24 See William Godwin, *Caleb Williams*, ed. David McCracken (Oxford: Oxford University Press, 1991), vol. i, p. 1.

25 William Godwin, 'Of Romance and History', unpublished essay, quoted in Kelly, 'The English Jacobin Novel', p. 322.

26 Thomas Holcroft, *The Adventures of Hugh Trevor* (1794–7), ed. Seamus Deane (London: Oxford University Press, 1973), p. 4.

27 Butler, *Jane Austen*, p. 75.

28 Godwin, *Caleb Williams*, vol. I, p. I.
29 Kelly, *The English Jacobin Novel*, pp. 192–3.
30 Austen, *Northanger Abbey*, p. 160.
31 Butler, *Jane Austen*, p. 61; Ty, *Unsex'd Revolutionaries*, p. 11.
32 Ty, *Unsex'd Revolutionaries*, p. 11.
33 William Godwin, *Enquiry Concerning Political Justice and its Influence on Morals and Happiness* (1793), ed. F. E. L. Priestley (Toronto: University of Toronto Press, 1946), vol. I, p. 79.
34 Godwin, *Caleb Williams*, vol. I, p. 303.
35 *Ibid.*, vol. I, appendix 1, p. 327.
36 *Ibid.*, vol. I, appendix 2, pp. 335–6.
37 Kelly, *The English Jacobin Novel*, pp. 193–4; cf. P. N. Furbank's suggestion that Caleb represents Godwin himself, 'Godwin's Novels', *Essays in Criticism*, 5 (1955), pp. 251–6.
38 Godwin, *Caleb Williams*, vol. I, p. 325.
39 Gary Kelly, *Women, Writing and Revolution, 1790–1827* (Oxford: Clarendon Press, 1993), pp. 95–6.
40 *Ibid.*, p. 104.
41 Mary Hays, *The Memoirs of Emma Courtney*, 2 vols., reprinted in facsimile with introduction by Jonathan Wordsworth (Oxford and New York: Woodstock Books, 1995), vol. II, p. 107.
42 J. G. A. Pocock, *The Machiavellian Moment* (Princeton: Princeton University Press, 1975), p. 466.
43 Elizabeth Inchbald, *Nature and Art*, 2 vols., reprinted in facsimile with introduction by Jonathan Wordsworth (Oxford and New York: Woodstock Books, 1994), vol. I, p. 81.
44 Mary Wollstonecraft, *A Vindication of the Rights of Woman* (1792) (Harmondsworth: Penguin, 1987), pp. 98–9.
45 *Ibid.*, p. 81.
46 *Ibid.*
47 Mary Wollstonecraft, *The Wrongs of Woman: Or, Maria. A Fragment* (1798) in *Mary and the Wrongs of Woman*, ed. James Kinsley and Gary Kelly (Oxford and New York: Oxford University Press, 1987), p. 73. Subsequent references will be incorporated in the text.
48 Butler, *Jane Austen*, p. 33.
49 Margaret George, *One Woman's 'Situation': A Study of Mary Wollstonecraft* (Urbana: University of Illinois Press, 1970), p. 148.
50 E.g. the character of Henry in *Mary*, and Maria's uncle in *The Wrongs of Woman*.
51 *Ibid.*
52 George, *One Woman's 'Situation'*, p. 10.
53 Ty, *Unsex'd Revolutionaries*, p. 37.
54 Sara Harasyn, 'Ideology and Self: A Theoretical Discussion of the "Self" in Mary Wollstonecraft's Fiction', *English Studies in Canada*, 12.2 (June 1988), p. 164; Mary Poovey, *The Proper Lady and the Woman Writer* (Chicago: Univer-

sity of Chicago Press, 1984), pp. 104–5; Laurie Langbauer, *Women and Romance* (Ithaca and London: Cornell University Press, 1990), pp. 93–100.
55 Langbauer, *Women and Romance*, p. 93.

8 CONCLUSION

1 Edward Copeland, *Women Writing About Money: Women's Fiction in England, 1790–1820* (Cambridge: Cambridge University Press, 1995), p. 3.

Bibliography

PRIMARY TEXTS

Addison, Joseph, Richard Steele and others, *The Spectator* (1711–12) reprinted in 4 vols., ed. Gregory Smith (London: Dent, 1979).

The Adventures of a £1000 Note (London, 1849).

The Adventures of a Silver Penny (London, [178?]).

The Adventures of a Watch (London, 1788).

The Aerostatic Spy: Or, Adventures with an Air-balloon (London, 1785).

Aristotle, *Works*, translated into English under the editorship of W. D. Ross, 7 vols. (Oxford: Clarendon Press, 1921, 1946, 1952).

Austen, Jane, *Emma*, ed. James Kinsley and David Lodge (Oxford: Oxford University Press, 1984).

    Northanger Abbey, in *Northanger Abbey, Lady Susan, The Watsons and Sanditon*, ed. John Davie (Oxford: Oxford University Press, 1980).

    Sense and Sensibility, ed. Claire Lamont and James Kinsley (Oxford: Oxford University Press, 1970).

Bage, Robert, *Man As He Is*, 4 vols. (1792), reprinted in facsimile (New York: Garland, 1979).

    Hermsprong: Or, Man As He Is Not, 3 vols. (1796), reprinted in facsimile (New York: Garland, 1979).

Barbon, Nicholas, A DISCOURSE CONCERNING COINING THE NEW MONEY LIGHTER (London, 1696).

Beattie, James, 'On Fable and Romance', in *Dissertations Moral and Critical* (London, 1783).

Bellers, John, *An Essay for Imploying the Able Poor: by which the Riches of the Kingdom may be greatly Increased* (London, 1714).

Berkeley, George, *An Essay towards Preventing the Ruin of Great Britain*, in *The Works of George Berkeley, Bishop of Cloyne*, ed. A. A. Luce and T. E. Jessop, 9 vols. (London: Thomas Nelson, 1953).

Blackmore, Richard, *Prince Arthur: An Heroick Poem in Ten Books* (1695), reprinted in facsimile (Menston, Yorks.: Scolar Press, 1971).

Blackwell, Thomas, *Enquiry into the Life and Writings of Homer* (London, 1735), reprinted in facsimile (Menston, Yorks.: Scolar Press, 1971).

Blair, Hugh, *A Critical Dissertation on the Poems of Ossian, the Son of Fingal*, in *Eighteenth-Century Critical Essays*, ed. Scott Elledge, 2 vols. (Ithaca: Cornell University Press, 1961).

Lectures on Rhetoric and Belles Lettres (London, 1783).

Bossu, Rene le, *Monsieur Bossu's Treatise of the Epick Poem* (London, 1695), reprinted in facsimile in *Le Bossu and Voltaire on the Epic*, ed. Stuart Curran (Gainesville, Fla.: Scholar's Facsimiles and Reprints, 1970).

Bridges, Thomas, *The Adventures of a Bank Note*, 4 vols. (London, 1770–1).

Britannia Languens: Or, A Discourse on Trade (1680), reprinted in *Early English Tracts on Commerce*, ed. J. J. McCulloch, first published by the Political Economy Club (London, 1856), reprinted for the Economic History Society (1952 and 1954), pp. 211–50.

Brooke, Henry, *The Fool of Quality: or, The History of Henry, Earl of Moreland* (Dublin, 1765–70), ed. E. A. Baker (London: Routledge, 1906).

Brown, John, *A Dissertation on the Rise, Union, and Power, the Progressions, Separations, and Corruptions, of Poetry and Music* (London, 1763).

Estimate of the Manners and Principles of the Times (1757), 6th edn (London, 1757).

Brunton, Mary, *Discipline* (London, 1842).

Burke, Edmund, *Reflections on the Revolution in France, and on the Proceedings in Certain Societies in London, Relative to that Event: In a Letter intended to have been sent to a Gentleman in Paris* (1790), in *The Works of the Right Honourable Edmund Burke*, 16 vols. (London: Rivington, 1826), volume v.

Burnet, James (Lord Monboddo), *Of the Origin and Progress of Languages* (Edinburgh, 1774).

Burney, Fanny, *Evelina: Or, The History of a Young Lady's Entrance into the World*, 3 vols. (1778), ed. Edward A. Bloom (Oxford: Oxford University Press, 1968, 1982).

Cantillon, Richard, *Essai sur la Nature du Commerce en Général, Traduit de L'Anglais* (London, 1755).

Carroll, John (ed.), *Selected Letters of Samuel Richardson* (Oxford: Clarendon Press, 1964).

Cary, John, *An Essay on the State of England in Relation to its Trade, its Poor, and its Taxes, for carrying on the present war against France* (Bristol, 1695).

Child, Sir Josiah, *A Tract Against Usurie, presented in the High Court of Parliament* (London, 1621), reprinted in facsimile in William Letwin, *Sir Josiah Child: Merchant Economist* (Boston, Mass.: Baker Library, 1959), pp. 59–76.

Brief Observations Concerning Trade and Interest of Money (London, 1688), reprinted in Letwin, *Sir Josiah Child*, pp. 39–58.

A Discourse About Trade, Wherein the Reduction of Interest of Money to 4 per centum is Recommended (London, 1690).

Cleland, John, *Memoirs of a Woman of Pleasure* (Harmondsworth: Penguin, 1985).

Monthly Review, 4 (March 1751).

Considerations on the east-india trade, reprinted in McCulloch, *Early English Tracts on Commerce*, pp. 541–629.

Coventry, Francis, *The History of Pompey the Little: Or, The Life and Adventures of a*

Lap-Dog (1751), ed. Robert Adams Day (Oxford: Oxford University Press, 1974).

[Francis Coventry?], *An Essay on the New Species of Writing Founded by Mr Fielding* (1751), ed. Alan Dugald McKillop, Augustan Reprint Society number 95 (Los Angeles: William Andrews Clark Memorial Library, 1962).

Crébillon, Claude Prosper Jolyot de, *The Sofa: A Moral Tale* (1742), trans. Bonamy Dobrée (London: George Routledge, 1927).

Critical Remarks on Sir Charles Grandison, Clarissa and Pamela (London, 1754), ed. Alan Dugald McKillop, Augustan Reprint Society number 21 (Los Angeles: William Andrews Clark Memorial Library, 1950).

Davenant, Charles, *Discourses on the Publick Revenues, and on the Trade of England*, 2 vols. (London, 1698).
 Political and Commercial Works, ed. Sir C. Whitworth, 5 vols. (London, 1771).

Davenant, Sir William, *Preface to Gondibert, An Heroick Poem* (1650).

Defoe, Daniel, *The Complete English Tradesman*, 2 vols. (London, 1725).
 The Farther Adventures of Robinson Crusoe (London, 1719).
 The History and Remarkable Life of the Truly Honourable Colonel Jacque, commonly call'd Col. Jack (1722), ed. Samuel H. Monk (Oxford: Oxford University Press, 1965).
 The Life and Strange Surprising Adventures of Robinson Crusoe (1719), ed. J. Donald Crowley (London: Oxford University Press, 1972).
 Serious Reflections During the Life and Surprising Adventures of Robinson Crusoe (London, 1720).

Dennis, John, *The Critical Works of John Dennis*, 2 vols., ed. Niles Hooker (Baltimore and London: Johns Hopkins University Press and Oxford University Press, 1939).
 Vice and Luxury Publick Mischiefs: Or, Remarks on a Book Intituled The Fable of the Bees: Or, Private Vices, Publick Benefits (1724).

Dryden, John, *Of Dramatic Poesy and other Critical Essays*, 2 vols., ed. George Watson (London and New York: Dent, 1962).

Elledge, Scott (ed.), *Eighteenth-Century Critical Essays*, 2 vols. (Ithaca: Cornell University Press, 1961).

England's *Great Happiness: Or, A* Dialogue Between Content *and* Complaint (London, 1677), reprinted in McCulloch, *Early English Tracts on Commerce*, pp. 251–74.

Enquiry Whether A General Practice of Virtue Tends to the Wealth or Poverty, Benefit or Disadvantage of a People (London, 1725).

Ferguson, Adam, *An Essay on the History of Civil Society, 1767*, ed. Duncan Forbes (Edinburgh: Edinburgh University Press, 1978).

Fielding, Henry, *Amelia* (1751), ed. Martin Battestin (Oxford: Oxford University Press, 1983).
 An Apology for the Life of Mrs Shamela Andrews (London, 1741) in *The History of the Adventures of Joseph Andrews and of his friend Mr Abraham Adams and An Apology for the Life of Mrs Shamela Andrews*, ed. Douglas Brooks-Davies (Oxford: Oxford University Press, 1980).

An Enquiry into the Causes of the Late Increase of Robbers and Related Writings, ed. Malvin T. Zirker (Oxford: Oxford University Press, 1988).

The History of the Adventures of Joseph Andrews and of his friend Mr Abraham Adams (London, 1741), ed. Martin Battestin (Oxford: Oxford University Press, 1967).

The History of Tom Jones: A Foundling (London, 1749), ed. Martin Battestin and Fredson Bowers, 2 vols. (Oxford: Oxford University Press, 1974).

The Jacobite's Journal and Related Writings, ed. W. B. Coley (Oxford: Oxford University Press, 1974).

A Proposal for Making Effectual Provision for the Poor, for Amending their Morals, and for Rendering them useful MEMBERS *of the Society* (London, 1753).

Fielding, Sarah, *The Adventures of David Simple, Containing an Account of his Travels through the Cities of London and Westminster in the Search of a Real Friend* (1744), ed. Malcolm Kelsall (Oxford: Oxford University Press, 1969).

Fortrey, Samuel, *England's Interest and Improvement, consisting in the Increase of the Store, and Trade of this Kingdom* (London, 1673), reprinted in McCulloch, *Early English Tracts on Commerce*, pp. 211–50.

Gerard, Alexander, *An Essay on Taste* (London, 1759).

Gildon, Charles, *The Golden Spy: Or, A Political Journal of the British Nights Entertainment*, 2 vols. (1709–10).

Glover, Richard, *Leonidas: A Poem* (London, 1737).

Godwin, William, *Enquiry Concerning Political Justice and its Influence on Morals and Happiness* (1793), ed. F. E. L. Priestley (Toronto: University of Toronto Press, 1946).

Things As They Are: Or, The Adventures of Caleb Williams, 3 vols. (1794), ed. David McCracken (Oxford: Oxford University Press, 1970).

Goldsmith, Oliver, *The Vicar of Wakefield: A Tale, supposed to be written by himself* (1766), ed. Arthur Friedman (Oxford: Oxford University Press, 1974).

Graves, Richard, *The Spiritual Quixote: Or, The Summer's Ramble of Mr Geoffrey Wildgoose, a Comic Romance* (1773), ed. Clarence Tracy (London: Oxford University Press, 1967).

Grew, Nehemiah, *The Meanes of a Most Ample Encrease of the Wealth and Strength of England in a Few Years* (1707), British Library, Landsdowne ms. 691.

[Guthrie, William,] *The Life and Adventures of a Cat* (1760).

Hales, John, *A Discourse of the Common Weal of this Realm of England*, ed. Elizabeth Lamond (Cambridge: Cambridge University Press, 1929).

Hamilton, Elizabeth, *Memoirs of Modern Philosophers* (1800).

Hamilton, Mary, *Munster Village* (London: Pandora, 1987).

Hayley, William, *An Essay on Epic Poetry* (1782) reprinted in facsimile (Gainesville, Fl.: Scholar's Facsimiles and Reprints, 1968).

Hays, Mary, *The Memoirs of Emma Courtney*, 2 vols. (1796), reprinted in facsimile with introduction by Jonathan Wordsworth (Oxford and New York: Woodstock Books, 1995).

Haywood, Eliza, *The History of Miss Betsy Thoughtless* (1751), with introduction by Dale Spender (London: Pandora, 1986).

The History of Sir George Warrington: Or, The Political Quixote (London, 1797).

Hobbes, Thomas, *Answer to Davenant's Preface to Gondibert* (1650).

Holcroft, Thomas, *The Adventures of Hugh Trevor* (1794–7), ed. Seamus Deane (London: Oxford University Press, 1973).

Anna St Ives (1792), ed. Peter Faulkner (Oxford: Oxford University Press, 1970).

Home, Henry (Lord Kames), *Elements of Criticism*, 9th edn, 2 vols. (Edinburgh, 1817).

Hume, David, *Enquiries Concerning Human Understanding and Concerning the Principles of Morals*, ed. L. A. Selby-Bigge, revised P. H. Nidditch (Oxford: Clarendon Press, 1975).

Essays Moral, Political and Literary, ed. T. A. Green and T. H. Grose, revised with variant readings, ed. Eugene Miller (Indianapolis: Liberty Classics, 1985).

A Treatise of Human Nature, ed. L. A. Selby-Bigge, revised P. H. Nidditch (Oxford: Clarendon Press, 1978).

Hurd, Richard, *Letters on Chivalry and Romance* (1762), reprinted in facsimile, ed. Hoyt Trowbridge, Augustan Reprint Society number 101–2 (Los Angeles: William Andrews Clark Memorial Library, 1963).

Hutcheson, Francis, *An Inquiry into the Original of our Ideas of Beauty and Virtue, in two Treatises* (London, 1725).

Reflections upon Laughter and Remarks on the Fable of the Bees (Glasgow, 1750).

Inchbald, Elizabeth, *Nature and Art*, 2 vols. (1796), reprinted in facsimile with an introduction by Jonathan Wordsworth (Oxford and New York: Woodstock Books, 1994).

A Simple Story (1791), with introduction by Jeanette Winterson (London: Pandora, 1987).

Johnson, Samuel, preface to *Dictionary*, in *Samuel Johnson*, ed. Donald Greene (Oxford: Oxford University Press, 1984).

The Works of Samuel Johnson, ed. Arthur Sherbo, 8 vols. (New Haven and London, 1963–).

Johnstone, Charles, *Chrysal: Or, The Adventures of a Guinea* (London, 1760–5), ed. E. A. Baker (London, 1907).

Kilner, Dorothy, *The Life and Perambulations of a Mouse* (*c.* 1785).

[Kilner, Dorothy,] *The Adventures of a Hackney Coach* (1781).

Kilner, Mary Ann, *The Adventures of a Pincushion* (London, [1790]).

The Adventures of a Peg-Top (London, [179?]).

King, Gregory, *Two Tracts: (a) Natural and Political Observations and Conclusions upon the State and Condition of England, 1696; (b) Of the Naval Trade of England 1688 and the National profit then arising thereby*, ed. George E. Barnott (Baltimore: Johns Hopkins University Press, 1936).

Law, John, *Money and Trade Considered, with a proposal for supplying the Nation with Money* (Glasgow, 1750).

Law, William, *Remarks on the Fable of the Bees* (1724).

Lennox, Charlotte, *The Female Quixote: Or, The Adventures of Arabella* (1752), ed. Margaret Dalziel (London: Oxford University Press, 1986).

Lewis, Matthew, *The Monk: A Romance* (1796), ed. Howard Anderson (Oxford: Oxford University Press, 1973).

Lloyd, Charles, *Edmund Oliver* (Bristol, 1798).

McCulloch, J. R., *Early English Tracts on Commerce: from the Originals of Mun, Roberts, North and Others*, first published by the Political Economy Club (London, 1856), reprinted for the Economic History Society (1952 and 1954).

Mackenzie, Henry, *Lounger*, 20 (18 June 1785).

 The Man of Feeling (1771), ed. Brian Vickers (Oxford: Oxford University Press, 1967).

Malynes, Gerard de, *Consuetudo, vel, Lex Mercatoria* (London, 1622).

 A Treatise of the Canker of England's Commonwealth (London, 1601).

Mandeville, Bernard, *The Fable of the Bees: Or, Private Vices, Publick Benefits* (1714), ed. F. B. Kaye, 2 vols. (Oxford: Clarendon Press, 1924).

 Letter to Dion [ie George Berkeley, Bp of Cloyne] occasion'd by his book call'd Alciphron, or the Minute Philosopher (1732).

Misselden, Edward, *The Circle of Commerce or the Ballance of Trade* (London, 1623).

 Free Trade: Or, The Means to Make Trade Flourish Wherein the Causes of the Decay of Trade in this Kingdom are Discovered (London, 1622).

Montagu, Lady Mary Wortley, *Complete Letters of Lady Mary Wortley Montagu*, ed. Robert Halsband and Isobel Grundy, 3 vols. (Oxford: Clarendon Press, 1967).

Moore, John, *Mordaunt: Sketches of Life, Characters and Manners in Various Countries* (1800) (London, 1965).

Mun, Thomas, *England's Treasure by Forraign Trade; Or, The Ballance of our Forraign Trade is the Rule of our Treasure* (London, 1664), reprinted in McCulloch, *Early English Tracts on Commerce*, pp. 115–210.

North, Sir Dudley, *Discourses upon Trade* (London, 1691).

Ogilvie, John, *Britannia* (1801), reprinted in facsimile (New Haven, n.d.).

 An Essay on the Lyric Poetry of the Ancients (London, 1762).

 Philosophical and Critical Observations on the Nature, Characters and Various Species of Composition, 2 vols. (London, 1774).

Opie, Amelia, *Adeline Mowbray: Or, The Mother and Daughter* (1804).

 The Father and Daughter (1801).

Percy, Thomas, 'Essay on the Ancient Metrical Romances', in *Reliques of Ancient English Poetry*, vol. III (Edinburgh, 1858).

Petty, Sir William, *The Economic Writings of Sir William Petty*, ed. Charles Henry Hull, 2 vols. (Cambridge, 1899).

Philips, John, *Cyder: A Poem in Two Books* (London, 1708).

Pinkerton, John [pseud. Robert Heron], *Letters of Literature* (London, 1785).

Pope, Alexander, *Poetical Works*, ed. Herbert Davis (Oxford: Oxford University Press, 1978).

 'On Epic Poetry', *Guardian*, 78 (19 June 1713).

Potter, William, *The Key to Wealth: Or, A New Way for Improving of Trade, Lawfull, Easie, Safe and Effectual* (1650).

Pye, Henry James, *A Commentary Illustrating the Poetic Works of Aristotle* (London, 1792).

Radcliffe, Ann, *The Italian: Or, The Confessional of the Black Penitents* (1797), ed. Frederick Garber (Oxford: Oxford University Press, 1991).

The Mysteries of Udolpho: A Romance (1794) ed. Bonamy Dobree (Oxford: Oxford University Press, 1966, 1980).

Rapin, René, *Reflections on Aristotle's Treatise of Poesie, Containing the Necessary, Rational and Universal* RULES *for Epick, Dramatick and Other Sorts of Poetry. With Reflections on the Works of the Ancient and Modern Poets. And their Faults Noted*, trans. Thomas Rymer (London, 1674).

Reeve, Clara, *The Progress of Romance Through Times, Countries, and Manners with Remarks on the Good and Bad Effects of it*, 2 vols. (Dublin, 1785).

Richardson, Samuel, *The Apprentice's Vade Mecum: Or, A Young Man's Pocket Companion, 1734, and A Seasonable Examination of Playhouses, 1735*, Richardsoniana 1 (London, 1974).

Clarissa: Or, The History of a Young Lady (1747–8), ed. John Butt, 4 vols. (London: Dent, 1962).

Clarissa: Or, The History of a Young Lady, ed. Angus Ross (Harmondsworth: Viking Penguin, 1985).

Clarissa: Preface, Hints of Prefaces and Postscript, ed. R. F. Brissenden, Augustan Reprint Society number 103 (Los Angeles: William Andrews Clark Memorial Library, 1964).

Correspondence, ed. Anna Laetitia Barbauld (London, 1804).

Familiar Letters on Important Occasions, ed. Brian W. Downs (London: Routledge, 1928).

The History of Sir Charles Grandison (London, 1753–4), ed. Jocelyn Harris, 3 vols. (Oxford: Oxford University Press, 1972).

Pamela: Or, Virtue Rewarded (1740), ed. Peter Sabor (Harmondsworth: Penguin, 1980).

Selected Letters of Samuel Richardson, 12 vols., ed. Leslie Stephen (London, 1883).

The Works of Samuel Richardson, introduced by Leslie Stephen (London, 1883).

Roberts, Lewes, *The Treasure of Traffike: Or, A Discourse of Foraigne Trade* (London, 1641).

Sage, Alain René le, *The Adventures of Gil Blas of Santillane*, 3 vols., translated by Tobias Smollett (London, 1881).

Scott, Helenus, *The Adventures of a Rupee* (1782).

Scott, Sarah, *A Description of Millenium Hall* (1762), ed. J. Spencer (London: Virago, 1986).

The Sedan (London, 1757).

Shaftesbury, Anthony Ashley Cooper, 3rd Earl of, *Characteristics of Men, Manners, Opinions, Times, etc.* (1714), ed. John M. Robertson, 2 vols. (Gloucester, Mass.: Peter Smith, 1963).

Smith, Adam, *An Inquiry into the Nature and Causes of the Wealth of Nations* (1776), 2 vols., ed. R. H. Campbell and A. S. Skinner, textual editor W. B. Todd (Oxford: Clarendon Press, 1976).

The Theory of Moral Sentiments, ed. D. D. Raphael and A. L. Macfie (Oxford: Clarendon Press, 1976).

'"Early Draft" of Part of *The Wealth of Nations*', in *Lectures on Jurisprudence*, ed. R. L. Meek, D. D. Raphael and P. G. Stein (Oxford: Clarendon Press, 1978), pp. 561–86.

Smith, Charlotte, *Emmeline: The Orphan of the Castle* (1788) (Oxford: Oxford University Press, 1971).

The Old Manor House (1793), ed. Anne Henry Ehrenpreis (Oxford: Oxford University Press, 1969).

Smollett, Tobias, *The Adventures of Peregrine Pickle*, ed. James L. Clifford, revised by Paul-Gabriel Boucé (Oxford: Oxford University Press, 1983).

The Adventures of Roderick Random (1748), ed. Paul-Gabriel Boucé (Oxford: Oxford University Press, 1979, 1981).

The Expedition of Humphry Clinker (1771), ed. Lewis M. Knapp (Oxford: Oxford University Press, 1966).

Smythies, Susan, *The Stage-Coach* (1753).

Sterne, Laurence, *The Life and Opinions of Tristram Shandy, Gent.* (1759–67), ed. Graham Petrie (Harmondsworth: Penguin, 1967).

Steuart, Sir James, *An Inquiry into the Principles of Political Oeconomy*, ed. Andrew Skinner, 2 vols. (Edinburgh and London: Oliver and Boyd, 1966).

Stewart, Dugald, *Collected Works*, 11 vols., ed. Sir William Hamilton (Edinburgh, 1854–60).

'Life of Adam Smith', in Adam Smith, *Essays on Philosophical Subjects*, ed. Joseph Black and James Hutton (London, 1795).

Swift, Jonathan, *The Examiner*, ed. Herbert Davis (Oxford: Oxford University Press, 1941).

Temple, Sir William, *Of Poetry* (1690).

'An Essay Upon Ancient and Modern Learning' (1690), in *The Works of Sir William Temple*, 2 vols. (London, 1720).

Thorold, John, *A Short Examination of the Notions Advanced in the Fable of the Bees* (1726).

Trapp, Joseph, *Lectures on Poetry Read in the Schools of Natural Philosophy at Oxford, Translated from the Latin with Additional Notes* (London, 1742).

Vanderlint, Jacob, *Money Answers All Things: Or, An Essay to Make Money Sufficiently Plentiful Amongst all Ranks of People, and Increase our Foreign and Domestick Trade* (London, 1734).

Voltaire, *An Essay upon the Epick Poetry of the European Nations from Homer down to Milton* (London, 1727), rpt. in *Le Bossu and Voltaire on the Epic* ed. Stuart Curran (Gainesville, Fl.: Scholar's Facsimiles and Reprints, 1970).

Walker, George, *The Vagabond: Or, Whatever is just is equal, but equality is not always just* (1799).

Warton, Thomas, *The History of English Poetry from the Eleventh to the Seventeenth Century* (London, 1778).

Wollstonecraft, Mary, *Mary: A Fiction* (1788) and *The Wrongs of Woman: Or, Maria, A Fragment* in *Mary and the Wrongs of Woman*, ed. James Kinsley and Gary Kelly (Oxford and New York: Oxford University Press, 1987).

A Vindication of the Rights of Woman (1792) (Harmondsworth: Penguin, 1987).

Wotton, William, *Reflections Upon Ancient and Modern Learning* (1694).
Young, Edward, *Conjectures on Original Composition: In a Letter to the Author of Sir Charles Grandison* (1759).

SECONDARY SOURCES

Appleby, Joyce Oldham, *Economic Thought and Ideology in Seventeenth-Century England* (Princeton: Princeton University Press, 1979).
Atkinson, R. D., 'Hume on "Is" and "Ought": A Reply to Mr MacIntyre', *Philosophical Review*, 70 (1961).
Barber, William J., *A History of Economic Thought* (Harmondsworth: Penguin, 1967).
Barker-Benfield, G. J., *The Culture of Sensibility: Sex and Society in Eighteenth-Century Britain* (Chicago and London: University of Chicago Press, 1992).
Barrell, John, *The Political Theory of Painting from Reynolds to Hazlitt* (New Haven: Yale University Press, 1986).
Barrell, John (ed.), *Painting and the Politics of Culture: New Essays on British Art, 1700–1850* (Oxford: Clarendon Press, 1992).
Battestin, Martin, *The Moral Basis of Fielding's Art: A Study of Joseph Andrews* (Middletown, Conn.: Wesleyan University Press, 1959).
The Providence of Wit: Aspects of Form in Augustan England and the Arts (Oxford: Clarendon Press, 1974).
Bellamy, Elizabeth, 'Private Virtues, Public Vices: Commercial Morality and the Novel, 1740–1800' (unpublished Ph.D. thesis, Jesus College, Cambridge, 1988).
Benjamin, Andrew E., Geoffrey N. Cantor and John R. R. Christie (eds.), *The Figural and the Literal: Problems of Language in the History of Science and Philosophy, 1630–1800* (Manchester: Manchester University Press, 1987).
Boucé, Paul-Gabriel, *Les Romans de Smollett* (1971), translated by Antonia White as *The Novels of Tobias Smollett* (London and New York: Longman, 1976).
Brissenden, R. F., *Virtue in Distress: Studies in the Novel of Sentiment from Richardson to Sade* (London: Macmillan, 1974).
Burns, Bryan, 'The Story-telling in *Joseph Andrews*', in *Henry Fielding: Justice Observed*, ed. K. G. Simpson (London: Vision Press, 1985).
Butler, Marilyn, *Jane Austen and the War of Ideas* (Oxford: Clarendon Press, 1975).
Romantics, Rebels and Reactionaries: English Literature and its Background, 1760–1830 (Oxford: Oxford University Press, 1981).
Campbell, T. D., *Adam Smith's Science of Morals* (London: Allen and Unwin, 1971).
Castle, Terry, *Clarissa's Ciphers: Meaning and Disruption in Richardson's Clarissa* (Ithaca: Cornell University Press, 1982).
Clark, J. C. D., *English Society 1688–1832: Ideology, Social Structure and Political Practice During the Ancien Régime* (Cambridge: Cambridge University Press, 1985).
Coats, A. W., 'Adam Smith and the Mercantile System', in Skinner and Wilson, *Essays on Adam Smith*, pp. 132–53

Collini, Stefan, Donald Winch and John Burrow, *That Noble Science of Politics: A Study of Nineteenth-Century Intellectual History* (Cambridge: Cambridge University Press, 1983).

Cook, Richard I., *Bernard Mandeville* (New York: Twayne, 1974).

Copeland, Edward, *Women Writing About Money: Women's Fiction in England, 1790–1820* (Cambridge: Cambridge University Press, 1995).

Copley, Stephen, 'Polite Culture in Commercial Society', in *The Figural and the Literal: Problems of Language in the History of Science and Philosophy, 1630–1800*, ed. A. Benjamin, G. Cantor and J. Christie (Manchester: Manchester University Press, 1987), pp. 176–201.

Copley, Stephen (ed.), *Literature and the Social Order in Eighteenth-Century England* (London: Croom Helm, 1984).

Cross, Wilbur L., *The History of Henry Fielding*, 3 vols. (New Haven: Yale University Press, 1918).

Curran, Stuart (ed.), *Le Bossu and Voltaire on the Epic* (Gainesville, Fl.: Scholar's Facsimiles and Reprints, 1970).

Davis, Lennard J., *Factual Fictions: The Origins of the English Novel* (New York: Columbia University Press, 1983).

Day, Robert Adams, *Told in Letters: Epistolary Fiction Before Richardson* (Ann Arbor: University of Michigan Press, 1966).

Dickinson, H. T., *Liberty and Property: Political Ideology in Eighteenth Century Britain* (London: Weidenfeld and Nicolson, 1977).

Dickson, P. G. M., *The Financial Revolution in England: A Study in the Development of Public Credit* (London: Macmillan, 1967).

Doody, Margaret Anne, *A Natural Passion: A Study of the Novels of Samuel Richardson* (Oxford: Clarendon Press, 1974).

Downs, Brian, *Richardson* (London: Routledge, 1928).

Dudden, F. H., *Henry Fielding: His Life, Works and Times*, 2 vols. (1952; rpt. Hampden, Conn.: Archon Books, 1966).

Dunn, John, 'From Applied Theology to Social Analysis: The Break between John Locke and the Scottish Enlightenment', in Hont and Ignatieff (eds.), *Wealth and Virtue*, pp. 119–36

Dussinger, John A., *The Discourse of the Mind in Eighteenth-Century Fiction* (The Hague: Mouton, 1974).

Eagleton, Terry, *The Function of Criticism: From The Spectator to Post-Structuralism* (London: Verso, 1984).

　The Rape of Clarissa: Writing, Sexuality and Class Struggle in Samuel Richardson (Oxford: Basil Blackwell, 1982).

Eaves, Duncan and Ben D. Kimpel, *Samuel Richardson: A Biography* (Oxford: Clarendon Press, 1971).

Ellis, Markman, *The Politics of Sensibility: Race, Gender and Commerce in the Sentimental Novel* (Cambridge: Cambridge University Press, 1996).

Erskine-Hill, Howard, *The Social Milieu of Alexander Pope: Lives, Example and the Poetic Response* (New Haven and London: Yale University Press, 1975).

Fiedler, Leslie A., *Love and Death in the American Novel* (London: Jonathan Cape, 1967).

Flew, Anthony, 'On the Interpretation of Hume', and 'Not Proven At Most', *Philosophy*, 38 (1963).

Flynn, Carol Houlihan, *Samuel Richardson: A Man of Letters* (Princeton: Princeton University Press, 1982).

Folkenflik, Robert (ed.), *The English Hero, 1660–1800* (London: Associated University Presses, 1982).

Forbes, Duncan, *Hume's Philosophical Politics* (Cambridge: Cambridge University Press, 1975).

Furbank, P. N., 'Godwin's Novels', *Essays in Criticism*, 5 (1955).

George, Margaret, *One Woman's 'Situation': A Study of Mary Wollstonecraft* (Urbana: University of Illinois Press, 1970).

Goldberg, Homer, 'Comic Prose Epic or Comic Romance: The Argument of the Preface to *Joseph Andrews*', *Philological Quarterly*, 43 (1964).

Goldberg, Rita, *Sex and Enlightenment: Women in Richardson and Diderot* (Cambridge: Cambridge University Press, 1984).

Goldsmith, M. M., *Private Vices, Public Benefits: Bernard Mandeville's Social and Political Thought* (Cambridge: Cambridge University Press, 1985).

Gonda, Caroline, *Reading Daughters' Fictions 1709–1834: Novels and Society from Manley to Edgeworth* (Cambridge: Cambridge University Press, 1996).

Hagin, Peter, *The Epic Hero and the Decline of Heroic Poetry: A Study of the Neoclassical English Epic with Special Reference to Milton's Paradise Lost* (Bern: Francke, 1964).

Harasyn, Sara, 'Ideology and Self: A Theoretical Discussion of the "Self" in Mary Wollstonecraft's Fiction', *English Studies in Canada*, 12.2 (June, 1988).

Heckscher, Eli F., *Mercantilism* (first published in Swedish, 1931), trans. by Mendel Shapiro, 2 vols. (London: Allen and Unwin, 1935).

Heidler, Joseph Bunn, *The History, from 1700 to 1800, of English Criticism of Prose Fiction*, Studies in Language and Literature, 13 (Urbana: University of Illinois Press, May 1928), no. 2.

Heimann, Eduard, *History of Economic Doctrines: An Introduction to Economic Theory* (London: Oxford University Press, 1945).

Hirschman, Albert O., *The Passions and the Interests: Political Arguments for Capitalism Before its Triumph* (Princeton: Princeton University Press, 1976).

Hohendahl, Peter Uwe, *The Institution of Criticism* (Ithaca: Cornell University Press, 1982).

Hont, Istvan and Michael Ignatieff, 'Needs and Justice in the *Wealth of Nations*: an Introductory Essay', in Hont and Ignatieff (eds.), *Wealth and Virtue*, pp. 1–44.

Hont, Istvan and Michael Ignatieff (eds.), *Wealth and Virtue: The Shaping of Political Economy in the Scottish Enlightenment* (Cambridge: Cambridge University Press, 1982).

Horne, Thomas A., *The Social Thought of Bernard Mandeville: Virtue and Commerce in Early Eighteenth-Century England* (London: Macmillan, 1978).

Hudson, W. D., 'Hume on "Is" and "Ought"', *Philosophical Quarterly*, 14 (1964).

Hunter, Geoffrey, 'Hume on Is and Ought', *Philosophy*, 37 (1962).

'Reply to Professor Flew', *Philosophy*, 38 (1963).

Hunter, J. Paul, *Before Novels: The Cultural Contexts of Eighteenth-Century English Fiction* (New York: Norton, 1990).

Ignatieff, Michael, *The Needs of Strangers* (London: Chatto and Windus, 1984).

Iser, Wolfgang, *The Implied Reader: Patterns of Communication in Prose Fiction from Bunyan to Beckett* (Baltimore and London: Johns Hopkins University Press, 1974).

Jackson, Rosemary, *Fantasy: The Literature of Subversion* (London and New York: Methuen, 1981).

Johnson, E. A. J., *Predecessors of Adam Smith: The Growth of British Economic Thought* (London: P. S. King, 1937).

Kelly, Gary, *English Fiction of the Romantic Period, 1789–1830* (London: Longman, 1989).

   The English Jacobin Novel, 1780–1805 (Oxford: Oxford University Press, 1976).

   Women, Writing and Revolution, 1790–1827 (Oxford: Clarendon Press, 1993).

   'The English Jacobin Novel and its Background, 1780–1805' (unpublished Ph.D. thesis, University of Oxford, 1972).

Keymer, Tom, *Richardson's Clarissa and the Eighteenth-Century Reader* (Cambridge: Cambridge University Press, 1992).

Kinkead-Weekes, Mark, *Samuel Richardson: Dramatic Novelist* (Ithaca and London: Cornell University Press, 1973).

Klein, Lawrence, *Shaftesbury and the Culture of Politeness: Moral Discourse and Cultural Politics in Early Eighteenth-Century England* (Cambridge: Cambridge University Press, 1994).

Kreissman, Bernard, *Pamela–Shamela: A Study of the Criticisms, Burlesques, Parodies, and Adaptations of Richardson's 'Pamela'*, University of Nebraska Studies number 22 (Lincoln, Nebr.: University of Nebraska Press, 1960).

Kristeva, Julia, *Desire in Language: A Semiotic Approach to Literature and Art*, ed. Leon S. Roudiez, trans. Thomas Gora, Alice Jardine and Leon S. Roudiez (Oxford: Basil Blackwell, 1980).

Langbauer, Laurie, *Women and Romance: The Consolations of Gender in the English Novel* (Ithaca and London: Cornell University Press, 1990).

Lawrence, Christopher, 'The Nervous System and Society in the Scottish Enlightenment', in Shapin and Barnes (eds.), *Natural Order*, pp. 19–40.

Leavis, F. R., *The Great Tradition: George Eliot, James and Conrad* (London: Peregrine Books, 1962, 1986).

Lehmann, William C., *Henry Home, Lord Kames and the Scottish Enlightenment: A Study in National Character and in the History of Ideas*, International Archives of the History of Ideas number 41 (The Hague: Martinus Nijhoff, 1971).

Letwin, William, *The Origins of Scientific Economics: English Economic Thought, 1660–1776* (New York: Doubleday Anchor, 1965).

   Sir Josiah Child: Merchant Economist, with a Reprint of Brief Observations Concerning Trade and Interest of Money (1668) (Boston, Mass.: Baker Library, Harvard Graduate School of Business Administration, 1959).

Locke, Don, *The Fantasy of Reason: The Life and Thought of William Godwin* (London: Routledge and Kegan Paul, 1980).

Lukacs, Georg, *The Theory of the Novel* (London: Merlin, 1962).

Macey, Samuel L., *Money and the Novel: Mercenary Motivation in Defoe and his Immediate Successors* (Victoria, B.C.: Sono Nis Press, 1983).

Macfie, A. L., *The Individual in Society* (London: Allen and Unwin, 1967).

Mackie, J. L., *Hume's Moral Theory* (London: Routledge and Kegan Paul, 1980).

MacIntyre, Alasdair C., 'Hume on "Is" and "Ought"', *Philosophical Review*, 68 (1959).

Maresca, Thomas E., *Epic to Novel* (Ohio: Ohio State University Press, 1974).

Marshall, Peter H., *William Godwin* (New Haven and London: Yale University Press, 1984).

McKendrick, Neil, John Brewer and J. H. Plumb, *The Birth of a Consumer Society: The Commercialization of Eighteenth-Century England* (London: Europa, 1982).

McKeon, Michael, *The Origins of the English Novel, 1600–1740* (London: Radius, 1988).

McKillop, Alan Dugald, *The Early Masters of English Fiction* (London: Constable, 1968).

  Samuel Richardson: Printer and Novelist (University of North Carolina, 1936; reprinted New York: Shoe String Press, 1960).

McVeagh, John, *Tradeful Merchants: The Portrayal of the Capitalist in Literature* (London: Routledge, 1981).

Meek, Ronald L. (ed.), *Precursors of Adam Smith* (London: Dent, 1973).

Meier, Thomas Keith, *Defoe and the Defense of Commerce*, English Literary Studies Monograph number 38 (Victoria, B.C.: University of Victoria, 1987).

Mossner, Ernest Campbell, *The Life of David Hume* (Edinburgh: Thomas Nelson, 1954).

Mullan, John, *Sentiment and Sociability: The Language of Feeling in the Eighteenth Century* (Oxford: Clarendon Press, 1988).

Napoleoni, Claudio, *Smith, Ricardo, Marx: Observations on the History of Economic Thought*, trans. J. M. A. Gee (Oxford: Blackwell, 1975).

Novak, Maximillian E., *Economics and the Fiction of Daniel Defoe* (Berkeley: University of California Press, 1962).

  Eighteenth-Century English Literature (London: Macmillan, 1983).

Nussbaum, Felicity and Laura Brown (eds.), *The New Eighteenth Century* (London: Methuen, 1987).

Paulson, Ronald, *The Beautiful, Novel and Strange: Aesthetics and Heterodoxy* (Baltimore: Johns Hopkins University Press, 1996).

  'The Pilgrimage and the Family: Structures in the Novels of Fielding and Smollett', in Rousseau and Boucé (eds.), *Tobias Smollett*, pp. 57–78.

Perry, Ruth, *Women, Letters and the Novel* (New York: AMS Press, 1980).

Phillipson, Nicholas, 'Adam Smith as Civic Moralist', in Hont and Ignatieff (eds.), *Wealth and Virtue*, pp. 179–202.

  'Culture and Society in the Eighteenth-Century Province: The Case of Edinburgh and the Scottish Enlightenment', in *The University in Society*, ed. L. Stone, 2 vols. (London: Oxford University Press, 1974), vol. II, pp. 407–48.

'Towards A Definition of "The Scottish Enlightenment"', in *City and Society in the Eighteenth Century*, ed. P. Fritz and D. Williams (Toronto: Hakkert, 1973), pp. 125–47.

Pinkus, Philip, 'Mandeville's Paradox', in Primer (ed.), *Mandeville Studies*, pp. 193–211.

Pocock, J. G. A., *The Machiavellian Moment: Florentine Political Thought and the Atlantic Republican Tradition* (Princeton: Princeton University Press, 1975).

'Between Machiavelli and Hume: Gibbon as Civic Humanist, and Philosophical Historian', *Daedalus* (Summer 1976).

'Cambridge Paradigms and Scotch Philosophers: A Study in the Relations between Civic Humanist and Civil Jurisprudential Interpretation of Eighteenth-Century Social Thought', in Hont and Ignatieff (eds.), *Wealth and Virtue*, pp. 235–52.

Poovey, Mary, *The Proper Lady and the Woman Writer: Ideology as Style in the Works of Mary Wollstonecraft, Mary Shelley and Jane Austen* (Chicago: University of Chicago Press, 1984).

Preston, John, *The Created Self: The Reader's Role in Eighteenth-Century Fiction* (London: Heinemann, 1970).

Primer, Irwin, 'Mandeville and Shaftesbury: Some Facts and Problems', in Primer (ed.), *Mandeville Studies*, pp. 126–42.

Primer, Irwin (ed.), *Mandeville Studies: New Explorations in the Art and Thought of Dr Bernard Mandeville (1670–1733)* (The Hague: Martinus Nijhoff, 1975).

Ray, William, *Story and History: Narrative Authority and Social Identity in the Eighteenth-Century French and English Novel* (Oxford and Cambridge, Mass.: Basil Blackwell, 1990).

Richetti, John, *Popular Fiction Before Richardson: Narrative Patterns, 1700–1739* (Oxford: Clarendon Press, 1969).

Robbins, Caroline, *The Eighteenth-Century Commonwealthman: Studies in the Transmission, Development and Circumstances of English Liberal Thought from the Restoration of Charles II until the War of the Thirteen Colonies* (Cambridge, Mass.: Harvard University Press, 1959).

Rogers, Pat, *Henry Fielding: A Biography* (London: Elek, 1979).

Literature and Popular Culture in Eighteenth-Century England (Brighton: Harvester, 1985).

Rousseau, George S. and Paul-Gabriel Boucé (eds.), *Tobias Smollett: Bicentennial Essays presented to Lewis Knapp* (Oxford: Oxford University Press, 1971).

Rubel, Margaret Mary, *Savage and Barbarian: Historical Attitudes in the Criticism of Homer and Ossian in Britain, 1760–1800* (Amsterdam: North-Holland, 1978).

Sales, Roger, *Jane Austen and Representations of Regency England* (London and New York: Routledge, 1994).

Schumpeter, Joseph A., *History of Economic Analysis*, ed. Elizabeth Boody Schumpeter (London: Oxford University Press, 1954).

Sekora, John, *Luxury: The Concept in Western Thought, Eden to Smollett* (Baltimore and London: Johns Hopkins University Press, 1977).

Shapin, Steven and Barry Barnes (eds.), *Natural Order: Historical Studies of Scientific*

Culture (London and Beverly Hills: Sage, 1979).

Shell, Marc, *The Economy of Literature* (Baltimore and London: Johns Hopkins University Press, 1978).

   Money, Language and Thought: Literary and Philosophical Economics from the Medieval to the Modern Era (Berkeley and London: University of California Press, 1982).

Simpson, K. G. (ed.), *Henry Fielding: Justice Observed* (London: Vision Press, 1985).

Skinner, Andrew S., and Thomas Wilson, *Essays on Adam Smith* (Oxford: Clarendon Press, 1975).

Smith, Grahame, *The Novel and Society: Defoe to George Eliot* (London: Batsford, 1984).

Solkin, David, *Painting for Money: The Visual Arts and the Public Sphere in Eighteenth-Century England* (New Haven: Yale University Press, 1993).

Spacks, Patricia Meyer, *Imagining a Self: Autobiography and Novel in Eighteenth-Century England* (Cambridge, Mass.: Harvard University Press, 1976).

Speck, W. A., *Society and Literature in England, 1700–1760* (Dublin: Gill and Macmillan, 1983).

Spencer, Jane, *The Rise of the Woman Novelist, from Aphra Behn to Jane Austen* (Oxford: Basil Blackwell, 1986).

Spender, Dale, *Mothers of the Novel* (London: Pandora, 1986).

Stephen, Leslie, *History of English Thought in the Eighteenth Century*, 2 vols. (London, 1876).

Swedenberg, H. T. (Jr), *The Theory of Epic in England 1650–1800*, University of California Publications in English number 15 (Berkeley: University of California Press, 1944; reissued New York: Russell and Russell, 1972).

   'Rules and English Critics of the Epic, 1650–1800', in *Studies in the Literature of the Augustan Age: Essays Collected in Honor of Arthur Ellicott Case*, ed. Richard Boys (Ann Arbor: Wahr, 1952, 1966), pp. 281–303.

Tanner, Tony, *Adultery in the Novel: Contract and Transgression* (Baltimore and London: Johns Hopkins University Press, 1979).

Tillyard, E. M. W., *The English Epic and its Background* (London: Chatto and Windus, 1954).

   The Epic Strain in the English Novel (London: Chatto and Windus, 1958).

Todd, Janet, *Sensibility: An Introduction* (London: Methuen, 1986).

   The Sign of Angellica: Women, Writing and Fiction, 1660–1800 (London: Virago, 1989).

Todd, William B. (ed.), *Hume and the Enlightenment: Essays Presented to Ernest Campbell Mossner* (Edinburgh: Edinburgh University Press, 1974).

Tribe, Keith, *Genealogies of Capitalism* (London: Macmillan, 1981).

   Land, Labour and Economic Discourse (London: Routledge and Kegan Paul, 1978).

Turner, Cheryl, *Living by the Pen: Women Writers in the Eighteenth Century* (London and New York: Routledge, 1992).

Ty, Eleanor, *Unsex'd Revolutionaries: Five Women Novelists of the 1790s* (Toronto and London: University of Toronto Press, 1993).

Tysdahl, B. J., *William Godwin as Novelist* (London: Athlone, 1981).

Van Sant, Ann Jessie, *Eighteenth-Century Sensibility and the Novel: The Senses in Social Context* (Cambridge: Cambridge University Press, 1993).

Warner, William Beatty, *Reading Clarissa: The Struggles of Interpretation* (New Haven and London: Yale University Press, 1979).

Watt, Ian, *The Rise of the Novel: Studies in Defoe, Richardson and Fielding* (London: Hogarth Press, 1987).

Wellek, René, *A History of Modern Criticism: 1750–1950* (London: Jonathan Cape, 1955).

Whitney, Lois, *Primitivism and the Idea of Progress in English Popular Literature of the Eighteenth Century* (New York: Octagon, 1973).

'English Primitivistic Theories of Epic Origins', *Modern Philology*, 21.4 (May 1924).

Williams, Ioan, *The Realist Novel in England: A Study in Development* (London: Macmillan, 1974).

Williams, Ioan (ed.), *The Criticism of Henry Fielding* (London: Routledge and Kegan Paul, 1970).

Wilson, Thomas and Andrew S. Skinner (ed.), *The Market and the State: Essays in Honour of Adam Smith* (Oxford: Clarendon Press, 1976).

Winch, Donald, *Adam Smith's Politics: An Essay in Historiographic Revision* (Cambridge: Cambridge University Press, 1978).

'Adam Smith's "enduring particular result": A Political and Cosmopolitan Perspective', in Hont and Ignatieff (eds.), *Wealth and Virtue*, pp. 253–69.

Wolff, Cynthia Griffin, *Samuel Richardson and the Eighteenth-Century Puritan Character* (Hampden, Conn.: Archon Books, 1972).

Wright, John P., *The Sceptical Realism of David Hume* (Manchester: Manchester University Press, 1983).

Wright, Walter, *Sensibility in English Prose Fiction, 1760–1814: A Reinterpretation* (Urbana: University of Illinois Press, 1937).

Index

British culture underwent radical change in
the eighteenth century with the emergence of
new literary genres and discourses of social
analysis. As novelists developed the fictional
form, writers of economic tracts and treatises
sought a language and a conceptual framework
to describe the modern commercial state. In
*Commerce, Morality and the Eighteenth-Century
Novel*, Liz Bellamy argues that the evolution of
the novel in eighteenth-century Britain needs to be
seen in the context of the discursive conflict
between economics and more traditional systems
of social analysis. In a series of fresh readings of
a wide range of novels, Bellamy shows how the
novel contributed to the debate over public and
private virtues and had to negotiate between
commercial and anti-commercial ethics. The
resulting choices were crucial in determining
the structure as well as the moral content
of the novel.